Sponsored by
The Consortium for Policy Research in Education

Rutgers, the State University of New Jersey
University of Southern California
Harvard University
Michigan State University
Stanford University
University of Wisconsin, Madison

Funded by
The Office of Educational Research and Improvement, U.S.
Department of Education, under cooperative agreement numbers
R117G10007 and R117G10039

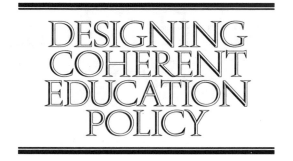

DESIGNING
COHERENT
EDUCATION
POLICY

Susan H. Fuhrman
Editor

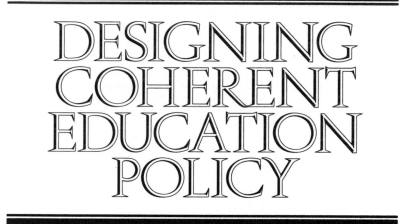

DESIGNING COHERENT EDUCATION POLICY

Improving the System

Jossey-Bass Publishers · San Francisco

Substantial discounts on bulk quantities of Jossey-Bass books are available to corporations, professional associations, and other organizations. For details and discount information, contact the special sales department at Jossey-Bass Inc., Publishers. (415) 433-1740; Fax (415) 433-0499.

For sales outside the United States, contact Maxwell Macmillan International Publishing Group, 866 Third Avenue, New York, New York 10022.

Manufactured in the United States of America

10% POST CONSUMER WASTE

The paper used in this book is acid-free and meets the State of California requirements for recycled paper (50 percent recycled waste, including 10 percent postconsumer waste), which are the strictest guidelines for recycled paper currently in use in the United States.

Library of Congress Cataloging-in-Publication Data

Designing coherent education policy : improving the system / Susan H. Fuhrman, editor.
    p.   cm. — (The Jossey-Bass education series)
    Includes bibliographical references and index.
    ISBN 1-55542-536-4
    1. Education and state—United States. 2. Education—United States—Aims and objectives. 3. Public schools—United States—Aims and objectives. I. Fuhrman, Susan. II. Series.
LC89.D47   1993
379.73—dc20   92-38852
                                                 CIP

FIRST EDITION
HB Printing   10 9 8 7 6 5 4 3 2 1   *Code 9339*

Contents

Preface

This book is about designing coherent education policy for public elementary and secondary schools. Its focus is primarily at the state level, where formal responsibility for public education lies, but it concerns federal and district policy and school practice as well. The word *coherent,* as defined by Webster's Dictionary, means "having the quality of holding together as a firm mass" and "logically consistent." Coherent education policies, therefore, need to be congruent, to send the same messages, and to avoid contradictions. The sense of a "firm mass" is especially pertinent to the issues in this book — policies must not only be compatible but they must also build on one another in some way to form a larger whole. The idea of coherent policy is not consistency for its own sake but consistency in service of specific goals for student learning. Coherent policy means giving a sense of direction to the educational system by specifying policy purposes. To the authors in this book, it means establishing high-quality goals about what students should know and be able to do and then coordinating policies that link to the goals.

Why is coherent policy important? Much of the failure of past policy efforts to improve education can be attributed to inconsistency and lack of unified purpose. Education policy in the United States has been characterized by a lack of coherence and an emphasis on low-level skills. The incoherence reflects our multilevel, fragmented governance structure; the high volume of education policy production at all levels, particularly in reform eras such as the 1980s; and a tendency to address each problem with a distinct special program. Policies and projects, often in conflict with one another, wash over the system without substantial impact on the conventional and unambitious content and pedagogy characterizing many classrooms. Efforts to integrate policies have been rare and generally focused on basic skills, not on more challenging learning goals. So when some urban school districts aligned their curriculum policies and assessment practices, they anchored them to minimal competencies. Many individual schools aim higher but find little support for their ambition from the larger system: from textbooks that water down content, from standardized tests that focus on isolated skills, from teacher preparation programs that emphasize credit collection over deep understanding of content and pedagogy. Less advantaged schools often lack the resources to buck the system, and even schools that do reform find it hard to sustain their efforts over time (Cohen, 1982; Smith and O'Day, 1991; Elmore, 1991).

Searching for more coherent policy has become part of the policy discourse surrounding elementary and secondary education. In the 1980s, leaders in California and a few other states called for ambitious, common goals of student learning and achievement and the close coordination of various elements of the policy infrastructure around the outcome expectations. Marshall S. Smith and Jennifer O'Day conceptualized and further refined what they termed a "systemic" vision of reform that would pair ambitious, coordinated state policies with restructured governance (Smith and O'Day, 1991). Numerous players at all levels of government, as well as associations, foundations, and other independent organizations, advocate and support this change (for example, National Governors' Association [NGA], 1991; Business Roundtable [BRT], 1992; National Council on Educational Standards and Testing [NCEST], Appendix G, 1992). Dozens of states as diverse as Arkansas, Arizona, Vermont, and Kentucky are involved, as well as national agencies such as the National Science Foundation and the U.S. Department of Education.

The Purpose of the Book

The purpose of this book is to expand the policy discussion by refining the definition of coherence and considering a number of complex questions raised by the notion of coherent policy. How politically feasible is the idea? What do we know about the effects of more coherent instructional policy on teaching and learning? How might the role of districts change if state policy became more coherent? Are there examples of coherence that provide lessons for K–12 education policy? What can we learn from examples of more coherent policy in private schooling or from discussions of more coherence among early childhood educators? How does the actuality of the classroom pose challenges for more coherent policy? How might more coherent policy direction serve all students, especially the neediest?

Before describing the chapters that address these questions, it is important to note that, even in a book about coherence, total congruence is lacking. It is a measure of the sophistication and complexity of the concept of coherent policy that there is divergence in how the authors use the term *coherence*. One difference concerns the extent to which the discussion of coherent policy focuses primarily on state-level instructional policies: curriculum frameworks, student assessment, instructional materials, and teacher professional development. Some authors propose that coherent policy should not only orchestrate these instruments but also expand governance in the concept of coherent policy. That is, although states would set ambitious expectations for students and coordinate instructional policies around those expectations, they would also undertake reforms to provide a great deal of freedom to schools in reaching those outcomes. Minimal standards regulations that currently make up much of education policy would be removed or revised so as not to restrict flexibility. State instructional policies would be sufficiently explicit so as not to be vague, but not so detailed that they would dictate day-to-day curriculum or constrain pedagogical choices. Other authors concern themselves primarily with coherent instructional guidance. Restructured governance is not a central topic of discussion, although these authors allude to various types of school flexibility within the more coordinated systems they describe. A third approach places instructional guidance somewhat in opposition to school-level flexibility, raising the notion that coherent curriculum policy can stifle school creativity and initiative. These different viewpoints indicate that decisions about allocation of responsibilities are central to current reform discussions. One wave of state-level reform in the 1980s focused on state-level mandates and a second on school-level reforms, while many of the current efforts to undertake "systemic" reforms center on combining the two trends and finding compatibility between central direction and school flexibility. Many of the chapters address the advantages and likelihood of simultaneous centralization and decentralization.

The authors also differ in the extent to which they extend the concept of coherence beyond interrelated policies to incorporate the match between policy and funding levels. Can policy be coherent if funding is insufficient to meet children's needs? Resource adequacy is addressed most squarely in Chapter Six; the gap between funding of and the national interest in early childhood education is termed an "external inconsistency." Resources are key to many of the proposals for improving elementary and secondary education, but the authors exhibit more concern for distributional or equity issues than for the adequacy of K–12 education funding. Does this mean that K–12 education resources are sufficient to support a more coherent, ambitious approach to instructional guidance? The truth is that we do not really know. In early childhood education, the measure of adequacy is the extent to which children are served. In elementary and secondary education, where schooling is theoretically universal, adequacy relates to quality of service, not to its presence or absence. We have had no way of judging whether resources are adequate because we have had no consensus on the goals we want to achieve and no standard by which to judge quality. One of the most interesting aspects of coherent policy as discussed in this book is the potential it offers for understanding the link between quality and resources. Once clear goals are established to provide direction for the system, we should have a basis for determining which features of schooling contribute to achievement of the goals and in what manner they exert their influence. Then it may be possible to understand the implications of school resources for student learning.

Overview of the Contents

In Chapter One, "The Politics of Coherence," I focus on whether more coherence can be expected from an extremely fragmented and chaotic political system. Our multilevel, multicentered governance structure and the electoral incentives that encourage policymakers to focus on discrete rather than integrated policies pose severe challenges to the design of coherent policy. These forces also suggest that even if policymakers are successful in crafting a set of intersecting ambitious policies, the consistency will erode over time as new concerns surface and new political leaders feel the need to make their mark. It might seem that only radical political reform aimed at rationalizing the system can create a climate hospitable to coherence. However, I find hope in recent policy efforts that provide proofs of coherence, in the general cultural thrust toward more coherent instructional guidance, in the willingness of states to experiment with new structures, and in the political and strategic appeal systemic reform has to unite policymakers and educators.

David K. Cohen and James P. Spillane widen the scope beyond the United States in Chapter Two, "Policy and Practice: The Relations Between Governance and Instruction." They contrast the dispersed authority and power structure in the United States with education governance in other nations. The authors then examine how various nations use a set of policy instruments (instructional frameworks, assessment of student performance, instructional materials, oversight of instruction, and requirements for teacher education and licensure) that come under the term "instructional guidance." They conclude that the consistency, prescriptiveness, and authority of instructional guidance is greater in other nations with more coherent governance systems. Can this make any difference in teaching and learning? The evidence to answer this question is sparse, but what little exists suggests that more coherent guidance can be a positive influence on teaching and learning, if other, nonstructural factors are supportive. The last third of the chapter explores how culture and social organization intertwine with formal governance to affect teaching and learning.

What if this nation does overcome political and other obstacles and create more coherent guidance at the state or national levels? How might local school districts respond and influence school reactions? Richard F. Elmore's chapter, "The Role of Local School Districts in Instructional Improvement," provides cautious optimism that more coherent higher-level policy would trigger a constructive district response. Research on the district role indicates that, historically, districts have not focused on instructional improvement. District personnel have not been staffed or organized in ways that promote attention to the issue; they have not spent significant amounts of time on the issue; they have overlooked opportunities to influence instruction; and they have passed key instructional decisions down the hierarchy to the classroom, without offering much support or reinforcement for what happens there. However, Elmore argues that it is quite likely that the incentive structure federal and state policies currently provide to districts influences them to attend more to fund accounting and rule compliance than to key issues of instruction. If states focus policies around ambitious instruction, districts will have greater incentives to shift to supporting schools in teaching and learning.

What examples do we have of more coherent approaches to elementary and secondary education? What elements do they include? In Chapter Four, William H. Clune's "Systemic Educational Policy: A Conceptual Framework" describes several historical problems with education policy: lack of improvement in student achievement; investment in practices, such as small decreases in class size, that are unrelated to achievement; and policy fragmentation. The author then develops a conceptual framework for systemic policy that grants a leading role to indicators of educational outcomes, inputs, and process. Differing somewhat from authors who emphasize challenging instructional standards as the anchor for coordinated policies, Clune argues that lagging uncertainty surrounding factors associated with student achievement necessitates comprehensive measures that alert us to problems and provide hints about solutions. The framework for systemic policy is then applied to the reforms of several states and to Chicago's restructuring.

The four chapters just summarized focus on the potential benefits and feasibility of more coherent policy in elementary and secondary education. The next two chapters take up examples outside of public elementary and secondary education that might inform the debate. In Chapter Five, "Student Incentives and Academic Standards: Independent Schools as a Coherent System," Arthur G. Powell discusses the system of independent schools and elite colleges guided by the College Board's common student standards and examination system that existed prior to World War II. The ambitious standards were expected of all students in these schools, who were diverse in ability though not in social class. Several linked elements accounted for the system's capacity to promote student achievement, including a sustained, general consensus about the content of academic standards; translation of the standards into credible examinations with predictable consequences; and the strong, direct influence of the examinations on school curriculum, teaching, and professional development. After the war, democratizing influences led to college selection based on talent, not preparation, and the system of common standards collapsed. An exception is the Advanced Placement Program, a systemic approach but only for the most able students.

In Chapter Six, "New Directions for Early Childhood Care and Education Policy," W. Steven Barnett illustrates that public policy regarding early childhood care and education (ECCE) is particularly fragmented and inconsistent. Internal inconsistencies are evident with respect to multiple programs, each of which has different rules for eligibility and participation and different service characteristics. Changes in public policy goals over time vastly enlarged target populations and the scope of public policy, but policy continues to be made in the context of existing agencies and through narrowly defined programs. External inconsistency concerns the mismatch between resources and programs and policy goals. Improving the coherence of

ECCE policy would require increased resources as well as restructuring of government's involvement in ECCE — moves that face serious problems of practical politics. However, demographic changes signal increased political clout for those who have a stake in enlarging and changing the structure of early childhood policy.

Chapter Seven concerns classroom realities that those who dream of more coherent policy must face. Milbrey W. McLaughlin and Joan E. Talbert's "How the World of Students and Teachers Challenges Policy Coherence" discusses students as context for what happens in school. Educators' subjective interpretations of the realities students bring with them to school influence every aspect of the school environment. Focusing on "nontraditional" students, the chapter describes the objective conditions of today's students that have an impact on the school and classroom and the subjective interpretations teachers construct of these student features, particularly their academic strengths and weaknesses. The authors argue that these different constructions pose challenges for more coherent policy, because similar policies affect students differently depending on the context in which they are carried out.

However, an important rationale for systemic reform is the hope it offers for greater equity, for improving the schooling of the nontraditional students that McLaughlin and Talbert discuss. Chapter Eight, "Systemic Reform and Educational Opportunity," provides a powerful argument for more coherence and higher standards. Jennifer A. O'Day and Marshall S. Smith argue that an emphasis on basic skills instruction and improved social and economic conditions contributed to a narrowing of the achievement gap between minority and white students, and to some extent between students at different levels of economic advantage, between 1960 and the mid 1980s. To continue such improvement, despite recent reverses in social and economic trends, O'Day and Smith believe it is essential to have a common set of high-quality standards for curricular content and student performance. Establishing standards would provide direction for the system, for students in disadvantaged as well as advantaged schools. Coordinated policies would provide the resources and other supports necessary for all to have an equal opportunity to reach the standards. Comparisons of resources and practices that are strongly related to achievement of the standards—such as the quality and appropriateness of curricular materials and the adequacy of teacher preparation— would expose inequitable differences between schools, suggest directions for assistance to low-performing schools, and strengthen legal mechanisms to ensure equity. Finally, O'Day and Smith argue that equal opportunity is served when there is sufficient participation in defining standards and enough local flexibility to facilitate a curricular balance between the common culture and diverse perspectives of subgroups. If we had common challenging standards, policy support in the way of well-trained teachers and adequate materials, and accountability tied to achievement on the standards, schools would be pressured and supported in developing programs that maximize achievement for all students.

Chapter Nine is a summary. While this introduction has focused on differences among the chapters in emphasis and approach to coherence, the summary concerns the common threads that span the various contributions. The conclusion focuses on the feasibility and sustainability of coherent policies. It asks how to create and use a supportive environment for more coherent policymaking to sustain the complicated process of instructional change envisioned by these new policies. It is our hope that the chapters in this book will advance understanding about these issues and provide insight into the design of coherent policy.

Acknowledgments

These chapters were written as part of a research project conducted by the Consortium for Policy Research in Education (CPRE). CPRE is a unique consortium of six institutions— Rutgers, the State University of New Jersey; the University of Southern California; Harvard University; Michigan State University; Stanford University; and the University of Wisconsin, Madison. Funded by the U.S. Department of Education's Office of Educational Research and Improvement (OERI), the consortium operates two separate but interconnected centers — the Policy Center and the Finance Center.

The authors gratefully acknowledge the advice and critiques they received from one another, as well as from additional individuals noted in specific chapters. Margaret Goertz, a senior research fellow at CPRE, was helpful in initial discussions that shaped the chapters. Special thanks go to Stacy Gands for organizing the contributions and for overseeing the process of compiling the manuscript for this book.

New Brunswick, New Jersey   Susan H. Fuhrman
February 1993

References

The Business Roundtable. *The Nine Essential Components: Putting Policy into Practice.* New York: Business Roundtable, 1992.

Cohen, D. K. "Policy and Organization: The Impact on State and Federal Educational Policy in School Governance." *Harvard Educational Review,* 1982, *52*(4), 474–499.

Elmore, R. F. "Innovations in Education Policy." Paper presented at the Innovation in the Public Sector Conference at Duke University, Durham, N.C., May 3, 1991.

National Council on Educational Standards and Testing. *Raising Standards for American Education.* Washington, D.C.: National Council on Educational Standards and Testing, 1992.

National Governors' Association. *From Rhetoric to Action: State Progress in Restructuring the Education System.* Washington, D.C.: National Governors' Association, 1991.

Smith, M. S., and O'Day, J. A. "Systemic School Reform." In S. Fuhrman and B. Malen (eds.), *The Politics of Curriculum and Testing.* Bristol, Pa.: Falmer Press, 1991.

The Editor

Susan H. Fuhrman is a professor of education policy at Rutgers, the State University of New Jersey, and director of the Consortium for Policy Research in Education (CPRE). Fuhrman is the author of numerous articles, research reports, and monographs on education policy and finance. She is the co-editor of *The Politics of Curriculum and Testing: Yearbook of the Politics of Education Association, 1990,* and serves on the editorial board of the *Phi Delta Kappan.* She has served on numerous task forces, including the Standards Task Force of the National Council on Educational Standards and Testing and the New Jersey Task Force on Educational Assessment and Monitoring. Fuhrman was a consultant to the Ford Foundation's program on educational management and finance for ten years. Between 1986 and 1992 she served on the school board in Westfield, New Jersey.

The Contributors

W. Steven Barnett is associate professor of economics and policy in the Graduate School of Education at Rutgers, the State University of New Jersey, where he is also a senior research associate at the Consortium for Policy Research in Education, Eagleton Institute of Politics. His research interests include early childhood care and education policy, long-term effects of education on human development and well-being, and the economics of education.

William H. Clune is Voss-Bascom Professor of Law at the University of Wisconsin Law School, director of the Wisconsin research group of the Consortium for Policy Research in Education (CPRE), a member of the executive board and faculty of the La Follette Institute of Public Affairs at Wisconsin, and co-director of the Wisconsin Center for Educational Policy (WICEP). His past research on education policy has included school finance, school law, implementation, special education, and public employee interest arbitration. His present research with CPRE concerns the effects of graduation requirements and other student standards, school site autonomy, regulation of the curriculum, systemic education policy, and the relationship between school finance and student achievement. He co-directed a conference on educational decentralization and choice for the La Follette Institute.

David K. Cohen has been the Hannah Professor of Education and Social Policy at Michigan State University since 1986. Previously, he was professor of education and social policy at Harvard University. His current research interests lie in the relations between policy and practice, the politics of education, and the nature of teaching practice.

Richard F. Elmore is professor of education and chairman of the Department of Administration, Planning and Social Policy at the Graduate School of Education, Harvard University. He is also a senior research fellow of the Consortium for Policy Research in Education. His research focuses on state-local relations in education policy, school organization, and educational choice. He teaches regularly in programs for public sector executives and holds several government advisory positions.

Milbrey W. McLaughlin is professor of education and public policy at Stanford University and director of the Center for Research on the Context of Secondary School Teaching. McLaughlin's interests focus on policy implementation, contexts for teaching and learning, and educational settings for urban youth. Her recent books include *Contexts of Secondary School Teaching* (1990, with J. E. Talbert and N. Bascia); *Teachers' Cultures: Individual and Collective Identities* (in press, with J. Warren Little); *Teaching for Understanding: Challenges for Policy and Practice* (1993, with D. K. Cohen and J. E. Talbert), and *Building Identities for Inner-City Youth: Beyond Ethnicity and Gender* (in press, with S. Brice Heath).

Jennifer A. O'Day is a research associate with the Pew Forum for Education Reform at Stanford University. In the past few years, O'Day has co-authored several published papers and articles on systemic school reform, on nationalizing trends in U.S. education, on research and policies in teaching and teacher education, and on quality of educational opportunity. An experienced teacher, she has also worked as an administrator, curriculum and assessment developer, and teacher educator in the field of second language acquisition.

Arthur G. Powell served the National Association of Independent Schools (NAIS) in several research capacities between 1978 and 1992. He was director of the NAIS Commission on Educational Issues and executive director of the commission's largest project, a study of high schools (1981–1985). He was senior author of one of the three books that emerged from the project, *The Shopping Mall High School: Winners and Losers in the Educational Marketplace* (1985). As senior research associate at NAIS, he directed a study of American independent schools, of which this chapter is one part. Prior to his work on independent schools, he was associate dean for academic affairs at the Harvard Graduate School of Education and author of the historical study, *The Uncertain Profession: Harvard and the Search for Educational Authority* (1980).

Marshall S. Smith is professor of education and dean of the School of Education at Stanford University. Prior to coming to Stanford in 1986, he directed the Wisconsin Center for Education Research and was professor of educational policy studies and educational psychology at the University of Wisconsin, Madison. Smith has extensive experience with federal education policymaking and implementation as executive assistant and chief of staff to the secretary of education, assistant commissioner of education for policy studies, associate director of the National Institute of Education, and chair of the Standards Task Force of the National Council on Education Standards and Testing. He is now the chair of the Board on Testing and Assessment of the National Academy of Sciences and the convener of the Pew Forum for Education Reform.

James P. Spillane's main research activities are in the area of education policy and its relationship to practice. He is particularly interested in the role of local government agencies and personnel in mediating state- and national-level educational policy, and in cross-national educational policy and practice.

Spillane worked as a primary school teacher with the Irish Department of Education from 1985 to 1988. Since 1988 he has been a doctoral candidate at the College of Education, Michigan

State University, where he has worked on research projects for the Consortium for Policy Research in Education and the Center for the Study of the Context of Secondary School Teaching, as well as teaching undergraduate and graduate education courses.

Joan E. Talbert is a senior research scholar and associate director of the Center for Research on the Context of Secondary School Teaching at Stanford University. Her current research examines the effects of embedded organizational and sociocultural contexts of schooling on teachers' professional lives and practice. She has published articles on teachers' career patterns, school organization, and professional communities among secondary school teachers. Her recent publications include two edited books: *Teaching for Understanding: Challenges for Policy and Practice* (1993, with D. K. Cohen and M. W. McLaughlin) and *The Contexts of Teaching in Secondary Schools* (1990, with M. W. McLaughlin and N. Bascia).

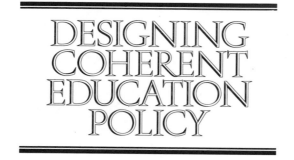

DESIGNING
COHERENT
EDUCATION
POLICY

1

The Politics of Coherence

Susan H. Fuhrman

The chapters in this book focus on the prospect of developing coordinated educational policies around ambitious outcome expectations, an approach a number of authors label "systemic reform." Many political observers greet this idea with strong skepticism. How can we expect such a rational approach — clear definition of student learning goals and the purposeful integration of key policies to support those goals — from a system that makes policies incrementally and in a disjointed fashion? (Lindblom, 1959; Wildavsky, 1974). Furthermore, the educational governance system is particularly disorganized. Education is funded and regulated by several levels of government, with multiple centers of authority at each level. Because each actor at each level has unique preferences, pressures, and timelines, coordinated policymaking would seem even harder to achieve in this policy area (Cohen, 1982). Even if an initial set of well-crafted and mutually reinforcing policies are enacted, one might expect that coherence would disintegrate over time as new policies are inevitably layered onto the system. After all, how can a policy process familiarly characterized by policy scholars as a "garbage can" (see Cohen, March, and Olsen's (1976) analysis of universities) produce anything resembling well-designed coherence?

This chapter explores the conditions under which we might expect coherent policymaking to occur and factors that

1

might enhance the political incentives for such policymaking. I begin by considering the idea of systemic reform from the standpoint of the political challenges it poses. I then evaluate the argument that these challenges reflect fundamental aspects of the American political system. I first consider the notion that only a fundamental redesign of the political system will create fertile ground for coherent policymaking and then reject that argument on several grounds. Finally, I explore opportunities for more coherent policymaking within the famework of our political structure.

Systemic School Reform and Politics

Systemic school reform, as explored in other chapters of this book, includes three major elements (Smith and O'Day, 1991; Consortium for Policy Research in Education, 1991). The first is the establishment of ambitious outcome expectations for all students, including specification of the knowledge and skills to be expected of every student. Standards would be set at a high level, requiring deep understanding of subject matter and sophisticated reasoning ability. The second is the coordination of key policies in support of the outcome expectations, which would be reflected in curriculum frameworks that lay out important topics and understandings. Student assessment, instructional materials, teacher licensing, and staff development would all be tied to the frameworks. In that manner, key policies would send coherent messages about instruction (see Cohen and Spillane, in this book). Third, the governance system would be restructured to support high achievement by according schools more flexibility in meeting the needs of their students. Higher levels of governance would focus on outcome definition and accountability and remove constraints on school practice. Schools would determine the instructional strategies most likely to foster student achievement of outcome goals.

All levels of governance—local school districts, states, and the federal government—might undertake outcome definition and coordination of key policy instruments. Presently many districts and states are making such efforts, and the governors and the administration have urged Congress to support a national-level standard-setting activity. Considerations about the politics of systemic reform are therefore relevant to several levels of government. However, my comments focus primarily on states, since they have both constitutional responsibility for education and the jurisdiction over both precollegiate and higher education necessary to achieve policy integration.

The approach suggested by systemic reform is relatively new in this country, where explicit consensus about outcomes has yet to be reached. In consequence, many individual schools aim for ambitious outcomes and are ultimately undermined by a system that fails to send clear signals in support of such learning (Smith and O'Day, 1991). But the idea of multiple policies coordinated around high-level expectations for student learning is embodied in the policy systems of many other industrialized nations (see Cohen and Spillane, in this book). In the few states that have embarked on this path, initial experience indicates that the new coordinated policies are exerting some positive leverage on classroom content (Marsh and Odden, 1991; Cohen, 1991). Furthermore, the idea has a strong rational appeal to it.

Systemic reform is built around two supremely logical notions: societal decision about outcome goals and coordination of important policy instruments.

Outcome Goals

The systemic reform strategy suggests that a policy decision be made at the state level about what society wants students to learn, departing from the current practice of leaving determination up to individual teachers and schools. At present schools and districts, more often than not, defer to textbook publishers' tables of contents for decisions about which topics to include in curricula and let standardized testing define the skills children should learn. Neither texts nor tests encourage a focus on high-level skills (Tyson-Bernstein, 1988; Fredericksen, 1984; Archbald and Newmann, 1988). In fact, in the absence of explicit consensus about outcomes, the system puts a de facto emphasis on low-level skills that are familiar and relatively easy to teach (Smith and O'Day, 1991). Furthermore, because clear direction is lacking, the system has no authentic means of judging its progress. Instead of deciding what level of performance students should attain and then judging the success of individuals, schools, and systems against that standard, we have relied on relative measures of performance. Standardized testing indicates how many are above and below average but not whether the average is good or what level of performance would be worth striving for. In addition, since the system lacks substantive goals, there is little substance in resource allocation decisions (Odden, 1991). Formulas or traditional expenditure patterns typically drive the allocation of spending increases and cuts, rather than decisions about how money should be used. The system has not yet determined how to use resources effectively because it has not defined effectiveness in education.

Policymakers have avoided central (for example, state-level) determination of outcome expectations by summoning up the hallowed educational tradition of local control. But in fact, deep conflicts over the purposes of education have made policymakers wary of opening goal discussions (Tyack, 1976, 1992). In our increasingly diverse society, there are many differences of opinion about what should constitute a core body of content learned by all students. Should it focus mainly on Western civilization; pay equal homage to the various histories, heroes, and heroines; permit choices about focusing on particular cultures, depending on location? By letting content expectations devolve to the school, policymakers can evade such difficult decisions. Furthermore, if, as some analysts assert, society's interest in education lies primarily in credentialing in a way that preserves economic and social inequity, there is little reason to bother with content expectations. (See, for example, Bowles and Gintis, 1976.) Others argue that since knowledge is tentative and constructed by individuals in specific contexts, it would be counterproductive to specify knowledge expectations for an entire society, no matter how worthy the expectations.

For the most part, educators have not challenged the status quo, the absence of policy-level outcome expectations. In fact, many have argued strongly against "policy interference" of this nature in the past (for example, Wise, 1979; McNeil, 1986). They are highly skeptical that policymakers can develop ambitious and challenging standards with respect to student achievement. The purpose of state-level standards or outcome expectations would be to spur the system, to set a goal toward which all students would aspire; yet politically determined standards are typically not challenging but minimal in nature.

Politicians set standards at levels fairly readily achieved with current capacity. When they are set too high, the backlash from implementors, who feel unfairly held to an impossible-to-attain standard, can be politically intolerable. Also, enforcing high standards would likely surpass the capacity of most regulatory bodies (McDonnell and Elmore, 1987). Furthermore, high standards may be met by demands for additional resources by those expected to meet the standards, making politicians apprehensive about launching the cycle.

In education, there are additional reasons to expect standards to be set at a minimal level. Since content or outcome expectations typically have been left up to individual schools and teachers, policymakers have focused educational standards on school processes and practices such as class size or course offerings. Many local educators, buoyed by the findings of education research that process requirements can interfere with the school-level discretion necessary for excellent practice, complain that such standards are intrusive. Policymakers have tried to minimize intrusion by setting process requirements at levels already exceeded by most districts.

Believing that government is incapable of making enlightened education policy, some educators have foresworn reform efforts that rely on policy and instead pin hopes for educational improvement on individual school efforts (Cuban, 1984). Mistrust of policymakers is balanced by belief in school-level personnel. Evidence from years of research on effective, improving, and restructured schools suggests that individual schools can develop highly stimulating learning environments without help from, or even in spite of, policy efforts (Cohen, 1983; Purkey and Smith, 1983; Elmore, 1990b). The best policy can do, many reformers argue, is to get out of the way, to remove the barriers to school excellence posed by excess process regulation. (See the request for proposals, New American Schools Development Corporation, for this view of policy and school improvement.) Some go further. Chubb and Moe (1990) argue that removing policy barriers is not sufficient; instead, the policy system, which they view as incapable of refraining from interference, must be removed from influencing schooling entirely. They propose market control as a substitute.

Of course, neither markets nor radical restructuring of the public system are likely to eliminate the need for regulation and policy, for equity reasons as well as others (Elmore, 1991b; Consortium for Policy Research in Education, 1992). More important than the issue of whether it would be feasible to dispense with policy, however, is the question of whether writing off policy is desirable. It is highly unlikely that a school-by-school approach to reform will lead to improvement in all 100,000 American schools. Without policy system support for ambitious outcomes, school-level efforts are rarely sustained. Changes in individual schools rarely spread to others (Elmore, 1991b). In addition, individual school reform comes last to the least advantaged schools, where time and resources are lacking. (See O'Day and Smith in this book.) To achieve improvement throughout the system in an equitable manner, therefore, requires policy support.

Finding a way to make policy leadership possible, to break the patterns of avoidance of goal consensus and the focus on minimal standards, becomes then a question of utmost importance for the entire educational system. Educators may believe it is in their self-interest to keep policymakers out of educational business, but what is truly in their self-interest is to support a conception of policy that would undergird rather than undermine school-based improvement. The alternatives may be grim: a few excellent schools amidst a failing system or even abandonment of the public system and the privatization of schooling.

Coordinated Policies

The systemic reform strategy also proposes that policies should be aligned with outcome expectations. It suggests departing from the current practice of fashioning a separate program for each educational problem because the individual projects, no matter how uniquely worthy, seldom reinforce one another and frequently send different, even conflicting, messages to schools. Education policy is characterized by contradiction and ambiguity. For example, most current teacher certification and evaluation requirements stress generic skills and not ability to teach the subject matter content students must know. Programs for students with special needs pull them away from the mainstream curriculum, fragmenting not only their education but the work of teachers and administrators. Staff development frequently consists of one-shot workshops on "hot" topics that are unrelated to each other or to the fundamental instructional and pedagogical issues teachers face daily.

The rationality of integrated policy based on deliberate goals is at once the appeal and the Achilles heel of systemic reform. The elements of consensual decision and policy coordination seem beyond the capacity of our political system. In fact, some argue that as our political system functions it deliberately thwarts decisiveness and coordination.

For politicians to lead consensus about outcomes and develop coordinated policy, they would have to favor agreement over unique positioning; open up deep value issues, for example, about multiculturalism in education, generally left hidden; refrain from making new policies that change direction and fashioning discrete projects that benefit key constituencies; take a long-term perspective that allows time for policies to exert effects before they are evaluated or changed; invest in capacity building for schools and teachers despite the absence of immediate, visible payoff from such investment; and work closely with education policymakers across branches and levels of government and sectors of education (Fuhrman, 1990; Fuhrman and Elmore, 1990a; McDonnell and Elmore, 1987). Admirable attributes such as restraint and patience are thought to be in short supply among political leaders, not because of any innate shortcomings but because the system provides incentives for opposing traits. The system attracts and rewards action, not restraint, and eagerness, not patience.

System Characteristics and Policymaking

At least four characteristics of the political system relate to fragmented policymaking: the segmented organizational structure;
the emphasis on elections; policy overload; and specialization.
The first is structural; the second is procedural; the third and
fourth have both structural and procedural aspects and are
closely intertwined with each other and with the first two aspects.

A Fragmented System

The fragmentation of our political system makes it very difficult
for policymakers to coordinate with one another or to develop
consensus across all levels. Separate branches of government
that check and balance one another exist at each level, each operating according to its own schedules and rules, its members
swayed by incentives related to institutional membership and
maintenance rather than the functioning of the entire system.
Opportunities to work with policymakers in other institutions
do not naturally occur or may require facilitation through the
creation of new institutions, further increasing the structural
complexity. Educational governance is particularly complex. Not
only are three levels of government (federal, state, and local)
making education policy but also separate structures at each level
that date from the Progressive era emphasize isolating education from partisan politics. So at the state level, both state legislatures and state boards perform legislative duties, and at the
local level, both municipalities and school districts influence
school governance and funding.

　　　The fragmentation by branches of government was a
deliberate invention of founders anxious to escape the tyranny
that had existed under English rule and prevent any aggrega-
tion of power, even democratically derived power. The ironies
resulting from such deliberate thwarting of coordination abound.
When institutions are not responsive (at least in part because
fragmentation impedes coordinated solutions to problems),
popular movements lead to new institutions that bypass the im-
penetrable structures. The new structures never go away but

add, like fossil layers, to the system's strata, increasing its fragmentation and, in turn, its unresponsiveness (Morone, 1990).
The fragmentation, reflecting pessimistic distrust of both people and government, frustrates but does not extinguish a con-
tinual popular yearning to use policy to solve societal problems,
reflecting a fundamentally optimistic view of government ruled
by people (Cohen, 1991).

Focus on Elections

A second characteristic of our system that thwarts rational policymaking is the emphasis on campaigning and election. The
"electoral connection," a priority on reelection above policy or
institutional improvement goals, is probably most apparent in
Congress where livelihood and career depend on staying in
(Mayhew, 1974; Fenno, 1973). However, as state legislatures
are in session longer and thus have more full-time, career politicians, and as the weakening of political parties makes elections more candidate centered, "the permanent campaign" is also
a characteristic of most state houses (Salmore and Salmore, 1990;
Rosenthal, 1989).

Although the phenomenon of emphasis on election is most
applicable to legislatures, especially lower houses where two-
year terms mean literally constant campaigns, executive-branch
elected officials face similar imperatives. Career politicians must
be reelected to keep their jobs and can no longer depend on parties, which have progressively lost strength in the face of a more
educated electorate, technologically sophisticated campaigns,
government largesse that makes machines redundant, increasing reliance on primaries for nominee selection, reform, and
reapportionment. Instead, candidates must make their own impressions on voters, using their policy and institutional roles in
office.

The priority put on elections has numerous consequences
for democratic governance. One frequently discussed is the campaign finance issue — as elections focus on the individual candidate's message and as the cost of getting that message across
rises, especially through media, candidates spend more time

raising money. The more money needed, and the more wide-ranging the fundraising efforts, the more the risk of conflicts of interest. Just as serious are the "electoral connection's" effects on policymaking and policy, which fall into three general categories.

Because impressions on constituents take priority, politicians seek ways to distinguish themselves from their colleagues rather than avenues to cooperate in group decisions. They deal in what Mayhew (1974, pp. 54–59) calls "particularized benefits," pork barrel projects or other "goodies" that particularly help their own constituencies and are clearly traceable to their originators, unique, discrete policies to which they can attach their name. Building on or fine-tuning an existing policy area brings less credit than doing something new and more visible. Taking a position is more important than resolving a problem (Mayhew, 1974) so they spend more energy getting on the record than in building coalitions and mobilizing support.

A second consequence of the preeminence of elections is the circumvention of controversial and difficult issues that upset elements of the electorate. Avoidance can take many forms, including deferring decisions to initiative and referendum, enacting vague legislation so that hard decisions are passed along to implementing bureaucrats, and transforming zero-sum or redistributive issues into unnecessarily expensive programs in which no one loses (Salmore and Salmore, 1990). The classic education policy example is the "hold harmless" approach to school finance reform. Equalization for poorer districts is generally attempted through leveling up with additional state aid. The alternative, removing aid from wealthier districts — or, even more extreme, recapturing some of the tax base of wealthier districts — is too politically difficult in most states. Only in the very recent past has severe state fiscal crisis pressured politicians to risk more redistributive approaches when courts mandate equalization. However, the politics of redistribution have been so acrimonious in Texas and New Jersey that leaders in other states may continue to seek non-zero-sum resolutions. Less than complete equity may result, but the damage to political careers may be contained. (See Clune, 1992, and Yudof, 1991, for discussions of "substantial equity" approaches.)

Finally, because of the emphasis on election, politicians are attracted to the type of policies that are most easily used as campaign issues: policies with immediate effects and clear benefits ("sound bites") are simpler to explain than longer-term efforts with more diverse or remote benefits. Subtlety loses out to flashiness; careful developmental efforts lose out to quick pushes that have less chance of success because the developmental groundwork was lacking.

Policy Overload

A third characteristic of the system that thwarts coordination is the overload of policy issues. As more and more areas of life become subject to governmental action, policymaking and implementing institutions become busier and more pressured. Issues — clean air and water are good examples — that were not even on the government's agenda as recently as a quarter century ago are now key subjects for debate and decision. Within education, over the last decade most states made policy on a number of important education issues — such as teacher salaries or the nature of student assessment — for the first time, subjects that had generally been left to local educators in the past. For example, although only a handful of states concerned themselves with teacher salaries prior to 1980, by 1986 thirty states had mandated minimum salaries (Darling-Hammond and Berry, 1988). During the 1984–1990 period, many states expanded the scope of or changed the design of their testing programs. By 1990, forty-seven states tested or required districts to test elementary and secondary students (Coley and Goertz, 1990).

Although states expanded their policy purview, local districts did not constrict their own activities in response. There was no zero sum game. Local districts made more policy as well (Fuhrman and Elmore, 1990b). More policy led to more policy. When so much is on the plate, each item gets less attention, and the sheer volume increases the likelihood that policies will tumble out, without any necessary connection to a long-range strategy or to one another. The expanding agenda is a procedural issue, but it has structural implications. One way to deal with the increase is to create new entities; hence, new regulatory bodies are established for environmental issues and states create boards and task forces for new education issues.

Specialization

A traditional strategy for managing the complexity that comes with too much work is specialization: the fourth system characteristic that promotes policy fragmentation. It reflects not only the expansion of the governmental role but also the emphasis on election. Specialization creates more arenas in which politicians can claim credit and impress voters. Consequently, legislative committees and subcommittees multiply and narrow their jurisdictions; special boards and commissions are created; new agencies are established. For example, in sixteen states, at least one legislative chamber has separate committees for higher education and for elementary and secondary education, and in five of those states, each house has separate committees for the levels of education. Constituencies reflect the jurisdictional splintering and specialize in the work of particular bodies. Whether legislative or administrative in origin, experts with increasingly narrow perspectives craft policies. Experts in a particular subfield have few incentives to consider interaction with policies in other specialized subfields or effects on other aspects of a policy area. Although bills often contain multiple provisions crossing many policy subareas, they are typically omnibus in nature, containing collections of discrete programs rather than integrated approaches to policy problems. Omnibus bills generally permit each collection of legislative specialists to make its impression on the electorate; unlike integrated approaches, such bills do not require trade-offs that allow some to get credit at others' expense.

The result of these factors is that a system designed to disperse power has evolved to further exacerbate the splintering. As parties weakened in the postwar era, so did much of the glue that bridged structural segmentation. A growing emphasis on election, an increasing policy burden, and the specialization that accompanies both have contributed to policymaking that focuses on narrow issue dimensions, avoids controversy, and attracts attention. It is not surprising that education policy, like other policy areas, is characterized by magic bullets rather than comprehensive strategies.

Systemic Reform Within the Current Political System

Daunted by the manner in which the system promotes fragmentation, some observers have relinquished ideals of coherent policymaking, taking on the comfortable cloak of skepticism many policy analysts come to wear. To avoid disappointment, they expect little and, forsaking dreams of societal improvement through policy, they set their sights low. They hope that the incremental, meager accomplishments dripping from a system they see as hopelessly muddled will at least, in the words of Hippocrates, "do no harm." Other reformers are much more ambitious. Equally dubious about the policymaking prospects of our political system, they turn not to despair but to invention and advocate redesigning our political system to make it less fragmented, more efficient.

Proposals for radical political reform take several forms. From time to time, reformers have looked wistfully at the parliamentary models of other democracies, which appear to offer greater coordination and accountability through the union of the legislative and executive branches. Although few would entirely abandon our founding principles, a number of approaches for greater interbranch coordination have been suggested. For example, our system could be modified to make House of Representative terms coterminous with presidential terms and place members on the same ticket with the president and vice president, or the president could select part or all of his cabinet from Congress (Cutler, 1980). Counterpart reform notions could be fashioned at the state level. In another approach to reform, some commentators have urged longer terms for House members and state legislators, arguing that it is the short term that exacerbates the emphasis on election (Sundquist, 1984; Rosenthal, 1989).

The current incarnation of radical reform is the movement to limit the terms of state legislators and members of Congress. Only three states, California, Colorado, and Washington, have imposed term limits as of this writing, but forty-five states considered such legislation in 1991. In 1992, term limitation appeared on the ballots of fourteen states (Kurtz, 1992). Reformers assert that limiting the number of elections in which incumbents are eligible will increase turnover, open up opportunities for women and underrepresented minorities, and provide pools of experienced politicians for other electoral offices. Term limits would improve policymaking, providing a periodic influx of fresh ideas and reducing the focus on pleasing narrow constituencies that comes with the constant quest for reelection. Reformers would break the electoral connection by eliminating the possibility that legislative service could become a career. Without the connection between office and livelihood, it is argued, politicians have more incentive to focus on policy accomplishment rather than credit claiming.

Each proposal for radical reform can be met by counterarguments suggesting that the link between such reforms and more logical policymaking is less than certain. Parliamentary systems may seem less messy and less likely to be gridlocked, yet a look at Great Britain indicates that party changes can bring dramatic policy reversals that undermine stability (Mann and Orenstein, 1981). The idea of lengthening House terms seems appealing until one looks at the Senate, which, according to columnist Al Hunt, offers "one clear refutation of the premise that longer terms produce a more thoughtful, farsighted legislative body" (1992, p. 273). Term limitation may detract from, not add to, the ability of legislators to reach consensus and develop consistent policy. For example, some argue that consensus building would suffer through the further weakening of legislative leadership, already a casualty of the decline of parties. Term limits would, it is asserted, undermine leadership strength by creating pressure for rotating leadership among short-termers all wanting a chance at a position and by curtailing the value of a remaining remnant of leadership power, control over legislative campaign fundraising (Rosenthal, 1989). Many worry that term limits would eliminate institutional memory, making the ideal of consistent policymaking over time patently unattainable. Either members would approach policy problems entirely de novo, exacerbating the project mentality that currently characterizes much policymaking, or they would defer to the greater experience of staffers and lobbyists, increasing the sway of nonelected officials at the expense of the people's representatives.

Concerns about the effects of radical reforms on the representativeness of government constitute a second major category of objections to the notion of political restructuring. No matter how uncoordinated, piecemeal, fragmented, project centered, and irrational our political system is, it is a very responsive system. The emphasis on reelection means that voters are important. Observers of the term limitation movement note that Costa Rican legislators, limited to only one four-year term, do virtually no casework on behalf of constituents (Kurtz, 1992). In contrast, American congressmen pay considerable attention to constituent service and thus, although they make policy less than neatly, they also hear public opinion, arguably a more important trait. As Mayhew (1974) asserts, "At voicing opinions held by significant numbers of voters back in the constituencies, the United States Congress is extraordinarily effective" (p. 106). Similarly, separation of powers may lead to stalemate when the president and Congress stand off, but the system does provide a variety of paths the expression of opinion. Mann and Orenstein (1981) say that, because of separation of powers, "many constituencies have a voice — and the outcomes, more often than not, are the better for it."

A third ground on which to reject the notion of radical reform rests on the "if it ain't broke, don't fix it" theory. In addition to being responsive, and flexible and resilient enough to see the nation through 200 years of history, the American political system is not so hostile to logical ideas that they never prevail. Despite the fragmentation and the muddle, logical solutions to policy problems are crafted, reforms occur, nonincremental change is made. For example, at the national level, Polsby (1990) identifies three periods of intense congressional activity over the last fifty years, periods when Congress "focuses its energies effectively, and undertakes policy innovation" (p. 30). He includes the New Deal (1933–1936), the creation of wartime agencies in Washington between 1939 and 1946, and the

New Frontier–Great Society (1963–1969). Although many years of stalemate fell in between, during these spurts of policymaking the Congress, the institution most criticized for overemphasis on elections and for fragmentation, showed "high productivity and strong coordination" (p. 29).

The power of ideas to influence the political process may be on the increase. To the extent that policymaking revolves around intellectual argument as opposed to constituency pleasing, it can be argued that the process is becoming more rational despite appearances to the contrary. It may be that as parties continue to weaken and as fragmentation related to candidate-centered politics and specialization increases, ideas become more important as a source of cohesion or glue. Ideas form a rallying point, a foundation for the formation of coalitions, one of the few remaining bases for unified action. Also, as policymaking becomes more complex and encompasses more technical and specific areas, the role played by experts who generate policy ideas increases.

Analysts are increasingly likely to attribute policy accomplishments to the strength of argument. For example, King (1990) argues that the "highly non-incremental lurches forward in public policy in the 1970s and 1980s," such as airline deregulation, were, in large measure, due to the climate of opinion, to the importance of ideas "whose time has come" (pp. 299–301). "Substantive policy information," in Sabatier's (1991) words, typically enlightens policy discussion, gradually changing decision makers' views of problems and solutions (Weiss, 1977; Lindblom and Cohen, 1979) and also directly contributing to policy decision (Derthick and Quirk, 1985). Those who trade most in policy ideas — policy professionals, specialists, or entrepreneurs — are influential in framing alternatives, latching solutions to problems, and identifying windows for action (Kingdon, 1984), although crises, dramatic changes in indicators, symbolic events, and the like can transform issues into problems waiting for solutions. Also, experts forge links across levels of government; they interact with people with shared expertise in specialized areas of policy. These "issue-skilled" individuals, inside and outside of government, share substantive knowledge in loose networks that help to overcome fragmentation (Heclo, 1978). Ironically, however, the very specialization that gives value to expert knowledge exacerbates the fragmentation that expert knowledge helps alleviate.

Evidence of the influence of ideas may be found in the increasing willingness of policymaker associations to traffic in them. Associations support the spread of policy ideas from state to state and among levels of government, giving them more airtime, exposure, and sway. During the education reform movement of the 1980s, specific reform ideas spread with unprecedented rapidity. For example, forty-one states increased high school graduation requirements between 1983 and 1985, a diffusion rate more than four times the historical rate for state policies without specific federal impetus. The uniformity in reform approach and the rapidity of spread reflects, in large measure, the work of national organizations that represent state policymakers. The Education Commission of the States (ECS), the National Governors' Association (NGA), and the National Conference of State Legislatures (NCSL) recommended specific policy directions, translated research, and provided technical assistance (McDonnell and Fuhrman, 1985).

For a number of general state government policymaker associations, a focus on substantive state-level policy solutions is relatively new. For example, the NGA used to concentrate on lobbying the federal government on behalf of states. In the 1970s it shifted toward improving governors' performance through publications and workshops on the process of governing. In the late 1970s, increasingly dissatisfied with relying on Washington for solutions to state problems, a number of governors began pressing the NGA for more information about state-based initiatives. Education was the first such issue to which the association turned its attention. In 1985, NGA chairman Lamar Alexander, who later became President Bush's secretary of education, convened a task force of all the governors to address education reform. His effort was the first NGA study to involve all fifty governors; education reform, by that time surrounded by growing urgency, was a popular choice (Fuhrman and Elmore, 1990a).

Association focus on policy ideas both reflects and reinforces the importance of ideas in the political process. The organizations would not invest significant resources in research, publication, networking, and technical assistance on the substance of important policy issues if their members did not view such information as increasingly necessary. In turn, by focusing on information dissemination of this type, the associations underline the fact that political skills can no longer suffice. Policymakers need ideas and substantive know-how as well.

Examples of coordinated policymaking offer a final answer to the hypothetical argument that radical political reform must precede rational policy reform. Systemic education reform efforts in a number of states indicate that challenging outcomes and coherent policymaking are possible without fundamental political reform. California, the nation's most diverse state, has over the last several years reached consensus on what should be taught in key subject areas. The resulting curriculum frameworks are the anchor to which student assessment, instructional materials adoption, and staff development are tied in an integrated fashion. Kentucky, given a clean slate by a court decision that invalidated the state's current education system, designed an education system based on challenging outcome expectations and linked accountability through new assessments of the outcome expectations. Although the court mandate greatly facilitated a systemic redesign by removing the entrenched status quo, the political system that produced a coherent and ambitious educational reform was not itself redesigned. It could have produced a piecemeal set of replacement reforms and structures, but it did not. Other states are moving on similar paths, without court rulings of the Kentucky variety. Arizona and Vermont are developing new assessment linked to ambitious student expectations; South Carolina is producing sophisticated curriculum frameworks around which to coordinate other state policies; Arkansas passed legislation calling for the development of standards and the integration of state policies in support of the standards. Almost all the states have applied to the National Science Foundation's Statewide Systemic Initiatives Program for support, to be matched by state dollars, to coordinate policies around ambitious goals in math and science. Recent state efforts bear watching to see if they will be sustained by the next set of leaders and those that follow them. But their very existence indicates that coherent policymaking of the type explored in this book is politically feasible within the current system. (See Levinson and Massell, 1992, for a review of these policy efforts.)

Radical political reform is neither desirable nor necessary as a precursor to more coherent policy development. Fundamental political reform proposals have uncertain effects and may undercut the greatest strength of our system, its responsiveness to the electorate. Furthermore, policy ideas — even highly rational ones — are enacted despite the system's fragmentation and irrationality. In fact, as power becomes increasingly dispersed, ideas exert increasing influence, particularly ideas that can bridge varied constituencies and offer some cohesion to the system. Systemic school reform may be the type of policy approach that forges links among constituencies and factions, an idea that will be explored in the following section. Even though the rationality of coherent policy seems at odds with American politics, recent policy efforts in several states offer existing proof of coordinated education policymaking in support of ambitious outcomes.

Opportunities for More Coherent Policymaking

If political reform is not the route to systemic school reform, do opportunities exist within our political system to foster more coherent policymaking? Since recent activities in a number of states suggest that policymakers can establish ambitious goals and reinforce them with coordinated policies, it is worth asking what factors contribute to these efforts and what forces promote them. Pending further study of the politics of reform efforts, it appears that strong leadership around a clear vision of reform, processes that promote public and professional involvement, and the examples of other states, which in turn are publicized by national groups and policymaker associations, are important in the development of systemic reform strategies (Fuhrman and Massell, 1992; Massell, 1992; Levinson and Massell, 1992). In addition, several other forces enhance the political chances of systemic reform. First, larger developments in the culture surround and support coherent policy, improving the destiny of policy efforts. Second, systemic reform efforts are prompting policymakers to experiment with new structures, which in turn offer an avenue for the maintenance of coherent reform over time. Third, systemic reform strategies speak to the strategic interests of educators and education policymakers, in enlarging support for education and in finding a way to promote common ground.

The first aspect of the current political scene that appears supportive of systemic reforms is pressure in the larger culture for more ambitious outcomes. The policy efforts to set outcomes and reinforce them with integrated instruments are only a portion of the movement toward upgraded instruction. The movement will proceed, influencing schools in states that never achieve more coherent policy and reinforcing the policy efforts in states that do.

For example, disciplinary associations of teachers have begun to reach consensus on challenging student outcomes. The National Council of Teachers of Mathematics (NCTM) began such an effort in the mid 1980s. By 1989, when its *Curriculum and Evaluation Standards* were published, other associations had begun to emulate them. The National Science Teachers Association is working with the American Association for the Advancement of Science and the National Academy of Sciences to do the same thing for science. Similar efforts are under way in history, geography, and English/language arts. These activities are influencing textbook publishers, testing efforts (such as the National Assessment of Educational Progress), and local districts. All over the nation, schools are said to be basing their mathematics curriculum on NCTM, in states that have formal curriculum frameworks embodying the NCTM standards and in those that do not (Hayes, 1992). Similarly, the NCTM's professional standards for teachers might well shape preservice and inservice education efforts, whether or not states act deliberately through licensing or staff development to reinforce NCTM's approach. Forty-one states are reporting changes in teacher preparation to coordinate with NCTM's recommendations (Ravitch, 1992). Furthermore, professional associations are not alone in deciding that it is time for societal definition of what students should know and be able to do. Business leaders have participated in the Secretary's Commission on Achieving Necessary Skills (SCANS), established by the labor department to determine the competencies necessary for the world of work.

If these nongovernmental efforts continue, they will provide support for the notion of challenging, communally identified outcomes. Surrounded by such broad, societal backing, policy efforts to establish and reinforce such outcomes take on increased authority. Broader support can nurture and buffer fragile political efforts that try to bridge traditional divisions and overcome short-term blinders in service of coherent policymaking. Equally important, policy need not carry the whole weight of reform but can provide leverage for professional efforts and make important marginal contributions. The political challenges facing systemic reform policies are still daunting, but working on them means joining an already established tide of educational reform, rather than fighting the current.

A second promising factor is state experimentation with ways to bridge fragmentation as they develop systemic reform strategies. Several states established broad-based processes to consult with the public and professionals on the development of standards for student learning. Vermont presented local forums; Kentucky used task forces and telephone surveys; South Carolina established a large, continuing curriculum congress (Massell, 1992). Texas created a Committee on Student Learning that represents higher education leadership, elementary and secondary education leadership, and political leaders. Kentucky's reform legislation vests oversight responsibility in a new Office of Accountability. Its placement in the Legislative Research Commission serves to cement legislative commitment to the reform act; legislators become the keepers of the act, charged with monitoring and fine-tuning it, and are less likely than otherwise to go off in new directions. Such efforts suggest that states might explore structural change as an approach to maintaining more coordinated policymaking over time.

Growing governmental specialization means that the arenas for policy consideration are increasingly narrow. The constituencies that form around narrow jurisdictions have limited

horizons. In turn, the policymaker seeking to please such interests, to provide them benefits, is more inclined to fashion discrete projects than to seek interaction across specific areas of
policy. For example, a legislator serving on an elementary and
secondary education committee is likely to define her constituency in terms of voters in her district and elementary and secondary education interest groups. Her legislative program is
primarily designed to please them, not to integrate with other
areas of state policy. Recognizing that her colleagues on other
committees have similar needs, she defers to their expertise in
their special areas just as they defer to her on K–12 issues.
Although all policy areas feed off the same budget and the appropriations process forces trade-offs, substantive integration
across committees is rare.

Broader policy arenas can be created by consolidating the
structure or work of existing entities. Elementary and secondary education committees and higher education committees can
merge; corresponding boards of education can also be unified.
Short of merger, opportunities might be found for these bodies
to hold joint meetings and hearings on a regular basis. Similarly, agencies and committees dealing with education and other
social service areas can review their jurisdictions to see how coordination can be improved (Kirst, 1992). Agencies might examine their structures to alleviate a project focus, including in their
review divisions built around programs for special-need students.
Seeking to assure that such programs serve the targeted populations and to keep funding streams clear, administrators at all
levels of government have segregated the management of these
programs. The result is more coordination among program
officials, such as special education directors, across levels of
government than among educators, general, and special education, at any one level of government (Meyer, 1979). Reor-
ganization supportive of integrated policy might group agency
specialists around key functions (such as research or technical
assistance) that cross programs.

New structures can also be considered. South Carolina's
1984 Education Improvement Act (EIA) created a number of
oversight entities: a Division of Public Accountability in the state

agency to report on reform effects, a Select Education Committee of key political leaders to oversee implementation, and a Business-Education Subcommittee. The latter, composed of twenty members — ten from the business community, six from education, and four from the legislature — includes many individuals who were prominent in shaping and selling the EIA. The subcommittee's charge is to monitor reform and suggest recommendations, including modifications to EIA over time.

The annual reports and the deliberations of the South Carolina bodies have kept public attention focused on reform. Citizens were regularly informed of implementation progress and effects and were continually reminded that the reforms would take time to bear full fruit. Policymakers showed their dedication to reform by serving on EIA oversight committees and commenting on the results shown in the mandated reports. As a consequence, no pressure was brought to follow EIA with other education reforms within its first five years of implementation. Instead, EIA was given time to work and its direction was maintained. South Carolina did not experience the shifts in emphasis and proliferation of projects that occurred in other states during the 1980s.

The South Carolina Business-Education Subcommittee is a particularly interesting structure because it represents a variety of key constituencies and consequently provides a forum for reaching consensus on policy directions, for negotiation across interests, before the recommendations enter the political arena. For example, South Carolina's 1989 reform legislation, Target 2000, which moves from EIA's focus on basic skills and mandates to stress more higher-order thinking skills and school flexibility, reflects committee deliberations over a long period of time on the accomplishments and shortcomings of EIA. The subcommittee functions much like task forces used by political leaders to shape important policy directions; it hears from educators and the public, develops specific recommendations, seeks compromise through trade-offs, balances the views of key interests in a way that leads to consensus, and builds support for the resulting policy. The difference is that the subcommittee is not ad hoc in the manner of task forces; it is a standing forum that functions as a permanent arena for consensus prior to the deliberation of political bodies. And unlike the political bodies to which its suggestions go, the subcommittee is likely to seek broad-based solutions that coordinate across specific interests. It is neither driven by electoral politics nor responsive to narrow constituencies.

Transposing the idea of a forum for coherence and consensus to the current discussion of systemic reform suggests an entity that includes teachers, university experts, parents, administrators, business and political leaders — all the constituencies interested in improving student achievement. States that are establishing broad-based, continuing curriculum/assessment committees appear to be moving in such a direction. Whether these entities are able to reach consensus about outcomes and protect the coherence of their approach over time will probably depend on a number of factors. To the extent that they include political leaders in their deliberations, their suggestions probably have a better chance of surviving through formal authorizing and appropriations processes. To the extent that they include practitioners, their decisions are more likely to reflect the realities of teaching and learning and enlist the support of teachers. If such bodies are to promote coherence, they need broad jurisdiction. For example, beyond the development of content expectations within subjects, they might consider the inter- and cross-disciplinary implications of subject matter experts' recommendations. Their deliberations might also encompass the array of policies that should be aligned in support of outcome recommendations.

Whether such structures are constituted as part of government or are somewhat independent is probably less important than their membership and scope of concern. Recommendations that need formal policy endorsement can be submitted to appropriate bodies subsequent to group deliberations. But whether embedded in policy or not, the groups' recommendations on content standards, teacher professional development, assessment strategies, and the like would take force from the expertise and representativeness of the membership. The group would be a vehicle for expression of respected opinion and for buy-in by key constituencies. In effect, the standards would influence educators much as design standards influence engineers; they would carry the "best practice" seal of approval granted by professional leaders.[1]

Such a group would not only set standards but also refine them over time, providing a mechanism for ensuring the incorporation of new knowledge and for adjusting to feedback provided by experience. With such flexibility in mind, it might be advantageous to avoid codifying standards by formal enactment but to rely instead on the continuing authority of a well-constituted and legitimate standards entity.

The National Education Goals Panel and its spinoff council on standards and testing has recommended that such an entity be established at the national level. The National Education Standards and Assessments Council, representing public officials, educators, and the general public, would "establish guidelines for standards-setting and assessment development and general criteria to determine the appropriateness of standards and assessments recommended" (National Council on Education Standards and Testing, 1992, p. 36). Because it is important to distinguish "national" efforts from "federal" activities, the new council should have as much independence from government as possible. Even where independence is not that critical an issue — for example, at the state level where there is no lurking specter of federal control to quash — it might be desirable to differentiate such an entity from governmental agencies. In maintaining distance from any one agency, the entity might exert more influence over various branches and agencies.

If consensus-reaching structures such as the new national council are to function, they must find grounds for reaching agreement. Systemic reform strategies may have the kind of political appeal necessary to bring together various interests and policymakers. First, they have strategic appeal to both professionals and education policymakers. State-level determination of outcome expectations would be a significant communal exercise, in which professionals and other educational interests would likely play a major role, as they certainly have in the states that have taken the lead in systemic reform approaches (Massell,

1992). Forging consensus around goals and establishing consistent policy direction would be the major policy game, one which would continue over time if content standards are to be refined and updated. The decisions about direction and reinforcing policies theoretically could exert much more influence over education than any other educational policy heretofore, since any single education policy in the past has most likely been contradicted or undercut by others. Should education interests concentrate their energies on these major decisions, they potentially could gain significant influence over the goals and nature of educational activities.

Determination of direction for education serves not just to orient policies but also to set priorities for the allocation of resources (National Council on Education Standards and Testing, 1992). Consensus about challenging education goals would clarify the need for educational spending, as opposed to spending on other services, and provide a sounder basis for assuring that all students in districts of varying wealth have equal opportunity to learn. The process of reaching consensus on goals or outcomes should include public participation that would serve to build public and political support for education spending. Support would not need to be rebuilt with every election or policy thrust. Consensus reframes the problem from one of generating new support to one of maintaining support for an agreed-upon direction. There would also be more faith in accountability built around outcome goal consensus than in current accountability systems that compare schools to one another rather than to a standard representing good schooling, bringing greater assurance that schools would be held accountable for using dollars wisely. This focus on outcomes rather than process appeals to both policymakers concerned about accountability and to practitioners who want to keep policymakers out of practice decisions.

Education is the largest single item in increasingly hardpressed state budgets, so the increased public support and clarity about what is being supported should benefit educational interests at budget time. Organizations would be better able to argue for additional support for education without the traditional charge of self-interest. This would alleviate some of the contentiousness that surrounds current funding requests. Similarly, education policymakers would find their support of education vis-à-vis other services strengthened.

The notions of more ambitious outcomes, coherent policy in support of those outcomes, and restructured governance reach across a number of traditional lines of division in a way that provides a basis for unification of those interested in educational improvement. The idea that consensus about outcomes should focus on a streamlined core body of knowledge and skills attracts educators who wish to leave determination of detailed curricula to the schools and foster the ability of schools to meet the needs of diverse student bodies. State curriculum frameworks and reinforcing policies would provide a protective structure that would undergird strategies for parental choice and other approaches to decentralizing school governance. As Smith and O'Day (1991) argue, "What is needed is neither a solely top-down nor a bottom-up approach to reform, but a coherent systemic strategy that can combine the energy and professional involvement of the second wave reforms with a new and challenging state structure to generalize the reforms to all schools within the state" (p. 234).

To the extent that systemic reform ideas form a platform for uniting diverse reform constituencies, they take on political power. The ideas that exert the greatest influence are those that balance political forces, finding ways to enlist existing interests as well as to open up new opportunities. Systemic reform has many of the properties of so-called "public ideas" (Moore, 1988; Reich, 1988). It challenges "society to perceive and deal with a problem differently" (Moore, 1988, p. 83) by changing the terms of the education reform debate. As argued above, education reform has been cast in terms of the incompatibility of policy and school-level improvement, of top down and bottom up. However, if policy is conceived as coherent and focused on ambitious outcomes instead of fragmented and focused on minimal standards, it can support school-level efforts, a support more likely than total reliance on school-by-school efforts to promote improvement in schools throughout the system. The reform debate changes from a focus on how schools can improve despite policy to how policies can help schools improve.

While state systemic reform efforts are too recent to judge

their staying power, the political forecast may be rosy, despite the political system's penchant for fragmentation. The larger cultural press for coherence on goals, the willingness of states to experiment with bridging structures that may have lasting benefits for education policy coherence, and the strategic and philosophical appeal of systemic reform to a wide variety of educators and policymakers offer encouragement for the development and maintenance of coherent policy.

Conclusion

A crisis of confidence surrounds education policy. Reformers despair of the failure of the "top-down reforms" of the early 1980s and of the unfulfilled promise of the "bottom-up," school-by-school change efforts of the later 1980s. The ability of the political system to deliver quality schooling is under attack. Many argue that policies should be abandoned altogether—by completely substituting market control or by removing policies so that schools can improve themselves unfettered.

However, the abandonment of policy does not offer hope of widespread improvement because schools cannot sustain self-generated change. Nor is school-by-school change likely to spread to all schools. The system must offer support. Systemic reform approaches suggest a way that the system can support school change, without either stifling school initiative or leaving schools to fare for themselves without help from the wider policy environment. Systemic reform approaches offer another possibility for those disappointed by policy, an approach to policy that combines centralized leadership around outcomes with decentralized decision making about practice.

The political appeal of an idea that redefines traditional top-down versus bottom-up or policy versus markets divisions may be strong enough to overcome the many aspects of our messy (albeit responsive) political system that have undercut coherent policymaking. The political attractiveness of coherent policymaking is bolstered by the larger cultural press for challenging student goals and the willingness of states undertaking systemic reform issues to tackle structural fragmentation. System reform efforts must be watched over time, of course, be-

fore any conclusions about their political legs can be drawn; at
the moment, however, the strong interest of states is encouraging. Some policy ideas emerge that change the politics over which
they triumph. Systemic reform may be one.

Note

1.   I am grateful to my colleague Richard Elmore for drawing
     the analogy.

References

Archbald, D. A., and Newmann, F. *Beyond Standardized Testing: Assessing Authentic Academic Achievement in the Secondary School.*
Reston, Va.: National Association of Secondary School Principals, 1988.

Bowles, S., and Gintis, H. *Schooling in Capitalist America: Educational Reform and the Contradictions of Economic Life.* New York:
Basic Books, 1976.

Chubb, J. E., and Moe, T. M. *Politics, Markets, and America's
Schools.* Washington, D.C.: Brookings Institution, 1990.

Clune, W. "New Answers to Hard Questions Posed by *Rodriguez:*
Ending the Separation of School Finance and Educational
Policy by Bridging the Gap Between Wrong and Remedy."
Connecticut Law Review, 1992, *24*(3), 1–42.

Cohen, D. K. "Policy and Organization: The Impact of State
and Federal Educational Policy on School Governance." *Harvard Educational Review,* 1982, *52*(4), 474–499.

Cohen, D. K. "Governance and Instruction: The Promise of
Decentralization and Choice." In W. H. Clune and J. F. Witte
(eds.), *Choice and Control in American Education.* Bristol, Pa.:
Falmer Press, 1991.

Cohen, D. K., and Ball, D. L. "Relations Between Policy and
Practice: A Commentary." *Educational Evaluation and Policy
Analysis,* 1990, *12*(3), 331–338.

Cohen, M. "Instructional Management, and Social Conditions
in Effective Schools." In A. Odden and L. D. Webb (eds.),
School Finance and School Improvement Linkage for the 1980s. Cambridge, Mass.: Ballinger, 1983.

Cohen, M., March, J., and Olsen, J. "A Garbage Can Theory of Organizational Choice." *Administrative Science Quarterly,* 1976, *17*(1), 1–25.

Coley, R., and Goertz, M. *Educational Standards in the 50 States: 1990.* Princeton, N.J.: Educational Testing Service, 1990.

Consortium for Policy Research in Education. "Putting the Pieces Together: Systemic School Reform." *CPRE Policy Briefs.* New Brunswick, N.J.: Consortium for Policy Research in Education, 1991.

Consortium for Policy Research in Education. "10 Lessons in Regulation and Schooling." *CPRE Policy Briefs.* New Brunswick, N.J.: Consortium for Policy Research in Education, 1992.

Cuban, L. "School Reform by Remote Control: SB813 in California." *Phi Delta Kappan,* 1984, *66,* 213–215.

Cutler, L. "To Make a Government." *Foreign Affairs,* 1980, *59*(4), 126–143.

Darling-Hammond, L., and Berry, B. *The Evolution of Teacher Policy.* A report for the Center for Policy Research in Education, Eagleton Institute of Politics, Rutgers University, and New Brunswick, N.J., RAND Corporation, Washington, D.C., 1988.

Derthick, M., and Quirk, P. *The Politics of Deregulation.* Washington, D.C.: Brookings Institution, 1985.

Elmore, R. F. *Community School District 4, New York City: A Case of Choice.* A report for the Center for Policy Research in Education, Eagleton Institute of Politics, Rutgers University, New Brunswick, N.J., 1990a.

Elmore, R. F. *Restructuring Schools: The Next Generation of Educational Reform.* San Francisco: Jossey-Bass, 1990b.

Elmore, R. F. "Innovation in Education Policy." Paper presented at the Innovation in the Public Sector conference at Duke University, Durham, N.C., May 3, 1991a.

Elmore, R. F. "Review of *Politics, Markets, and America's Schools* by John Chubb and Terry Moe." *Journal of Applied Public Policy and Management,* 1991b, *10*(4), 687–694.

Fenno, R. *Congressman in Committees.* Boston: Little, Brown, 1973.

Fredericksen, N. "The Real Test Bias: Influences of Testing on Teaching and Learning." *American Psychologist,* 1984, *39,* 193–202.

Fuhrman, S. "Legislatures and Education Policy." Paper prepared for the Symposium on the Legislature in the Twenty-First Century, Williamsburg, Va., Apr. 27–29, 1990.

Fuhrman, S., and Elmore, R. F. "Governors and Education Policy in the 1990s." Paper presented at the annual research conference of the Association for Public Policy and Management, San Francisco, Oct. 20, 1990a.

Fuhrman, S., and Elmore, R. F. "Understanding Local Control in the Wake of State Education Reform." *Educational Evaluation and Policy Analysis,* 1990b, *12*(1), 82–96.

Fuhrman, S., and Massell, D. "Issues and Strategies in Systemic Reform." Paper prepared for the Consortium for Policy Research in Education, Eagleton Institute of Politics, Rutgers University, New Brunswick, N.J., 1992.

Hayes, L. "News and Views." *Phi Delta Kappan,* 1992, *73*(10), 806–807.

Heclo, H. "Issue Networks and the Executive Establishment." In A. King (ed.), *The New American Political System.* Washington, D.C.: AEI Press, 1978.

Hunt, A. R. "In Defense of a Messy Congress." In R. H. Davidson (ed.), *Governing: Readings and Cases in American Politics.* (2nd ed.) Washington, D.C.: Congressional Quarterly Press, 1992.

King, A. "The American Polity in the 1990s." In A. King (ed.), *The New American Political System.* (2nd ed.) Washington, D.C.: AEI Press, 1990.

Kingdon, J. W. *Agendas, Alternatives & Public Policies.* Boston, Mass.: Little, Brown, 1984.

Kirst, M. "The Evolving Context of California Education." *Comparative State Policies,* 1988, *10*(5).

Kirst, M. "Financing School-Linked Services." *USC Center for Education Finance Policy Briefs,* no. 7. Los Angeles: University of Southern California, 1992.

Kurtz, K. T. "Limiting Terms—What's in Store?" *State Legislatures,* 1992, *18*(1), 32–34.

Levinson, C., and Massell, D. "Systemic Reform: A Literature Review." Paper prepared for the Consortium for Policy Research in Education, Eagleton Institute of Politics, Rutgers University, New Brunswick, N.J., 1992.

Lindblom, C. "The Science of Muddling Through." *Public Administrative Review,* 1959, *19*(2), 79–88.

Lindblom, C., and Cohen, D. K. *Usable Knowledge.* New Haven, Conn.: Yale University Press, 1979.

McDonnell, L., and Elmore, R. "Getting the Job Done: Alternative Policy Instruments." *Educational Evaluation and Policy Analysis,* 1987, *9*(2), 133–152.

McDonnell, L., and Fuhrman, S. "The Political Context of Reform." In V. D. Mueller and M. P. McKeown (eds.), *The Fiscal, Legal, and Political Aspects of State Reform of Elementary and Secondary Education.* Cambridge, Mass.: Ballinger, 1985.

McNeil, L. *Contradictions of Control.* New York: Routledge & Kegan Paul, 1986.

Mann, T., and Orenstein, N. "Congress and the President: A Letter to the Editor." *Foreign Affairs,* 1981, *60*(1), 418–420.

Marsh, D., and Odden, A. "Implementation of the California Mathematics and Science Curriculum Frameworks." In A. Odden (ed.), *Education Policy Implementation.* Albany: State University of New York Press, 1991.

Massell, D. "Achieving Consensus: How States Develop Consensus on State Instructional Policies." Paper prepared for the Consortium for Policy Research in Education, Eagleton Institute of Politics, Rutgers University, New Brunswick, N.J., 1992.

Mayhew, D. *Congress: The Electoral Connection.* New Haven, Conn.: Yale University Press, 1974.

Meyer, J. W. *The Impact of the Centralization of Educational Funding and Control on State and Local Organizational Governance (NIE Contract P-79-0086).* Stanford, Calif.: Institute for Research on Educational Finance and Governance and Department of Sociology, Stanford University, 1979.

Moore, M. "What Makes Public Ideas Powerful?" In R. Reich (ed.), *The Power of Public Ideas.* Cambridge, Mass.: Ballinger, 1988.

Morone, J. A. *The Democratic Wish.* New York: Basic Books, 1990.

National Council on Education Standards and Testing. *Raising Standards for American Education: A Report to Congress, the Secretary of Education, the National Education Goals Panel, and the Ameri-*

can People. Washington, D.C.: U.S. Government Printing Office, 1992.

New American Schools Development Corporation. "Designs for a New Generation of American Schools" (request for proposals). 1991.

Newmann, F. "Beyond Common Sense in Educational Restructuring: The Issue of Content and Linkage." *Educational Researcher,* forthcoming.

Odden, A. "School Finance in the 1990s." *Phi Delta Kappan,* 1991, *73*(6), 455–461.

Polsby, N. "Political Change and the Character of the Contemporary Congress." In A. King (ed.), *The New American Political System.* (2nd ed.) Washington, D.C.: AEI Press, 1990.

Purkey, S. C., and Smith, M. "School Reform: The District Policy Implications of the Effective Schools Literature." *Elementary School Journal,* 1983, *85*(4), 353–389.

Ravitch, D. Remarks to OERI/OECD at Conference on Education Research and Development, Washington, D.C., June 1–2, 1992.

Reich, R. (ed.). *The Power of Public Ideas.* Cambridge, Mass.: Ballinger, 1988.

Rosenthal, A. "The Legislative Institution: Transformed and at Risk." In C. Van Horn (ed.), *The State of the States.* Washington, D.C.: Congressional Quarterly Press, 1989.

Sabatier, P. "Toward Better Theories of the Policy Process." *Political Science and Politics,* June 1991, pp. 144–147.

Salmore, S., and Salmore, B. "Campaigns and Elections and the Legislature." Paper prepared for the Eagleton Institute of Politics for the Symposium on the Legislature in the Twenty-First Century, Williamsburg, Va.: Apr. 1990.

Smith, M., and O'Day, J. "Systemic School Reform." In S. Fuhrman and B. Malen (eds.), *The Politics of Curriculum and Testing.* Bristol, Pa.: Falmer Press, 1991.

Sundquist, J. W. "Whither the American Party System—Revisited." *Political Science Quarterly,* Winter 1984, *98,* 573–593.

Tyack, D. "Public School Reform: Policy Talk and Institutional Practice." *American Journal of Education,* 1992, *100*(1), 1–19.

Tyack, D. "Ways of Seeing: An Essay on the History of Compulsory Schooling." *Harvard Educational Review,* 1976, *46*(3), 355–389.

Tyson-Bernstein, H. "The Academy's Contribution to the Impoverishment of America's Textbooks." *Phi Delta Kappan,* 1988, *70*(3), 193–198.

Weiss, C. *Using Social Research in Public Policy Making.* Lexington, Mass.: Heath, 1977.

Wildavsky, A. *The Politics of the Budgetary Process.* Boston: Little, Brown, 1974.

Wise, A. *Legislated Learning:* Berkeley: University of California Press, 1979.

Yudof, M. "School Finance Reform: Don't Worry, Be Happy." *The Review of Litigation,* 1991, *10*(3), 585–598.

2

Policy and Practice: The Relations Between Governance and Instruction

David K. Cohen
James P. Spillane

Introduction

Ours is a time of remarkable ferment in U.S. education. The recent school reform movement initially focused on the "basics" but then took off in a dramatically new direction in the middle 1980s. Reformers started to demand more thoughtful and intellectually ambitious instruction. Leaders in politics and business argued that students must become independent thinkers and enterprising problem solvers. Educators began to say that schools must offer intellectually challenging instruction that is deeply rooted in the academic disciplines.

These ideas are a dramatic change. For most of this century, politicians and businessmen ignored public education, or supported only minimum programs for most students. And most leaders in education long have been inclined to the view that

This chapter was originally published as "Policy and Practice: The Relations Between Governance and Instruction." *Review of Research in Education,* 1992, *18,* 3–49. Copyright 1992 by the American Educational Research Association. Reprinted by permission of the publisher. We are grateful to Carol Barnes, Linda Darling-Hammond, Robert Dreeben, Robert Floden, Susan Fuhrman, Harry Judge, James Kelly, Magdalene Lampert, Barbara Neufeld, Andrew Porter, Daniel Resnick, Brian Rowan, Lauren Sosniak, Marshall Smith, Gary Sykes, Teresa Tatto, Suzanne Wilson, and Rona Wilensky for comments on earlier drafts of this essay. Gerald Grant and Linda Darling-Hammond offered especially helpful suggestions on the next to last draft.

students need basic and practical education, rather than more high-flown and demanding stuff. These tendencies were entirely representative. Though the American people have been enthusiasts for schooling, few have been keen on intellectually ambitious education.

More unusual still, recent reformers have proposed fundamental changes in politics and policy to achieve the new goals. They argue for the creation of state or national curricula, to push instruction to new heights. Or they advocate state or national tests or examination systems, to pull instruction in the same direction. Or they propose to link examinations and curricula to gain even more leverage on teaching and learning. Prominent politicians, businesspeople, and professors have endorsed one or another of these proposals, and several state and national agencies have begun to implement them. Major efforts are under way to mobilize much more consistent and powerful direction for instruction from state or national agencies.

These developments seem hopeful to some and unwise to others. But everyone agrees that they mark an astonishing reversal, and many therefore wonder whether the new proposals are attainable. One set of problems concerns politics. Power and authority have been extraordinarily dispersed in U.S. education, especially in matters of instruction. Could state or national agencies actually mobilize the influence required to steer teaching and learning in thousands or hundreds of thousands of far-away classrooms? That would require extensive new state or national infrastructure in education, as well as a radically new politics of education. Are such things possible?

A second set of problems concerns instructional practice. The new proposals envision much more thoughtful, adventurous, and demanding instruction, but most instructional practice in the United States is quite traditional. Teachers and students spend most of their time with lectures, formal recitations, and worksheets, intellectual demands generally are modest, and a great deal of the work is dull. Only a modest fraction of public school teachers have deep knowledge of any academic subject. Hence, even if state or national agencies accumulated the infrastructure and influence required to steer teaching and learning, could they be steered so sharply away from long-established practice?

To answer these questions about how things might change, one must ask others about how they now work. How do instructional policies made in state and national agencies play out in local classrooms? What are the relations between policy and practice? What might it take to change them? Have central agencies ever tried to promote innovative and adventurous teaching? If so, with what results? These seem crucial issues for America today and tomorrow, but our knowledge about them is limited by what we did yesterday. The dispersed organization of American education rendered the connections between policy and instruction inconsequential for most of our history. The topic barely entered educational inquiry because it seemed so distant from educational reality. There is little American evidence about the structure or consequences of much greater state or national control. Similarly, American disdain for intellectually challenging education has left us with only modest evidence on how such education might turn out in this nation's schools. In order to learn much about such matters, we must look beyond the U.S. education mainstream and to studies of other national school systems.

We tackle the issues in four chunks. First, we probe the relations between state and national government on the one hand and instruction on the other. We explore how the structure and activities of central government affect classroom practice. But in some systems, key decisions about instruction, like what texts to read, or what tests to use, are made by no central agency. Hence, in the second chunk of the chapter we identify the specific sources of guidance for instruction, including tests, texts, and other things. We explore how they interact with governance structures, and we probe their effects on classroom practice.

In the third chunk of the chapter we scrutinize change in classroom practice. The recent U.S. reforms propose ambitious shifts in instructional purposes, processes, and content: we inquire about the prospects for such change in teaching.

Finally, we consider nongovernmental influences on instruction. Recent reformers have proposed radical changes in

policy, politics, and instructional guidance, seeing these as potent influences on classroom work. Yet studies of schooling here
and abroad often suggest that social and cultural influences may
be no less significant. For instance, some researchers report that
Japanese families tend to support children's hard work and academic achievement, while Americans tend not to. Such differences may account for many of the effects often ascribed to policy
and institutions.

Government Structure and Policymaking

The formal institutions of government are widely supposed to
shape the relations between education policy and instructional
practice. In France and many other nations, central agencies
have enormous authority and power (Lewis, 1985; Holmes,
1979). Ministries of education make most policy for local education, and they often do so in great detail. But the U.S. political system was specifically designed to frustrate central power.
Authority in education was divided among state, local, and federal governments by an elaborate federal system, and it was
divided within governments by the separation of powers. These
divisions were carefully calculated to inhibit the coordinated action of government, and they gained force from the country's
great size and diversity (Kaufman, 1969).

   The U.S. federal government thus has had a relatively
weak influence on education, as a matter of both law and tradition. But since World War II the central government has accumulated increasing influence on state and local decisions about
funding, education for disadvantaged groups, civil rights and
civil liberties in schools, research, and curriculum improvement.
Despite these changes, direct federal governance of education
is marginal. Federal agencies directly operate few schools and
contribute only a little more than 6 percent of school operating
budgets, on average (U.S. Bureau of the Census, 1989).

   State governments are the constitutional center of U.S.
education, but most states have delegated most authority to localities, for most of their history. States supported the establishment of public schools with enabling statutes and, sometimes,

a bit of money, in the nineteenth century, but most of the pressures to establish public schools lay outside of state government. There has been some variability in states' influence in education. Hawaii has no local districts, and southern states have tended to be stronger than those elsewhere (Wirt and Kirst, 1982). But until fifteen years ago, the general pattern was extensive delegated state power. Most state agencies were small and weakly staffed (McDonnell and McLaughlin, 1982; Murphy, 1974). State governments have begun to exercise more power during the last decade (Cantor, 1980), but most are still far from what, in world perspective, could be called central control.

Such weakness in higher-level agencies is quite unusual. In many nations the national ministry is the senior and often sole partner, managing all educational programs and paying most or all operating costs. In modern France, the schools have until recently been a creature of the national government in Paris, not of local or departmental governments (Cameron and others, 1984b; Holmes, 1979; Lewis, 1985). Even state or provincial governments in other federal systems have much greater power and authority. Australian state governments hold most constitutional authority in education, as they do in the United States, but the six Australian states also are the basic operating units in education (Boyd and Smart, 1987; Cameron and others, 1984a). Each state operates all the public schools within its boundaries, performing all the functions that Americans associate with both state and local school government.

The United States thus has a remarkably fragmented governance system. Many important educational decisions are made in the nation's roughly 110,000 individual schools (U.S. Bureau of the Census, 1989), including decisions about educational program, student assignment, teacher assignment, and resource allocation among students (Wirt and Kirst, 1982). One result is remarkable variation across schools (Cusick, 1983; Powell, Farrar, and Cohen, 1985). Recent efforts at local "restructuring" and "school-based management" will almost certainly enhance the influence of many schools.

Local districts are the fundamental governance agencies, by tradition and practice. There are some 15,000 local districts

(U.S. Bureau of the Census, 1989), and their influence is extraordinary in world perspective. Despite the recent growth of state and national power, these districts make a great range of decisions, including those that bear on levels of funding, the nature of educational program, and the teachers to be hired (Travers and Westbury, 1989). Financial support for most U.S. schools is still tied to local tax bases and taxation decisions, which produces enormous variation in educational resources and, thus, instructional programs. The key role of local districts builds many differences into U.S. education (Firestone, 1989).

Individual schools and districts have had much less influence in many other nations (Travers and Westbury, 1989). The French and Singaporean ministries of education have until recently monopolized decisions about educational programs, teacher assignment, and resource allocation (Cameron and others, 1984b, 1984d). Local schools have had little leeway within central guidelines, a condition that some nations have begun trying to change (Cohen, 1990a; Resnick and Resnick, 1985, 1989), and many nations simply have no local districts. Australian state education departments deal directly with each school (Cameron and others, 1984a), though some use regional offices for some administrative purposes. Funding decisions typically are made by national or state agencies, greatly reducing or eliminating fiscal and programmatic variation among schools. Some nations with strong central governments do have local jurisdictions that are supposed to play a large role in education. The postwar Japanese constitution guarantees local authority in such educational decisions as teacher hiring and curriculum (Cameron and others, 1984c), but the influence of local prefectures is constrained both by the broad authority of national agencies and by centuries-old habits of deference to the center. The result limits educational variation of many sorts (Cameron and others, 1984c).

In most nations, the relations between policy and practice are framed by systems of central power, or by a small number of powerful state or provincial governments. The authority of the state is immense, and in many cases, theoretically unlimited. Schools are creatures of the nation-state or the province, and usually were created in the process of consolidating those entities (Meyer, 1983; Ramirez and Rubison, 1979; Ramirez and Boli, 1987). The connection between central power and public education is a world pattern to which the local mobilization of schooling in the United States is one of the few great exceptions. Despite growing state and federal power, local government still is the key element in U.S. schooling. And the relations between policy and practice are framed by sprawling government structures in which fragmented power and authority express a considered mistrust of government.

If government structure frames the formal relations between central policy and classroom practice, policymaking fills that frame with specific content. The two are often at odds. Although the design of American government incarnates a deep mistrust of state power, the design of most education policy expressed an abiding hope for the power of government and a wish to harness it to social problem solving. Collisions between the two were precipitated by the proliferation of state and federal education policies and programs in the last three decades. These included federal efforts to improve curriculum and instruction in the 1950s and early 1960s and to eliminate the racially dual school system throughout the South in the 1960s and 1970s. They also included federal and state efforts to improve education for disadvantaged students, to reform the education of handicapped students, to provide bilingual education for non-English-speaking students, and to ensure sex equity in schools across the nation. Nearly all of these policies and programs sought to solve problems that crossed jealously guarded jurisdictional boundaries among and within governments.

To speak of the relations between policy and practice in the United States is thus to speak both of collisions between policy and governance and of the consequences in educational institutions. Those collisions have affected the relations between policy and practice in several ways. New educational policies expanded central authority and drew the agencies of policy and practice closer together, but these policies did not commensurately reduce the autonomy of lower-level agencies. The flood of state and federal policies and programs coursed through a

large and loosely jointed governance system, yet agencies throughout the system retained much of their operating independence.
For instance, the states depend on localities for political support and policy execution, as any higher-level agent depends
on subordinates. State governments, therefore, should be constrained by what localities will accept, yet the states often act
with remarkable independence. The state education reforms of
the last ten years were in some respects quite offensive to local
educators, but many were enacted with little difficulty (Fuhrman, Clune, and Elmore, 1988). Similarly, the national government has only a modest constitutional role in education, and
it has long deferred to state and local authorities. Nonetheless,
federal agencies have taken various dramatic initiatives designed
to greatly change state and local education, many over local and
state opposition, some over fierce and even violent opposition
(Orfield, 1969). Despite the constraints that lower-level agencies can impose on their superiors, agencies above have regularly pushed far beyond the presumed limits.

      The same phenomenon obtained in reverse: state and local
autonomy has been only modestly constrained by higher-level
policy. Researchers have documented the states' great flexibility in responding to the dramatic federal policies and programs
of the 1950s and 1960s (Murphy, 1974). Researchers also have
shown that local schools and districts retain considerable latitude in coping with state and federal policies (Berman and
McLaughlin, 1978; McLaughlin, 1987). Despite the increasing flow of higher-level requirements, advice, and inducements,
lower-level agencies have much room to interpret and respond.
Relations among state, federal, and local agencies therefore remain quite attenuated despite decades of effort to bring them
closer together. Centers of organization and governance are
widely dispersed and weakly linked, despite the growth of policy.
Central agencies can make serious demands on others with relative ease; they need only mobilize the political resources to enun-
ciate a policy or begin a new program. But the costs of enforcing
demands are much greater. A great distance remains between
state or federal policymaking and local practice (Firestone, 1989).

      Yet policymaking has complicated educational organization. In order to make contact with local educational organizations, state and federal agencies have had to bridge vast political chasms artfully designed to frustrate central power. To increase general governance authority in education was politically unthinkable for the federal government. What is more, federal agencies were weak. They had no general capacity in curriculum, instruction, school personnel, or assessment, since both the Constitution and political practice were thought to forbid it. State agencies had much more authority, but with a few exceptions they had little more capacity. A majority of states had delegated most operations to local governments and private test and text publishers. Traditions of decentralization, suspicions about central power, and deference to local authority meant that higher-level authority could only grow by way of individual, free-standing programs, each of which promised to solve a specific educational problem (Bankston, 1982; Meyer, 1983). But these individual programs were located in agencies that had little general operating capacity in the "technical core" of education.

Hence, when weak federal and state agencies tried to implement such ambitious programs as Head Start and Title I of the Elementary and Secondary Education Act (ESEA) (1965), in a vast and decentralized polity, each program had to be outfitted with its own minimum core of administrative operations (budget, personnel, evaluation, and the like). Furthermore, each program had to coordinate operations across many levels of government, owing to the lack of general administrative capacity above the local level. Lacking general central authority and capacity, leaders of each program had to establish their own systems. How else could they hope to mobilize tens or hundreds of thousands of educators, in hundreds or thousands of jurisdictions, across several levels of government?

Work in such policies and programs therefore was confined within specialized administrative subunits organized around oversight tasks within each program (Wise, 1979). Administrative capacity grew, but within programs rather than across entire governments. Administrative burdens therefore multiplied as the same or similar administrative work was repeated across programs (Bankston, 1982; Cohen, 1990a; Meyer, 1983; Rowan,

1982, 1983). Central agencies grew, but in a fragmented fashion (Clark, 1965; Scott and Meyer, 1983; Stackhouse, 1982), and the administrative expansion added little to central capacity in the core areas of education such as curriculum and instruction. The collisions between optimistically designed policies and cautiously designed government produced fractured and duplicative administration.

These fractures were reflected in the organization of agencies outside of government. As policies and programs took shape, networks of interested agencies — advocacy organizations, professional groups, and special purpose research and development agencies, among others — grew up around them. Examples include the loose network that helped build support for the legislative proposals that became PL 94-142 and Title I of the 1965 ESEA (now Chapter 1). Each network has helped to coordinate and stabilize program operations and mobilize support for programs across governments and among many sorts of agencies (Cohen, 1982; Peterson, 1981; Peterson, Rabe, and Wong, 1986). Like the programs and policies that they grew up around, these policy networks are ingenious, for they support state and national efforts to solve local problems in a political system that was designed to frustrate such efforts (Kaufman, 1969). But these clever inventions also encourage political fragmentation and multiply administrative work (Bankston, 1982; Cohen, 1982; Meyer, 1983; Rogers and Whetten, 1982), for the networks support fractured authority within education agencies, as managers in each program attempt to build their own bridges across great political chasms. The ingenious devices that cope with fragmentation among governments tend to exacerbate fragmentation within them.

Collisions between cautious designs of government and hopeful designs for policy also complicated local educational practice, because administrative work grew as localities coped with increasing state and federal policies and programs. Since higher-level authorities are so distant from local practice, they are rarely held accountable for their actions there, hence state and federal initiatives were generated with little regard for the relations among them, or for their cumulative local effects (Kimbrough and Hill, 1981; Kirst, 1988; Wise, 1979). Indeed, some of the most potent local effects of state and federal programs or policies had no intended programmatic content. The best example is underfunded mandates: federal legislation for handicapped students placed unaccustomed procedural and substantive burdens on local education agencies, but the legislation carried less than half the estimated costs of compliance. Although it was thought that full funding would soon follow, it never did, yet federal requirements were never relaxed. Local and state school agencies had to allocate their own funds to this area of program support, often with grave results for other educational activities.

Yet requirements have limits. State and federal officials rarely can effectively oversee local program implementation. No state or federal education agencies have the inspectorates found in Britain, France, and their former colonies. At best, U.S. state and federal agencies use oversight-at-a-distance, such as written program evaluations, grant recipients' reports on operations, and the like. Such processes multiply work without producing fruitful contacts among public servants at different levels of government (Bardach and Kagan, 1982), and local schools retain considerable autonomy. Administrators and teachers usually can tailor higher-level programs to local purposes and conditions if they have the will and take the time (Berman and McLaughlin, 1978). Often they can cope with such directives simply by ignoring them, a ubiquitous management tool (Kiesler and Sproull, 1982) that can be especially efficient in a fragmented governance system.

These patterns contrast sharply with many foreign education systems. The ministries of education in France and Singapore deal with schools on a broad range of educational matters, as do the state departments in Australia and provincial governments in Germany. The administrative subunits in these agencies are broadly defined by the key areas of schools' operation (curriculum, instruction, personnel, and the like). The subunits have extensive general authority and new initiatives typically subsist within them, rather than being set aside in independent units, because the operating units make the key decisions about education and have the resources. As might be expected in nations founded on etatist traditions, policy initiatives are not organized as though they were at war with government, or on the assumption that they can have little to do with the core operations of education.

The collisions between rapidly expanded policymaking and fragmented governance are a hallmark of U.S. education. Few nations have such dispersed authority and power in education, yet few nations have such intense higher-level policymaking. Americans complain more than any other people about state interference with education and centralizing forces in schools, but authority and power are more dispersed here than in nearly any other nation. Perhaps that is why we complain more.

Instructional Guidance

State and federal governments have made many efforts to improve instruction: they offer financial aid to local districts, sponsor child health and nutrition programs, and support efforts to improve education for the disadvantaged. Yet such policies rarely make broad or close contact with instruction. Teaching and learning are more directly affected by the texts that students and teachers use, the examinations that assess students' academic accomplishments, the standards teachers must satisfy in order to secure a post, and the like. These instruments comprise the means so far invented to guide classroom work. We lump them under the rubric of instructional guidance and sort them into five categories: instructional frameworks, assessment of student performance, instructional materials, oversight of instruction, and requirements for teacher education and licensure.

Nations use these instruments very differently. In some cases guidance is designed and deployed by governments, while in others private agencies play a large role. Additionally, the arrangement of government-sponsored guidance varies greatly across nations (Broadfoot, 1983), and although all school systems adopt some stance toward guiding instruction, often that stance includes offering little advice.

Instructional guidance also mediates the effects of other

policies that seek to affect practice. For the effects of all government policies that try to influence instruction, including those that do so by offering extra aid to the disadvantaged or holding schools "accountable," are mediated by such things as instructional materials, teachers' professional capacities, and methods of student assessment. Intentionally or not, the aggregate of instructional guidance is a medium in and through which many other educational policies and programs operate.

In what follows we compare instructional guidance in the United States with its counterparts in other national school systems. We focus on the instruments of guidance; although these are governed in many different ways in national school systems, we do not try to describe that variety here. Instead we use a few key categories that describe variations in instructional guidance, variations produced by many different governmental and administrative arrangements (see Porter and others, 1988). One category is *consistency*. Given different domains of guidance, an important issue is the extent of agreement within and among domains. In some systems instructional frameworks are consistent internally and consistent with texts or teacher education, but in other systems they are not. Another category is *specificity or prescriptiveness*. Teaching and learning are complex enterprises, and there are many different ways to enact them. Teachers and students are offered clear and detailed guidance about content coverage or pedagogy in some systems, while in others guidance is very general or vague. A third category is *authority and power*. To offer guidance is not to decide what weight it carries. Advice for instruction is presented in ways that have great authority with students and teachers in some systems, but in others it is presented in ways that carry little weight.

Instructional Frameworks

Instructional frameworks are general designs for instruction (that is, broad conceptions of the purposes, structure, and content of academic work). Frameworks can set the terms of reference for the entire enterprise. In some school systems they guide course structure and content, the nature of textbooks, the purposes and content of examinations, and the like. They can be quite prescriptive. In some former French and British colonies such frameworks offer extensive and focused guidance about instructional content and in some cases approaches to teaching as well. In France many curriculum decisions are made by the national ministry of education (Horner, 1986), which often details the topics to be studied, the teaching materials and methods to be used, and even time allocations (Beauchamp and Beauchamp, 1972; Lewis, 1989). The Japanese central ministry issues frameworks for each subject (Kobayashi, 1984), prescribing content and detailing the sequence of topics (Kida, 1986; Organization for Economic Cooperation and Development, 1971).

Such guidance often seems to carry great authority and power. In France, many central curriculum decisions are made by the national assembly, while others are ministry decrees. But authoritative guidance need not be governmental. In Holland it is offered by autonomous agencies that are supported by government but are not part of it.

Frameworks have been unusual in the United States. The most common instructional designs have been bare listings of course requirements by state or localities. Apart from the New York State Regents it was long uncommon for state agencies to offer advice about the material to be covered within particular subject areas, or about the structure of courses. This passivity was not unique to state governments. Until quite recently, few local systems prescribed topics within courses or curricula, and guidelines about pedagogy have been even more rare. Relatively weak state and local guidance concerning course content and pedagogy has meant that students and teachers had great latitude in shaping the content and purposes of their courses (Cusick, 1983; Porter and others, 1988; Powell, Farrar, and Cohen, 1985; Schwille and others, 1983; Sedlak, Wheeler, Pullin, and Cusick, 1986).

A few states recently have moved more aggressively into instructional design. Florida, South Carolina, and a few other southern states instituted statewide basic skills curricula in efforts to improve students' performance during the past decade. These included guidance for content coverage and pacing and, at least implicitly, for teacher education. Several states have published evaluations that claim gains in student achievement, although no independent evaluations seem to have been done. At the same time several other states have pressed guidance for a radically different sort of content. In 1985, California issued the first of a series of curriculum frameworks that were intended to make teaching and learning intellectually much more ambitious and demanding. Arizona and Michigan have taken similar steps, as has Connecticut.

Some local school systems also began to move toward instructional frameworks in the 1970s and 1980s, with the news that test scores were declining and mounting demands that schools get "back to the basics." Local districts came under unfamiliar pressure to improve performance, and some began to devise minimum instructional programs in response — Washington, D.C., Chicago, and Philadelphia among them. There is little systematic research on these matters, so we cannot gauge the depth or extent of these changes. Additionally, several cities that adopted such schemes recently announced their demise. But officials in a few districts that we recently visited reported a move to greater central control. Schools can no longer determine their own instructional programs, and central offices have written rudimentary curriculum frameworks, usually blueprints for "essential skills."

Instructional Materials

Texts and other materials are found in all systems, but the extent of guidance for their content and use varies enormously. In Japan and many other systems the national ministry sets the terms of references for text content and/or authorizes the textbooks to be used on curriculum frameworks (Kida, 1986; Organization for Economic Cooperation and Development, 1973). In such cases, there is a good deal of consistency between the guidance teachers receive from textbooks and from national curriculum frameworks. In some nations ministries actually publish texts, while in others texts are privately published, but in either event, materials are powerfully influenced by curriculum frameworks.

Decisions about instructional materials have been much more fragmented in the United States. Since there have been few instructional frameworks until recently, publishers had little or no consistent, content-oriented guidance. Instead, they were guided by what had been done before, by official and unofficial expressions of state or local preferences, and by their own sense of the market. Texts have improved in many ways over those that were available in the 1920s, but most commentators regard most texts as intellectually shallow. Many states and localities officially adopt textbooks, and Americans often have thought this to be highly prescriptive for instruction. But lacking much official guidance for topic coverage within texts, save for such matters as evolution, these texts seem not to have been highly prescriptive for topic coverage (Floden and others, 1988). Researchers report that many texts mention many more topics than can be dealt with, which leaves open extensive topic choice by teachers (Tyson-Bernstein, 1988). Additionally, there seem to be appreciable inconsistencies in content coverage among the different texts for most subjects at most grade levels (Freeman and others, 1983). Hence, texts have offered many opportunities for teachers and students to vary the content they cover (Freeman and Porter, 1989; Porter and others, 1988; Schwille and others, 1983).

As several states recently moved toward more explicit instructional designs, they tried to make them count for textbooks. California used its new curriculum frameworks in mathematics, literature, and language arts to press publishers to revise texts. Publishers were told that if they did not make satisfactory revisions, their texts would not be approved for adoption. But the state's guidance still was general. The mathematics framework, for instance, offered little specific guidance about topic coverage, and studies of mathematics texts and framework suggest only modest change thus far (Putnam, Heaton, Prawat, and Remillard, 1992). Casual comparisons of the new and old literature and language arts texts with the revised framework suggest that the state has won some significant changes, although systematic analysis remains to be done.

Some local districts also have begun trying to promote

greater consistency between instructional frameworks and materials. Several that devised such frameworks also specified the knowledge and skills that students and teachers should cover in texts and other materials, often doing so in compilations of "essential skills." In at least one case, local officials tied their guidance to recently published texts that seemed to fit with the local instructional frameworks. The district specified the material to be covered in the common text, and when it should be covered. That constitutes an extraordinary change for U.S. schools, but we have found no studies that gauge its breadth or depth.

Assessment of Results

Assessment of instructional results is an essential element of instructional guidance in most school systems. Though assessment practices are changing in European systems (Kellaghan and Madaus, 1991; Madaus, 1991), many nations tie assessment closely to curriculum. In France and many former French and British colonies, examinations are referenced to national curricula, instructional frameworks, or both. The examinations thus provide both a visible target for instruction and a means of checking on its results (Madaus, 1991; Resnick and Resnick, 1985, 1989). The nature of assessment in these cases varies greatly among nations, but it all differs from American approaches. The examinations probe students' performance in specific curricula. Many systems mix multiple-choice questions with extended essay or problem-solving performances, though some — Japan, for instance — rely entirely on multiple-choice questions (Cheney, 1991). In contrast, U.S. schools employ standardized tests that are referenced to national norms and are designed to be independent of curricula, with performance limited to answering multiple-choice questions (Noah and Eckstein, 1989).

In France, Great Britain, and Japan, examinations count in very specific ways. Students' promotion and further education depend partly or entirely on their exam performance (Eckstein and Noah, 1989). Indeed, many school systems that employ examinations are highly selective and the exams are the key agent of selection (Kellaghan and Madaus, 1991). In Singapore, exams are used to make nearly irrevocable decisions about streaming in both the primary and secondary grades, and thus to influence decisions about students' careers and further education. This use of examinations sharply limits students' opportunities to recoup earlier poor performances. (The United States lacks such a selective examination system, which is one reason why students here have more "second chances" than they do in any other nation.) The use of examinations for student selection enhances the examinations' authority (Madaus, 1988, 1991; Madaus and Kellaghan, 1991; Resnick and Resnick, 1985, 1989). In New South Wales, Australia, for example, students' performance on the school leaving exam determines their opportunities for further education; differences of a tenth of a point in exam scores can be crucial. In Japan, scores on both national secondary school leaving exams and university extrance exams decide which high school students will go on to university, as well as the quality and prestige of the universities that students will attend (Ohta, 1986; Organization for Economic Cooperation and Development, 1973; White, 1987). Secondary schools' prestige also is tied to students' success in examinations for prestigious universities (Organization for Economic Cooperation and Development, 1971). The social and economic significance of exam performance thus offers many incentives for students and teachers to take them seriously.

Matters are very different in the United States: there is a great deal of assessment, but it has an uncertain bearing on instruction. One reason is that most tests have been designed to minimize their sensitivity to specific curricula (Madaus, 1989; Resnick and Resnick, 1985; Smith and O'Day, 1991). What is more, many different tests are designed, published, and marketed by many different private testing agencies, and most decisions about which test to use have been made by thousands of local and state school agencies, each of which adopts tests of its own liking independent of the others' decisions. All of this has made for inconsistent guidance from assessment.

Variation in content coverage has been another source of inconsistency in the guidance that U.S. tests offer for instruction. Standardized tests often have been seen as interchangeable, but one of the few careful studies of topical agreement among tests raised doubts about that view. Focusing on several leading fourth grade mathematics tests, the authors observed that "our findings challenge . . . th[e] assumption . . . that standardized achievement tests may be used interchangeably" (Freeman and others, 1983). The authors maintain that these tests are topically inconsistent and thus differentially sensitive to content coverage.

Inconsistency has been further enhanced by the widespread local practice of using one publisher's test in one grade and others' in other grades. This problem has been magnified by the increase in testing during the past several decades, as local and state-sponsored minimum competency and essential skills tests have spread. American students are now tested much more often than they were twenty years ago but with more different tests.

Thus, established U.S. approaches to assessment would have impeded consistency among the elements of instructional guidance, had consistency been sought. Until recently, however, it was not. The guidance for instruction that tests offered was general, and probably more a matter of the form of knowledge (that is, it exists in multiple-choice formats and is either right or wrong) than its content. This guidance also was vague, since the test results were rarely known. They were even kept from teachers, partly on the designers' view that they were not designed to guide instruction.

Indeed, decisions about test design, marketing, and adoption typically have been made apart from knowledge of specific school curricula, teacher education, and the like. Test theory and practice have held that such independence is crucial to test validity, but this has further weakened consistency between tests and instructional materials. Research seems to bear out the weak relations between the subject matter content of standardized tests and of texts. Several investigators concluded that "if a fourth-grade teacher limits instruction to one of the four books analyzed, students will have an adequate opportunity to learn or to review less than half of all topics that will be tested" (Freeman and others, 1983, p. 511).

To the extent that tests guide instruction, they have done

so inconsistently. This has weakened the instructional authority of the tests. It is thus not surprising that many teachers report they rarely take test results into account in instruction (Floden, Porter, Schmidt, and Freeman, 1978; MacRury, Nagy, and Traub, 1987; Ruddell, 1985; Salmon-Cox, 1981; Sproull and Zubrow, 1981).

There have been a few exceptions to these patterns, notably the New York State Regents exams and the Advanced Placement Program (AP). The AP Program is a special subsystem within public education, in which high-achieving students take advanced courses. The AP exams seem to strongly influence instruction, in part because they are tied to a suggested curriculum and readings. The exams also seem to be taken seriously by most students and teachers, partly because the scores count for college entrance as well as college course taking, but these have been anomalies in American education (Powell, 1991).

These patterns have begun to change. Rising public interest in testing and other political pressures led many states and localities to begin publishing scores in the early 1970s, after decades of secrecy. By now, many do so as a matter of course and often conviction. State and local school agencies also increasingly turned to tests in efforts to improve instruction. The favored method was to institute "accountability" schemes, often based on minimum competency tests. Many of these included only a high school graduation requirement, but some also included tests for promotion. Some were hastily contrived under political pressure, so that the tests often were adapted from standardized norm-referenced tests designed for other purposes.

State and local use of tests to guide instruction marked a dramatic turn in assessment practices, but the fragmentation characteristic of U.S. education was evident here as well. Many minimum competency tests were unrelated to other elements of instructional guidance, such as curriculum. The tests effectively became the curriculum in some cases (Darling-Hammond and Wise, 1985). Recently, however, that has begun to change as well, as some publishers have brought out text series that are accompanied by criterion-referenced test systems, linking curriculum and instruction to testing. In several cities that we have studied, these test and text series are the heart of the instructional program. Students' performance is monitored by regular testing that is keyed to text pages, and sometimes students are retested until they achieve "mastery." We have discovered no studies that probe the frequency of such practices, though they seem to be found chiefly in cities with many disadvantaged students, where tests offer much more specific and prescriptive guidance than ordinarily has been the case in the United States.

How does such testing affect instruction? There has been surprisingly little research on the issue. Several researchers assert that the tests have had a powerful effect on teaching (Darling-Hammond, 1987; Darling-Hammond and Wise, 1985; Resnick and Resnick, 1989; Romberg, Zarinnia, and Williams, 1989). Competency tests are said to drive instruction in a mechanical and simplistic direction. Teachers orient instruction to the test items, and if students do poorly on the test, remediation consists of drill on the items they do not know (Kreitzer, Madaus, and Haney, 1989; Madaus, 1988). A recent U.S. Department of Education report claims that "accountability systems . . . are very powerful policy tools that have changed school-level planning and teaching activities" (Office of Educational Research and Improvement, 1988, p. 31).

But it also is often said that these claims only hold for situations in which the tests carry "high stakes" (that is, they count for students' academic progress or for schools or teachers). This condition does not hold for many minimum competency testing programs (Ellwein, Glass, and Smith, 1988), or for many students in high-stakes testing programs. It also seems to be accepted that such tests are much more likely to affect poor and minority group children, since more advantaged students pass the tests with little effort. These considerations suggest that the effects of minimum competency testing have been quite uneven and are salient only for a particular segment of the school population. Additionally, we do not know how salient the tests have been, because there have been no observational studies of teachers' responses. The little research on competency testing thus far is based on interviews with teachers who describe the effects of testing in rather global terms, and the evidence they present is very mixed (Office of Educational Research and Improvement, 1988; Romberg, Zarinnia, and Williams, 1989).

The effects of testing are complicated by recent reforms. Minimum competency testing has come under sharp attack, and standardizing testing itself is the object of unprecedented criticism. Several states recently have begun to use novel testing programs in efforts to strengthen and radically change guidance for instruction. The California state education department has begun revising its statewide testing program in an effort to align the state's tests with its ambitious new curriculum frameworks. State officials hope that if the tests are changed to assess thinking and understanding rather than facts and memorization, they will drive instruction in the new directions. Connecticut has been making similar changes, although it seems to rely on tests much more than on instructional designs. Florida has dropped its minimum competency testing program in favor of a radically different approach to reform. Proposals for performance assessments have become common, and many educational agencies claim to be implementing them. This ferment is quite unprecedented, but the developments are so recent that little is known about the operation of innovative assessments, let alone their effects.

Monitoring Instruction

The inspection of students' work, the observation of teaching, and other monitoring constitute a fourth type of instructional guidance. Monitoring also varies dramatically among nations. French and British central school agencies long included inspectorates, whose duties extended to checking on the topics that teachers covered, their pedagogy, and the materials they used. British inspectors visited schools to maintain standards of work and offer advice on content and pedagogy. Although this role has fallen into disuse in Britain, they still publish reports and conduct continuing professional education for teachers (Lawton and Gordon, 1987). Such arrangements were adopted in one form or another in many former French and British colonies.

Monitoring has been extremely modest and inconsistent in the United States. Few states and localities systematically monitored either teachers' coverage of curriculum or the quality of classroom work. There were no education inspectorates, nor was it common for principals to keep tabs on students' and teachers' academic work (Schwille and others, 1983). Indeed, it was uncommon for students to keep the detailed records that would permit such monitoring. Even if such records were kept, few principals involved themselves in instruction. Hence there have been few checks on what materials are used, how they are used, or what instruction is provided. In this respect, U.S. teachers have had quite extraordinary autonomy.

Many observers believe that U.S. teachers nonetheless teach more or less the same thing. They often point to the use of textbooks, believing that the text determines instruction in most classrooms. If teachers use the same text, it is expected that they will teach the same subject matter. Though there has been little research on this matter, the assumed homogeneity of content coverage is unsupported by the available evidence. Even when teachers use the same texts, their content coverage seems to vary greatly (Putnam, Heaton, Prawat, and Remillard, 1992; Schwille and others, 1983). The authors of one study concluded that "this investigation challenge[s] the popular notion that the content of math instruction in a given elementary school is essentially equal to the textbook being used" (Freeman and Porter, 1989, p. 418).

There are some recent signs of change. Many state and local systems attempt to monitor instruction with minimum competency tests, though the evidence suggests that these efforts are quite inconsistent and often ineffective. But at least one local school system that we visited went further: as it adopted more centralized instructional guidance, the district also devised a way to monitor teachers' coverage of it. Teachers fill out forms that report chapter and page coverage in required texts, and the forms are read by principals and central office officials. Some states also have begun monitoring of a sort. South Carolina has used test scores to identify both low-performing schools and districts that need special attention and high-performing schools and districts that can be released from various state requirements. But there are few studies of these schemes, and we could find no investigations of their effects on instruction.

Teacher Education and Licensing

Guidance for instruction in teacher education also varies greatly among nations. In many countries, this is quite consistent with other sorts of guidance. One key connection is with the schools' curriculum; for instance, in Singapore, teachers' professional education is closely tied to the curriculum of the schools. Additionally, in many nations the requirements for licensure are national rather than local, and teacher education is consistent across institutions. That is true at the national level in France, partly because the ministry's inspectors play a central role in the preparation of elementary school teachers in the École Normale (Lewis, 1985). This tends to create consistency in the professional education of teachers and in the messages they receive from different elements of the system.

Such guidance is more of a hodgepodge in the United States. States are the agency for licensure of virtually all occupations; however, unlike medicine, teacher certification requirements are inconsistent across states and often within them. Chicago and New York City, for instance, have different certification requirements than do the states in which they are located. The interstate differences are so considerable that one recent study concluded that "a teacher certified in one state is unlikely to meet the certification requirements in another" (Haggstrom, Darling-Hammond, and Grissmer, 1988, p. 12).

Most requirements for certification focus on teachers' education, and virtually all concern higher education. But the state agencies that set certification standards are remote from the colleges and universities that conduct most teacher education. Moreover, certification agencies usually have little connection with the state agencies that govern colleges and universities and, in addition, have acted purely in terms of course requirements rather than course content or students' performance. Hence there is room for considerable variation in how colleges and universities interpret the same requirements.

Another source of inconsistency is the loose relation between college and university requirements for teacher education and the schools' curricula, which vary within states, as well

as within local districts. The variety of local instructional programs cannot be accounted for by teacher education departments, and in many cases members of those departments regard
the schools' curricula as a collection of errors that intending
teachers must learn to avoid.

   Against this background, the mere idea of consistent
guidance for teacher education and licensing seems revolutionary, yet recently there have been moves in that direction. Most
notable is the National Board for Professional Teaching Standards (NBPTS), which has begun efforts to develop a voluntary national examination system for teachers. If successful, this
could lead to a partial national system for teacher certification,
which could profoundly affect teacher education.

Instructional Guidance: An Overview

Instructional guidance in the United States has been inconsistent and diffuse. Many private and public agencies issue advice for instruction, but few take account of each other's advice;
hence much guidance for instruction has been unrelated, divergent, or contradictory and also largely decoupled from government. Public agencies have extensive authority to guide instruction, but they delegate most of it to private firms or local schools.
The influence of U.S. school governments pales when compared
with central or provincial agencies in other countries.

   Instructional guidance also filters the effects of other initiatives that aim to influence classrooms. Prolific and inconsistent guidance in the United States has muffled and diffused such
initiatives. Since government officials could not turn to an established system of guidance, individual programs or policies
could not exert a powerful and consistent influence on instruction. Each was on its own, each competing with a buzz of other
advice. Federal and state policymakers dealt with this problem
by trying to mobilize special arrangements (for example, program guidelines, evaluation, and technical assistance), but these
are ancillary to the core instruments of guidance and have been
no more than modestly influential.

   The result is paradoxical. Public and private agencies

produce guidance more prolifically than in societies with much more potent advice for instruction. But this does not press instruction in any consistent direction, because when guidance is inconsistent and diffuse, no single test, curriculum, or policy or program is likely to have a broad or marked effect. Many teachers and students are aware of different sorts of advice, but few are keenly aware of most of it. Many know that most guidance is either weakly supported or contradicted by other advice and that much can safely be ignored, which opens considerable latitude to those who work within it.

Teachers' habits and decisions are important in any system of instruction, but when clear and strong guidance is absent, they become unusually important. The result in U.S. classrooms is curiously mixed. The forms of instruction are generally traditional and the intellectual level usually low, but the specific content is remarkably variable. There are many reasons for the variation, including differences in students' inclinations and teachers' judgment, but one important reason is that students' and teachers' preferences are not informed by a clear system of common purposes and content. Classrooms around the world are of course traditional in form as well, often much more so than in the United States, but classrooms here exhibit a distinctive sort of diffuse, academically relaxed traditionalism. The content is highly variable. Teachers' work is guided more by inherited practices and individual decisions than by any clear and common view of what is to be covered, how it is to be covered, and why. In this sense, American schools have the worst of both worlds.

Our point is not that instructional guidance has been irrelevant in U.S. schools. Rather, it has been relevant only when someone chose to notice it and to do something about it. In a sense, this is true anywhere: teachers in Singaporean or French schools must notice guidance and choose to do something about it before it can shape instruction, but its consistency, prescriptiveness, and authority increase the chances that teachers will notice the same advice. In contrast, teachers' and students' autonomy have been enhanced in the United States because they work in such a diffuse system of instructional guidance. The classroom doors behind which teachers labor are no thicker here than elsewhere, but teachers receive fewer strong and consistent messages about content and pedagogy. Hence, they and their students have found it relatively easy to pursue their own preferences once the doors have closed behind them.

The situation has begun to change as recent school reformers seek to cure the ills of U.S. education by mobilizing more consistent guidance for instruction. We know little about the effects of these efforts, but the cures bear an uncanny resemblance to the disease. Several states and localities are trying to promote some form of consistent guidance, but quite naturally do so independently of each other. Federal education officials, as well as several national groups — the National Governors' Association, the National Board for Professional Teaching Standards, the National Council of Teachers of Mathematics, and others — recently have begun trying to create more consistent guidance for instruction, but their efforts so far have been independent of many state and local endeavors. Some professional associations also have taken up the idea, as have several academic disciplines; however, there is modest contact among these endeavors as well, and little relation to state and local initiatives. We live in a blizzard of different, divergent, and often inconsistent efforts to create more consistent guidance.

There also are deep divisions over the content of the recent reforms. Proposals for more lively and demanding instruction are circulating in various political, disciplinary, and educational circles, but there are many versions of the new ideas. These novel schemes also compete with established ideas and practices, for "back to basics," "effective schools," and "direct instruction" all are alive, well, and firmly rooted in school and classroom practice.

All of this is par for the American course. Government structure has not been changed by recent reforms, nor has political practice. The power of our ingeniously fragmented political system is evident even in efforts to cure fragmentation. Some attack fragmentation as a barrier to more effective instruction, but others celebrate it as a source of vitality in American institutions. Similarly, today's disagreements about the aims and methods of education are only the most recent expression of old tensions between our practical and anti-intellectual bent and our occasionally more elevated aspirations. The dispute has deep roots in both popular culture and the institutions of education, and it would be astonishing if it were settled easily or soon.

Effects of Instructional Guidance

If instructional guidance is worth noticing, it must be because it makes a difference to teaching and learning. But does it? Many educators around the world would think the answer obvious and affirmative. That guidance affects instruction is the working assumption of many European and Asian school systems. But many U.S. social scientists argue that it is difficult or impossible to steer education toward consistent practices or results, owing to weak knowledge of educational processes and other uncertainties (Berlak and Berlak, 1989; Floden and Clark, 1988; Jackson, 1968; Lampert, 1985; Lortie, 1975). John Meyer and his associates contend that school systems therefore create elaborate rituals, building a "logic of confidence" to replace evidence of rational relations between educational resources and processes on the one hand and results on the other (Scott and Meyer, 1983). School systems "buffer" themselves by offering evidence on attendance and degrees instead of on performance. Oddly, there is little evidence on these contending assumptions. For all the variation in instructional guidance, there is little research on its effects.

Effects on Teaching

Many scholars assert that guidance affects teaching. In writing of the effects of the French baccalaureat examinations, for instance, Patricia Broadfoot notes that the "examination questions virtually become the [schools'] syllabus" (Broadfoot, 1984, p. 210). But guidance from one source can be offset by guidance from another. Hence we put the issue more specifically: Is teaching more consistent in school systems with more consistent instructional guidance? The only direct way to answer the question would be to connect evidence on the structure and content of guidance in education systems to evidence on teaching within them. The only study that permits such comparisons is the IEA's Second International Mathematics Study (SIMS), but while SIMS contained evidence on math teaching and curriculum for fifteen nations, it offered few data on system structure. David Stevenson and David Baker (1991) compiled such data, focusing on the degree of central curriculum control, which they tied to SIMS data on the consistency of topic coverage among teachers within nations. They found that cross-national differences in the degree of central curriculum control were positively related to consistency in the topics that teachers reported that they taught. Teachers in nations with more centralized curriculum control reported greater agreement on topics taught than did teachers in systems with less. More centrally controlled systems also had fewer teachers who reported teaching little of the prescribed curriculum. There was less within-system variation in the amount of mathematics instruction in systems with more national curriculum control than in those with local or provincial control. Finally, teachers in more locally controlled systems were more likely to report that they adjusted instruction to local conditions, including their perceptions of students' ability and mastery of mathematics (Stevenson and Baker, 1991). Although modest, these differences all suggest an effect of consistent guidance, but Stevenson and Baker point out that they had no direct measures.

SIMS seems to be the only data set in which system-level effects can be explored, but instructional guidance operates at many levels of education. Many recent studies of school effectiveness have focused attention on school-level consistency in guidance. The studies are of varying quality, but they show that schools differ widely. Some adopt a laizzez-faire style, permit diverse offerings and approaches, and thus create many choices for teachers about what to teach and how, and for students about what to study and how much. Others offer more consistent instructional guidance, thus limiting both instructional offerings and faculty and student choices (Cusick, 1983; Powell, Farrar, and Cohen, 1985; Bryk, Lee, and Smith, 1990).

What explains the effects of instructional guidance on teaching? Researchers who study individual schools offer varied answers to the question. Some point to school heads' leadership in forging consensus about goals and methods; others focus on school "climate," or shared norms for instruction among faculty and students (Bryk, Lee, and Smith, 1990), and others offer levels of faculty collegiality and cooperation (Purkey and Smith, 1983). But other analysts point as much to structural as cultural factors; that is, some schools are committed to less differentiation in the curriculum and thus to fewer choices for students and teachers, creating more consistency by organizing curriculum around a common core of courses (Powell, Farrar, and Cohen, 1985). Not surprisingly, such schools tend to be smaller (Bryk, Lee, and Smith, 1990), which suggests another influence on consistency. Researchers who study school systems offer a different sort of answer: more central control of curriculum produces more consistent topic coverage (Stevenson and Baker, 1991). But it is possible that such consistency only expresses what teachers learned as students. If elementary and secondary schools are the prime agencies of teacher education, as many scholars argue, then the curriculum that teachers present may reflect their earlier school learning, rather than current official directives. The difference could be consequential for reform: if official directives are a potent influence on teachers' actions, then recent state and national reforms might quickly affect classroom work, but if consistency is more the result of inattentive curricular hand-me-downs, then changes in policy could take much longer to find their way into classroom practice.

Effects on Learning

Our interest in the effect of instructional guidance on teaching is partly instrumental: we want to know if it affects learning. There is, unfortunately, no cross-national evidence on this issue, nor do we expect anything persuasive soon, for researchers would have to connect evidence on the large structure of educational systems with evidence on the fine structure of teaching, and connect both of those to learning. Furthermore, they would have to do so across many different nations with different school systems. It would be an immensely complex task to make those connections while also taking other salient influences into account. If the prior history of research on school effects is any precedent, knowledge will grow slowly.

But many U.S. schools have tried to improve learning by increasing guidance for instruction, and many researchers have investigated the effects. One body of evidence arises from studies associated with the movement for "effective schools." Researchers reported that students' achievement improved or was higher than expected in schools in which leaders focused on common goals and faculty had high expectations for students (Purkey and Smith, 1983; Rowan, 1990). But these studies usually involved only a few schools, and most offered very limited data on school organization and culture (Purkey and Smith, 1983).

More systematic evidence on the effects of school-level guidance arises from reanalyses of the High School and Beyond data set. Bryk and Driscoll (1988) probed the relations between various measures of schools as "communities" and students' performance. Community included shared values, common curriculum and other activities, and an ethos of caring for students. Schools that were high on these dimensions had significantly lower dropout rates and absenteeism and slightly higher gains in mathematics achievement. Lee and Bryk (1989) used the same data set to probe differences in schools' constraint of curricular choices. Schools that channeled most work into a common curriculum created consistency by increasing the amount of work that students did in common. Lee and Bryk argued that such schools tended to reduce performance differences among students over time, particularly for minority students. In a later article they wrote that schools can "minimize the normal differentiation effects that accompany wide latitude in course choices. . . . [I]nitial differences among students' [performance] can be either amplified or constrained" (Bryk, Lee, and Smith, 1990, p. 178).

John Chubb and Terry Moe also reanalyzed High School and Beyond and stressed consistent instructional guidance even more. They argued that high-performing high schools are marked by "coherence," in which principals "provide a clear vision of

where the schools are going . . . [and] encourage . . . cooperation and collegiality." These attributes add up to "organizational
coherence" (Chubb and Moe, 1990, p. 91). They also found
that students performed better when school staffs had a coherent vision of academic goals and were collegial and cooperative, although the magnitude of the effect was quite modest.

Summary of Effects

What can we conclude about the effects of instructional guidance? For one thing, consistency is a construct with quite different dimensions. One line of thought focuses on culture and
values, another on the organization of curriculum choice, and
a third on leadership. For another, most research on the effects
of instructional guidance is recent, and the evidence is modest.
One cross-national study seems to show that more central curriculum control is modestly associated with greater topical consistency in teaching, and various U.S. school studies claim that
more consistent instructional guidance is associated with more
consistent instruction. But no field studies make a convincing
case for the causal power of guidance, and no cross-system
studies connect consistency at the system level with student performance. Both are crucial gaps. A diverse body of research
shows that more consistent instruction and instructional guidance
in schools are associated with higher student achievement, but
the causal ambiguities remain, and there are significant problems in inferences from schools to systems. Additionally, although
most studies reveal only modest effects, scholars argue fiercely
about them (Witte, 1990).

Even if the studies were more extensive and convincing,
there is another problem: the measure of student achievement
in all this research has been traditional standardized tests. These
tests entail a version of academic accomplishment that is said
to depend heavily on recall of isolated facts and mastery of routine mental operations—just the sort of work that recent reformers wish schools to put aside in favor of more sophisticated
endeavors. Can we assume that a positive effect of consistent
guidance on such tests would hold for more challenging ver-

sions of achievement? It seems doubtful. Some would argue that the ambitious academic work recent reformers seek would be inimical to consistent guidance. With Theodore Sizer, they would say that if schools are to cultivate sophisticated and independent instruction, they must be sophisticated and independent.

Do we conclude that instructional guidance affects teaching and learning? Plainly it does, somehow, but how? Are the effects of guidance fragmentary or systemic? Specifically, are teaching and learning more consistent in systems that have more consistent guidance for instruction? Evidence on this question is thin. There is some support for the idea in one cross-national study, as well as in many smaller studies of schools, but these studies are limited in many ways, and the authors of the cross-national study caution their readers against making too much of the results (Stevenson and Baker, 1991). There is, for example, no evidence that would permit us to distinguish the effects of formal guidance from teachers' earlier learning. Research on this matter does not offer much support for recent U.S. efforts to use instructional guidance to press teaching and learning toward greater consistency.

Change in Teaching

Uncertainty about the effects of instructional guidance looms even larger when we consider the content of guidance that reformers wish to offer teachers and students. They propose to transform teaching from relatively dull and routine practices into exciting and intellectually demanding ones. To this end many argue for novel assessments that are tied to both new curriculum frameworks and radically revised instructional materials, a combination seen as a way to dramatically change learning and teaching. Would that happen? The studies discussed thus far have little to say on this point, for they all concern the present and past operations of schools and school systems. What do we know about how teachers might change in response to more consistent and ambitious guidance for their work?

Precious little, if we want a direct answer. We have found no studies of school systems that attempted to shift from local autonomy and traditional teaching to more centrally controlled and intellectually ambitious instruction. None of the national school systems that currently exhibit great consistency did so. Some evolved over the course of several centuries, others were hastily created in the wake of decolonization, but in neither case were teachers required to change from well-established traditional practice to novel and much more adventurous practice.

Some have studied efforts to turn teaching in a more adventurous direction. Larry Cuban found that American classrooms remained traditional despite progressive reforms (Cuban, 1984). He argued that teaching changes at a glacial pace and in fragmentary fashion. In most cases teachers borrowed bits and pieces of progressive ideas and practices and integrated them into standard classroom formats. That conclusion fits with the studies of other investigators in the United States and the United Kingdom, who all concluded that efforts to make teaching more ambitious produced change at the margins but little else (Goodlad, Klein, and Associates, 1974; Popkewitz, Tabachnick, and Wehlage, 1982; Stevens, 1912).

It might be objected that progressivism was only a program. There were many ideas, books, articles, pamphlets, and even a few teacher education agencies devoted to the "new education," and some professors taught courses. But there were no curricula, no assessments, no instructional frameworks that might have helped teachers to learn a different pedagogy. From this perspective, the 1950s curriculum reforms were an improvement, for there were many new textbooks, and teachers had many opportunities to learn about the curricula. Some of the new texts were widely adapted, and many teachers took advantage of opportunities to learn. But reports of great change in teaching were few and far between. Some teachers dramatically changed their approach to instruction in the early years of reform, but many more struggled to understand and change (Sarason, 1977). Most teachers made only marginal changes, grafting bits of reform ideas and practices onto established, traditional teaching. There is indirect evidence that these were major changes for the teachers involved (Cohen, 1990b; Cohen and Ball, 1990), but the difficulty of such change was not appreciated by most (Sarason, 1977). Measures that might have supported more change thus were not contemplated, much less taken, and changed educational priorities soon swept away opportunities for teachers to learn more. A subsequent National Science Foundation (NSF)-sponsored study found few classroom traces of the curriculum reforms (Stake and Easley, 1978).

Would not the recent reforms be much more potent? Instead of new texts and opportunities for further education, there would be an entire guidance system: new instructional frameworks reflected in novel sorts of assessment, in new curriculum materials, and in new approaches to teacher licensing and education. Would not "systemic reform" (Smith and O'Day, 1991) offer much more structure for teaching, much richer opportunities for teacher learning, and a chance for professional community in teaching? Would not more direction offer more support and pressure for change?

The idea has some appeal. But if greater structure and consistency would offer a more substantial basis for change in teaching, it does not follow that change would be easy or swift, for the greater structure would frame new and ambitious purposes, content, and methods. The agenda for teacher change would be vast, even with greater guidance. Consider, for example, studies of the "new math" in Europe. Some European school systems that adopted the new math had more consistent guidance for instruction than did others or the United States, but those differences did not seem to effect change in teaching. The research is spotty, but the most detailed study argues that the processes of reform were strikingly similar across systems with very different structures (Moon, 1986). Reports about change in teaching also were quite homogeneous across systems. Participants and researchers reported that classroom practice changed only a little, and for the most part in fragmentary ways (Damerow, 1980; Howson, 1980; Moon, 1986; Oldham, 1980a, 1980b; Van der Blij, Hilding, and Weinzweig, 1980). The new math seemed to fare little differently in the French system of consistent guidance structures than in the less consistent British or U.S. systems (Welch, 1979).

We are inclined to think that some versions of systemic

reform could offer more support for radical change in teaching than purely decentralized arrangements, but there is no evidence on the relative rates or depth of change under various organizational conditions. More important, there is growing evidence of several fundamental obstacles to the changes that reformers currently urge, none of which are structural in nature. One concerns teachers' knowledge. The recent reforms demand a depth and sophistication in teachers' grasp of academic subjects that is far beyond most public school teachers. For instance, although math is a leading area in the current reforms, most elementary school teachers have a very modest understanding of the mathematics they teach (Post and others, 1988; Thompson, 1984). They would need to learn a great deal more if the reforms were to have any chance of success. More important, teachers would have to shed established modes of understanding and adopt more modern, constructivist versions of knowledge. Such change is not just a matter of learning more—it could fairly be termed a revolution, and scholarship in several fields has shown that intellectual revolutions are very difficult to foment (Cohen, 1990b; Cohen and Ball, 1990; Fiske and Taylor, 1984; Markus and Zajonc, 1985; Nisbett and Ross, 1980; Kuhn, 1970).

Another obstacle lies in teaching. Even if teachers knew all that they needed, the reforms propose that students become active, engaged, and collaborative. If so, classroom roles would have to change radically. Teachers would have to rely on students to produce much more instruction, and students would have to think and act in ways they rarely do. Teachers would have to become coaches or conductors and abandon more familiar and didactic roles in which they "tell knowledge" to students (Lampert, 1988; Newmann, 1988; Roehler and Duffy, 1988; Scardamalia, Bereiter, and Steinbach, 1984; Sizer, 1984). Researchers have studied only a few efforts at such change, but they report unusual difficulty, for teachers must manage complex interactions about complex ideas in rapid-fire fashion. The uncertainties of teaching multiply phenomenally, as does teachers' vulnerability (Cohen, 1988; Cuban, 1984; Lampert, 1988; Roehler and Duffy, 1988; Newmann, 1988).

Because the recent reforms would require much teacher learning, they would require many changes in teachers' opportunities to learn — a third obstacle to change. Those who presently teach would need many educational opportunities on the job as well as off in colleges, universities, and other agencies. Yet few schools now offer teachers many chances to learn while they teach, and what they do offer is generally deemed weak at best. Most continuing education in universities has a dismal reputation among teachers and researchers. In addition, intending teachers would require fundamentally revamped undergraduate disciplinary and professional education. Few intending elementary teachers can major in an academic subject, and few intending teachers of any sort can learn new approaches to subject matter or pedagogy, since college and university educators rarely teach as reformers now intend (Boyer, 1987; Cohen, 1988; Cuban, 1984; McKeachie, Pintrich, Lin, and Smith, 1986).

More consistent guidance for instruction could not solve these problems although, under some conditions too complex to spell out here, it might help. But fundamental change in teaching also would require fundamental reform of the education of intending and practicing teachers, and equally fundamental changes in schools and universities to support such learning. Even with those reforms, deep change in teaching probably would be slow and difficult.

Beyond Formal Structure

Guidance for instruction never stands alone. School systems contain not only rules and formal structures but also beliefs about authority, habits of deference and resistance, and knowledge about how things work. Culture and social organization intertwine with formal structure. The success of school systems in Europe and Asia that offer consistent guidance may owe more to the influences of culture and society than to government or system structure. Because U.S. society often undermines academic effort, the attention to system structure in our current reform movement may be misplaced.

Social Circumstances of Schooling

Higher education and business firms are the two largest consumers of schooling in most societies. Hence, their consumption patterns send signals concerning the qualities and accomplishments they find desirable in students. The consumption patterns of American colleges and universities send mixed but generally weak signals about the importance of strong academic performance. Only a small group of highly selective colleges and universities has demanding admissions standards, so only a few students can enter them. A much larger fraction has very modest requirements: students need only a thin record of academic accomplishment in high school, often only a "C" or low "B" average, to be acceptable for admission. Only high school graduation is required for admission in still another large group of institutions, and not even high school graduation is required in another large group. There is something to celebrate in this, for many students have a second or third chance to make good despite previous failures. But these arrangements also signal that it is irrational for most high school students to work hard in order to get into college or university (Bishop, 1989a, 1989b; Powell, Farrar, and Cohen, 1985; Trow, 1961, 1988).

A similar situation holds for the employment practices of most U.S. businesses. Few firms ask for students' high school transcripts or references from teachers when considering them for employment, and even when they do request transcripts, only a tiny fraction of schools supply them (Bishop, 1989a, 1989b). The lack of employer interest deters students from thinking that grades, effort, or behavior count for jobs, and it deters teachers from thinking that their judgments about students could make a difference (Rosenbaum and Kariya, 1989). Hence it would be irrational for students who intend leaving high school for work to do their best in school. Thinking deeply is difficult, and only a small fraction of students seem intrinsically motivated to do it. If students can get jobs without presenting evidence of their grades, school behavior, and teachers' evaluations of their work, why should they work hard?

Colleges and universities in Japan, France, and many other nations, on the other hand, lay great weight on students' performance in high school or on high school leaving and university entrance exams. If students wish to enter a university, it is essential to work hard in school and get good grades, prepare for the exams, or both (Rosenbaum and Kariya, 1987).

There are many troublesome features of such systems, including the exclusion of able students who do not do well on exams, but they leave no doubt in any minds about the importance of hard work and good school performance.

Employers in many nations also pay close attention to students' secondary school records in hiring decisions. This is true in Japan, New South Wales, Australia, Singapore, and West Germany (Bishop, 1987, 1989a, 1989b; Clark, 1985; Kariya and Rosenbaum, 1987; Rosenbaum and Kariya, 1989). Employers routinely review transcripts and teacher references when high school graduates or early school leavers apply for jobs. In some cases, schools and employers work closely in placing students in apprenticeship or regular work situations. Teachers know this, as do students, so it is understood that students who do not apply themselves and behave decently in school will have difficulty finding good jobs. Hence there are important rewards for academic effort and good behavior, even for students who have no ambitions for further education.

Culture

Incentives are not the whole story. The values attached to learning and teaching differ among societies, as do attitudes toward authority and habits of child rearing. Such beliefs, values, and habits may support the guidance that issues from formal agencies in some cases and subvert it in others.

Americans have long been ambivalent about intellectual work: anti-intellectualism is a prominent feature in American culture (Hofstadter, 1963), and we are inclined to value experience over formal education. Americans also value practical rather than intellectual content within formal education (for example, learning to "get along") and job-related knowledge and skills (Cusick, 1983; Lynd and Lynd, 1929; Powell, Farrar, and Cohen, 1985). Eighty-one percent of the respondents in a recent Gallup poll said that the chief reasons people want their children to get a formal education are job opportunities, preparation for a better life, better paying jobs, and financial security. Only 15 percent said that the chief reason was to become more knowledgeable or to learn to think and understand (Elam and Gallup, 1989). Relatively few American mothers report working closely with their children on academic tasks or offering support for hard work and success in school (Stevenson and others, 1985; Stevenson, Lee, and Stigler, 1986).

Intellectual work and academic accomplishment appear to be more highly regarded in other societies. In Japan and China, for instance, parents take education very seriously and hold teachers in high esteem. Investigators report that Japanese mothers play a central role in their childrens' academic success (Holloway, Kashiwagi, Hess, and Hiroshi, 1986; Lebra, 1976; Shimahara, 1986; White, 1987). They encourage children and work closely with them on assignments, creating an environment conducive to learning (Holloway, Kashihagi, Hess, and Hiroshi, 1986; Stevenson and others, 1985; Stevenson and Lee, 1990; White, 1987). Similar practices are found among Chinese parents (Stevenson and Lee, 1990). Japanese and Chinese mothers also seem to hold higher standards for their children and to have more realistic evaluations of their achievement than American mothers (Stevenson and Lee, 1990).

Family life and values may support successful schooling in Japan while impeding it in the United States. One researcher noted that "it would be quite impossible to take account of Japanese formal education without recognizing that — in many ways — it lives in close symbiosis with that culture" (King, 1986, p. 75; see also White, 1987). American commentators often have offered similar explanations of weak work in school here (Coleman, 1961; Cusick, 1983; Lynd and Lynd, 1929; Powell, Farrar, and Cohen, 1985).

Habits of association and attitudes toward authority also may help to explain why formal guidance for instruction seems to be treated more seriously in some societies than in others. Since Alexis de Tocqueville, observers have noted Americans' distinctive individualism: their preoccupation with personal autonomy and their focus on individual expression and development. These qualities often have been contrasted with more cooperative and deferential behavior in other societies, in which people seem more preoccupied with how they can fit in, work with others, and advance collective values. For instance, Japanese teachers carefully foster cooperative work on common tasks, build habits of collaboration and conflict resolution, and teach accommodation to group preferences. They exercise great patience in encouraging students to work with groups and use groups to regulate behavior, manage conflict, and support desired attitudes. In the process, Japanese teachers accommodate "discipline" problems that would be intolerable to most Americans. But they build many centers of support for the values and behavior that they wish to inculcate rather than assuming the entire burden themselves. Many "discipline" problems are therefore managed by other students rather than the teacher alone (Boocock, 1989; Peak, 1989).

Many American teachers instead foster individual work on individual tasks, cultivate little or no group activity, and rarely build group strength. They do not support accommodation to group preferences but tend to impose their own preferences. They manage all discipline problems themselves and have little patience with misbehavior. American students learn little about alternative ways to manage conflict or about collaborative work.

Thomas Rohlen (1989) framed these comparisons in a broad analysis of differences in organizational life. He viewed Japanese classrooms as marked by more respect and deference than those in the United States but as less hierarchical and teacher centered. The Japanese emphasis on accommodation to group values and cooperative work helps to explain the coexistence of two things that strike Americans as inconsistent: deference to authority and enormous capacity for productive work in decentralized organizations. Rohlen notes that these qualities are found in all sorts of organizations, from primary classrooms to business and government. "The result is an overall social structure that is in many respects centrifugal in terms of affiliation and the capacity to order events. Social contexts and organizations are built up from the bottom (or the outside), so to speak, in a way that invests the peripheral entities with great stability. The locus of social order is in the lower-level, subordinate groupings. . . . These entities gain a degree of autonomy from the fact that internally they are strengthened by the pattern of attachment we are considering" (Rohlen, 1989, pp. 31–32).

Americans have few alternatives between individualism and imposed authority. We often fluctuate between centralized hierarchies and decentralization. The result makes it difficult for central authority to succeed, while also precluding the development of alternatives. The remarkable consistency in Japanese education may owe as much to deference to authority, habits of accommodation, and extraordinary pressures for cooperation at all levels as to formal guidance.

Conclusion

Most schemes for fundamental change present a paradox. They offer appealing visions of a new order but also contain a devastating critique of existing realities, which, if pursued, reveals the lack of many capacities that would be required to realize and sustain the new vision. Reformers can imagine a better world in which those capacities would be created, but their problem is more practical: how to create the new world when those capacities are lacking.

Recent reform proposals offer a version of this puzzle, for they entail two dramatic departures from American political and instructional practice. One is that schools should promote a new instructional order marked by deep comprehension of academic subjects, in which students are active learners rather than passive recipients and in which teachers practice a much more thoughtful and demanding pedagogy. The other is radical reform in school governance and instructional guidance to produce the desired changes in classrooms. These reforms include a national examination or testing system, national curricula, a national system of teacher certification, and many equally dramatic reforms at the state level. Although different in important ways, all of these plans and proposals move sharply toward greater state, national, or federal control of education. All seek to realize new and ambitious sorts of teaching and learning in ordinary classrooms. Hence all represent an effort to much more powerfully guide instructional practice with policy. These are astonishing, even revolutionary, proposals that are appealing in many respects. But we have pointed to weak capacities for change in several crucial departments.

One is politics. Reformers seek much greater state, national, or federal control of education and a consequent tightening of the links between central policy and local practice. But the entire fragmented apparatus of American government weighs against such ventures. Past efforts have met with extremely limited success, and they produced organizational side effects that have greatly complicated governance and administration.

These reforms sketched above seem unlikely to succeed unless the governance and organization of U.S. education is either greatly streamlined or simply bypassed. Streamlining has much appeal, including relief from the burdens consequent upon past efforts to reform local practice with state or federal policy. But streamlining would entail an unprecedented reduction of existing policies and programs, and thus a reduction in existing governmental authorities at all levels. It would spell the end of many state and local government functions in education, even though it could ease many administrative and organizational problems. What would induce local and state officials to accept the diminishment or demise of their domains? Visions of a better school system? Barring fiscal catastrophe or a sustained mass movement for fundamental change in education, we see no sign of the requisite inducements.

Bypassing government appeals to many partly because the prospects for streamlining seem so bleak. The creation of nongovernmental or quasi-nongovernmental authorities that may design a national examination system already is under way. A similar course of action has been taken by the National Board on Professional Teaching Standards in its efforts to create a national system of teacher examination and certification. Such bypass operations have great short-run appeal, for avoiding government sponsorship and operations could greatly ease the work of designing and developing national education systems of one sort or another. But the systems thus created would only work in the medium and long run if government were streamlined, for national curricula, examinations, or teacher certification systems could operate efficiently only if many extant policies and programs regarding testing, curriculum, instruction, and teacher licensing fell into disuse. Of course, that would require many existing state and local government authorities to fade away, the difficulties of which we just touched upon.

Instructional practice is a second realm in which the capacity for change is weak. Reformers seek much more thoughtful, adventurous, and demanding teaching and learning, and they envision new instructional guidance to produce it. But nearly the entire corpus of instructional practice weighs against it. Teachers and students spend most of their time with lectures, recitations, and worksheets. Intellectual demands generally are modest, and a great deal of the work is dull. Only a modest fraction of public school teachers have deep knowledge of any academic subject. Research and experience both show that past efforts to fundamentally change teaching have had modest effects at best. Most often, they have resulted in fragmentary adoption of new practices, or translation of new practices into old ones, or both.

Solutions to these capacity problems would require fundamental redevelopment in education. An intellectually ambitious system of instructional guidance would be one key element, but few Americans have had the education or experience that would prepare them to understand such guidance or put it to appropriate use. To build new capacities for education would be to reeducate many Americans. That is obviously true for teachers, but teachers' efforts would not prosper if parents and political leaders did not understand and support their work. Additionally, few teachers work in schools that could support radically different approaches to instruction, let alone teachers' efforts to learn such things. Building new capacity would require that schools become places in which teachers could learn and teach very differently.

Such redevelopment would be an immensely ambitious endeavor. The creation of new instructional guidance arrangements would be an extraordinary research and development task, surely the largest ever in U.S. education. For example, new examinations would have to be invented, to assess a broader range of academic knowledge and skills than conventional tests. The exams also would assess students' skill and knowledge in more diverse ways, for example, writing essays in English, explaining and justifying answers in chemistry, and offering nonnumerical representations of mathematical problem solving. Because examinations of this sort would invite students to use and display a broad range of knowledge and skill (Nickerson, 1989), the results would be difficult and time consuming to evaluate, especially for a large and diverse population. Such things are possible, and approximations can be found here and there in the United States and some other nations (Resnick and Resnick, 1989). But the approach has been little tried in the United States, although specialists are just beginning to invent examples and a few states are beginning to experiment with them (California State Department of Education, 1985). A few problems with such exams have already been suggested (Porter, 1990), but many others are likely to appear if they actually are developed and widely used.

New curricula also would be needed for any guidance system keyed to deep understanding of academic subjects. Instructional frameworks, texts, and other materials would have to be devised, along with curriculum guides that focused attention on key elements of each academic subject. These materials would have to be accessible to a large and diverse population of teachers and learners, and they would be most useful if designed in a way that teachers could learn from them while teaching, preparing to teach, and reconsidering their teaching. Such materials would be most helpful to teachers and students if subject coverage were integrated across the grades. Though such things seem possible, they are entirely unfamiliar in the U.S. A few states are just beginning to develop more demanding and thoughtful curricula, but it seems reasonable to expect that such a novel endeavor would take a long time to develop and longer to mature.

Neither new exams nor new curricula would work unless teachers understood them, and as things now stand, most teachers would not. This problem might be solved in part if teachers were extensively involved in building new frameworks, curricula, and assessments and in grading students' work. Such activities could be extraordinarily educative if they were designed with that end in view, but to do so would greatly complicate the development tasks. Additionally, these activities would reach only a fraction of the teaching force and touch only part of the reeducation need. Teacher education itself would have to be greatly improved, which would require fundamental changes in college and university education, to deepen both professional and subject matter education and focus much more closely on the content of schooling. Such daunting changes might be encouraged by the examination system that the National Board for Professional Teaching Standards has proposed. Intending teachers' grasp of subject matter and pedagogy could be fairly assessed, then the exams might offer college and university programs sensible targets for their educational efforts. If the targets were accepted, if teacher education programs were revised accordingly, and if school systems used the exam results as hiring criteria, the quality of teaching might be greatly improved. But note that such changes would be immense: the examinations do not now exist, and it would take colleges and universities at least a generation to make the required instructional reforms. The National Board is just beginning to develop some exams, and current estimates are that it will take at least three years to produce an initial prototype in a single subject for a grade or two. The NBPTS staff hopes that a full set of examinations will be developed by the year 1997, though no one really knows how long it will take. Here too Americans are relatively inexperienced. Even if the exams were developed roughly on schedule, it would be prudent to assume that many adjustments would be required as the exams came into use, and only a handful of professors have given any thought to the reforms of higher education that might dramatically improve the education of intending teachers.

It would be no mean feat to solve any one of these research and development problems by itself. But the recent reforms are "systemic"; that is, they seek to link assessment of students' performance to the content and form of curriculum guides and course materials, and to tie both of them to teacher education. Hence the research and development tasks sketched above should be undertaken jointly, which would be an extraordinarily demanding and time-consuming effort.

Although changes in instructional guidance are crucial,

they would not work all by themselves. Americans are well used to local control of education, and they have been less and less inclined to defer to teachers. Radical reform of instruction would be unlikely to get very far unless parents and political leaders supported it, yet to do so these Americans would have to embrace very different conceptions of knowledge, teaching, learning, and schooling than they currently do. That is possible. For instance, administrators, political leaders, and parents could learn about new examinations by participating in their development, in field trials, and in revisions. Though such work probably would increase conflict in the short run, it might increase the long-run chances that the finished exams would be understood, accepted, and used appropriately. But the learning would be a great change for parents and political leaders, no less difficult than for teachers and students, and to give administrators, parents, and politicians opportunities to learn would complicate, slow down, and alter the development of new exams.

Finally, the reforms we have been discussing would require changes in individual school operations and organization. One reason is that teachers and administrators would have a great deal to learn. It is unlikely they could offer the intellectually ambitious instruction that reformers seek unless they had ample time to learn on the job. Another reason is that the new instruction would be much more complex and demanding than the common fare in schools today. It is unlikely that teachers could do such work unless they had the autonomy to make complicated decisions, to work with colleagues, and to revise as they went. Still another reason is that teachers could hardly contribute to the development of a common instructional system unless they had much more time and opportunities to work with others in education beyond their school. How could these changes be made in the context of reforms that entail much greater central authority and power? This could not be done easily, unless the reforms were carefully designed to enhance such autonomy, and unless the capacities to exercise it were nurtured at all levels of education. Marshall Smith and Jennifer O'Day (1991) have sensibly argued that systemic reform would require a combination of "bottom-up" and "top-down" change. But given the present organization of U.S. schools and school governments, and the work habits of policymakers, teachers, and administrators, that would be a great change indeed.

These observations suggest that the recent reforms might have more chances of success if the entire venture were conceived and executed as a great educational enterprise, one in which state and national leaders had as much to learn as teachers and students. That seems appropriate to a set of proposals that would require such radical change in individuals and institutions and the cultivation of so many new capacities. But the recent reforms began to catch Americans' imagination just as economic and social problems further constrained the capacities for change. States and localities are struggling with a massive fiscal crisis, and many confront staggering social problems.

What happens when grand visions of change collide with limited capacities? The most common consequences are incremental alteration at the margin of institutions and practices, or self-defeating results, or both. For example, education reformers could relatively easily add streamlining mandates and a layer of streamlining agencies to the existing accumulation of mandates and organizations. But they would find it much more difficult and costly to replace the present cluttered and fragmented structure with one that was much simpler and more powerful. Similarly, bypass operations could easily add complexity and confusion rather than reducing them. Governments would not sit still: experience suggests that they would respond by regulating the bypassing agencies, or by finding roles for themselves in interpreting and managing the functions generated by the bypassing agencies, or by taking over the bypass agencies without closing down the authorities that were to have been bypassed, or some combination of the above. Similarly, it would be relatively easy and cheap for reformers to add mandates for more thoughtful teaching and learning on top of extant mandates for teaching basic skills, informing students about drugs and AIDS, remedial education, bilingual education, and programs for cooperative learning and improving students' self-concepts. It would be much more difficult and costly to replace the present cluttered and fragmented accumulation of instructional guidance with a system that was simpler, more focused, and more powerful. It would be even more difficult to redevelop education in ways that would enable most educators to take advantage of such changes.

But uncommon results are always possible. For instance, the recent reforms might succeed by a sort of osmosis. If reformers kept up the pressure for several decades, much more consistent and demanding instruction might result. Indeed, the extraordinary fragmentation of American institutions may create a porosity that would permit such change. That sort of osmosis seems to have occurred in the spread of basic skills instruction during the 1970s and 1980s. Vastly more time and pressure would be required for the more difficult reforms that we have discussed here, and most reform movements in education are notoriously brief. But the fragmentation of American government could open many opportunities to persistent reformers.

We also may underestimate the ingenuity of policymakers and educators. Perhaps they will seize on the growing social and financial crisis to turn schools in the direction that reformers wish. Streamlining, simplification, and consistency could be appealing slogans in an era of falling budgets and rising problems. Perhaps the crippling legacy of the Reagan years in public finance and the economy will become an opportunity to press ahead with its nationalizing legacy in education.

No one knows how the story will turn out. But if American politics and education run true to form, reformers will do better at addition than subtraction. They will introduce many different schemes to make education more consistent, but they will be less able to produce consistency among those schemes, to greatly reduce the clutter of previous programs and policies, or to fundamentally change teaching. If so, current efforts to reduce fragmentation would only add several new and unrelated layers of educational requirements and instructional refinements on top of many old and inconsistent layers. The new ideas would have their day, but only at the expense of further clutter and inconsistency.

References

Bankston, M. *Organizational Reporting in a School District: State and Federal Programs.* Stanford, Calif.: Institute for Finance and Governance, School of Education, Stanford University, 1982.

Bardach, E., and Kagan, R. A. *Going by the Book: The Problem of Regulatory Unreasonableness.* Philadelphia: Temple University Press, 1982.

Beauchamp, G. and Beauchamp, H. *Comparative Analysis of Curriculum Systems.* Willmette, Ill.: The Kagg Press, 1972.

Berlak, A., and Berlak, H. *Dilemmas of Schooling.* New York: Routledge, Chapman & Hall, 1989.

Berman, P., and McLaughlin, M. *Federal Programs Supporting Educational Change.* Vol. VIII: *Implementing and Sustaining Innovations.* Santa Monica, Calif.: RAND Corporation, 1978.

Bishop, J. *Information Externalities and the Social Payoff to Academic Achievement.* Ithaca, N.Y.: Center for Advanced Human Resource Studies, Cornell University, 1987.

Bishop, J. *Incentives for Learning: Why American High School Students Compare So Poorly to Their Counterparts Overseas.* Ithaca, N.Y.: Center for Advanced Human Resource Studies, Cornell University, 1989a.

Bishop, J. "Why the Apathy in American High Schools?" *Educational Researcher,* 1989b, *18*(1), 6–10.

Boocock, S. "Controlled Diversity: An Overview of the Japanese Preschool System." *Journal of Japanese Studies,* 1989, *15*(1), 41–66.

Boyd, W., and Smart, D. *Educational Policy in Australia and America: Comparative Perspectives.* Bristol, Pa.: Falmer Press, 1987.

Boyer, E. *The Undergraduate Experience in America.* New York: HarperCollins, 1987.

Broadfoot, P. "Assessment Constraints on Curriculum Practice: A Comparative Study." In M. Hammersley and A. Hargreaves (eds.), *Curriculum Practice: Some Sociological Case Studies.* Bristol, Pa.: Falmer Press, 1983.

Broadfoot, P. "Form Public Examinations to Profile Assessment: The French Experience." In P. Broadfoot (ed.), *Selection, Certification, and Control.* Bristol, Pa.: Falmer Press, 1984.

Bryk, A., and Driscoll, M. *The High School as a Community: Contextual Influences and Consequences for Students and Teachers.* Madison, Wis.: National Center for Effective Secondary Schools, 1988.

Bryk, A., Lee, V., and Smith, J. "High School Organization and Its Effects on Teachers and Students: An Interpretive Summary of the Research." In W. H. Clune and J. F. Witte (eds.), *Choice and Control in American Education.* Vol. 1. Bristol, Pa.: Falmer Press, 1990.

California State Department of Education. *Mathematics Framework.* Sacramento, Calif.: California Sate Department of Education, 1985.

Cameron, J., and others (eds.). *"Australia." International Handbook of Educational Systems.* New York: Wiley, 1984a.

Cameron, J., and others (eds.). *"France." International Handbook of Educational Systems.* New York: Wiley, 1984b.

Cameron, J., and others (eds.). *"Japan." International Handbook of Educational Systems.* New York: Wiley, 1984c.

Cameron, J., and others (eds.). *"Singapore." International Handbook of Educational Systems.* New York: Wiley, 1984d.

Cantor, L. "The Growing Role of States in American Education." *Comparative Education,* 1980, *16*(1), 25–31.

Cheney, L. *National Tests: What Other Countries Expect Their Students to Know.* Washington, D.C.: National Endowment for the Humanities, 1991.

Chubb, J. E., and Moe, T. M. *Politics, Markets, and America's Schools.* Washington, D.C.: Brookings Institution, 1990.

Clark, B. "Interorganizational Patterns in Education." *Administrative Science Quarterly,* 1965, *10,* 224–237.

Clark, B. "The High School and the University: What Went Wrong in America, Part II." *Phi Delta Kappan,* Mar. 1985, *66,* 472–475.

Cohen, D. K. "Policy and Organization: The Impact of State and Federal Educational Policy on School Governance." *Harvard Educational Review,* 1982, *52*(4), 474–499.

Cohen, D. K. *Teaching Practice: Plus ca Change. . . .* East Lansing, Mich.: National Center for Research on Teacher Education, Michigan State University, 1988.

Cohen, D. K. "Governance and Instruction: The Promise of

Decentralization and Choice." In W. H. Clune and J. F. Witte (eds.), *Choice and Control in American Education.* Bristol, Pa.: Falmer Press, 1990a.

Cohen, D. K. "A Revolution in One Classroom: The Case of Mrs. Oublier." *Educational Evaluation and Policy Analysis,* 1990b, *12,* 311–330.

Cohen, D. K., and Ball, D. L. "Relations Between Policy and Practice: A Commentary." *Educational Evaluation and Policy Analysis,* 1990, *12*(3), 331–338.

Coleman, J. *The Adolescent Society.* New York: Free Press, 1961.

Cuban, L. *How Teachers Taught: Constancy and Change in American Classrooms, 1890–1980.* New York: Longman, 1984.

Cusick, P. *The Egalitarian Ideal and the American High School.* New York: Longman, 1983.

Damerow, P. "Patterns of Geometry in German Textbooks." In H. G. Steiner, *Comparative Studies of Mathematics Curricula — Change and Stability, 1960–1980.* Haus Ohrbeck (FRG): Institut fur Didaktik der Mathematik der Universitat Bielefeld, 1980.

Darling-Hammond, L. "The Over-Regulated Curriculum and the Press for Teacher Professionalism." *NASSP Bulletin,* Apr. 1987, pp. 22–29.

Darling-Hammond, L., and Wise, A. E. "Beyond Standardization: State Standards and School Improvement." *Elementary School Journal,* 1985, *85*(3), 315–336.

Eckstein, M., and Noah, H. "Forms and Functions of Secondary School Leaving Examinations." *Comparative Education Review,* 1989, *33*(3), 295–316.

Elam, S. M., and Gallup, A. M. "The 21st Annual Gallup Poll of the Public Attitudes Toward the Public Schools." *Phi Delta Kappan,* 1989, *71,* 41–54.

Ellwein, M. C., Glass, G. V., and Smith, M. L. "Standards of Competence: Propositions on the Nature of Testing Reforms." *Educational Researcher,* 1988, *17*(8), 4–9.

Firestone, W. "Educational Policy as an Ecology of Games." *Educational Researcher,* 1989, *18*(7), 18–24.

Fiske, S., and Taylor, S. *Social Cognition.* Reading, Mass.: Addison-Wesley, 1984.

Floden, R. E., and Clark, C. "Preparing Teachers for Uncertainty." *Teachers College Record,* 1988, *89,* 505–524.

Floden, R. E., Porter, A. C., Schmidt, W. H., and Freeman, D. J. *Don't They All Measure the Same Thing? Consequences of Selecting Standardized Tests.* Research Series no. 25. East Lansing, Mich.: Institute for Research on Teaching, Michigan State University, 1978.

Floden, R., and others. "Instructional Leadership at the District Level: A Closer Look at Autonomy and Control." *Educational Administration Quarterly,* 1988, *24*(2), 96–124.

Freeman, D. J., and Porter, A. C. "Do Textbooks Dictate the Content of Mathematics Instruction in Elementary Schools?" *American Educational Research Journal,* 1989, *26*(3), 403–421.

Freeman, D., and others. "Do Textbooks and Tests Define a National Curriculum in Elementary School Mathematics?" *Elementary School Journal,* 1983, *83*(5), 501–514.

Fuhrman, S. "Diversity Amidst Standardization: State Differential Treatment of Districts." In W. H. Clune and J. F. Witte (eds.), *Choice and Control in American Education.* Bristol, Pa.: Falmer Press, 1990.

Fuhrman, S., Clune, W., and Elmore, R. "Research on Educational Reform: Lessons on the Implementation of Policy." *Teachers College Record,* 1988, *90*(2), 237–257.

Goodlad, J., Klein, M., and Associates. *Looking Behind the Classroom Door.* New York: McGraw-Hill, 1974.

Haggstrom, G., Darling-Hammond, L., and Grissmer, D. *Assessing Teacher Supply and Demand.* Santa Monica, Calif.: RAND Corporation, 1988.

Hofstadter, R. *Anti-Intellectualism in American Life.* New York: Vintage Books, 1963.

Holloway, S., Kashiwagi, K., Hess, R., and Hiroshi, A. "Casual Attributions by Japanese and American Mothers and Children About Performance in Mathematics." *International Journal of Psychology,* 1986, *21*, 269–286.

Holmes, B. *International Guide to Education Systems.* Paris: UNESCO, 1979.

Horner, W. "Curriculum Research in France and Luxembourg." In U. Hameyer, K. Frey, H. Haft, and F. Kuebart (eds.), *Curriculum Research in Europe.* Strasbourg: Council of Europe, 1986.

Howson, A. "Some Remarks on the Case Studies." In H. G. Steiner, *Comparative Studies of Mathematics Curricula — Change and*

Stability, 1960–1980. Haus Ohrbeck (FRG): Institut fur Didaktik der Mathematik der Universitat Bielefeld, 1980.

Jackson, P. *Life in Classrooms.* New York: Holt, Rinehart & Winston, 1968.

Kariya, T., and Rosenbaum, J. "Self-Selection in Japanese Junior High Schools: A Longitudinal Study of Students' Educational Plans." *American Journal of Sociology,* 1987, *60,* 168–180.

Kaufman, H. "Administrative Decentralization and Political Power." *Public Administration Review,* 1969, *29*(1), 3–15.

Kellaghan, T., and Madaus, G. "Proposals for a National American Test: Lessons from Europe." Unpublished manuscript, Boston College, 1991.

Kida, H. "Educational Administration in Japan." *Comparative Education,* 1986, *22*(1), 7–12.

Kiesler, S., and Sproull, L. "Managerial Responses to Changing Environments: Perspectives on Problem Sensing from Social Cognition." *Administrative Science Quarterly,* 1982, *27,* 548–570.

Kimbrough, J., and Hill, P. *The Aggregate Effects of Federal Education Programs.* Santa Monica, Calif.: RAND Corporation, 1981.

King, E. "Japan's Education in Comparative Perspective." *Comparative Education,* 1986, *22*(1), 73–82.

Kirst, M. W. "Who Should Control Our Schools: Reassessing Current Policies." Stanford, Calif.: Center for Education Research, Stanford University, 1988.

Kobayashi, V. "Japanese and U.S. Curricula Compared." In W. Cummings and others (eds.), *Educational Policies in Crisis.* New York: Praeger, 1984.

Kreitzer, A. E., Madaus, G. F., and Haney, W. "Competency Testing and Dropouts" Unpublished paper, Boston College, 1989.

Kuhn, T. *The Structure of Scientific Revolutions.* Chicago: University of Chicago Press, 1970.

Lampert, M. "How Do Teachers Manage to Teach? Perspectives on Problems in Practice." *Harvard Educational Review,* 1985, *55*(2), 178–194.

Lampert, M. *Teachers' Thinking About Students' Thinking About Geometry: The Effects of New Teaching Tools.* Cambridge, Mass.: Educational Technology Center, 1988.

Lawton, D., and Gordon, P. *The HMI.* New York: Routledge & Kegan Paul, 1987.

Lebra, T. *Japanese Patterns of Behavior.* Honolulu, Hawaii: University Press of Hawaii, 1976.

Lee, V., and Bryk, T. "A Multilevel Model of the Social Distribution of High School Achievements." *Sociology of Education,* 1989, *62,* 172–192.

Lewis, H. *The French Education System.* London: Croom Helm, 1985.

Lewis, H. "Some Aspects of Education in France Relevant to Current Concerns in the U.K." *Comparative Education,* 1989, *25*(3), 369–378.

Lortie, D. *Schoolteacher: A Sociological Study.* Chicago: University of Chicago Press, 1975.

Lynd, R., and Lynd, H. *Middletown: A Study in Modern American Culture.* Orlando, Fla.: Harcourt Brace Jovanovich, 1929.

McDonnell, L. M., and McLaughlin, M. W. *Education Policy and the Role of the States.* Santa Monica, Calif.: RAND Corporation, 1982.

McKeachie, W., Pintrich, P., Lin, Y., and Smith, D. *Teaching and Learning in the College Classroom: A Review of the Research Literature.* Ann Arbor, Mich.: National Center to Improve Postsecondary Teaching and Learning, 1986.

McLaughlin, M. "Learning from Experience: Lessons from Policy Implementation." *Educational Evaluation and Policy Analysis,* 1987, *9*(2), 171–178.

MacRury, K., Nagy, P., and Traub, R. E. *Reflections on Large-Scale Assessments of Study Achievement.* Toronto: Ontario Institute of Technology, 1987.

Madaus, G. F. "The Influence of Testing on the Curriculum." In L. Tanner (ed.), *Critical Issues in Curriculum.* Chicago: University of Chicago Press, 1988.

Madaus, G. F. "The Distortion of Teaching and Testing: High-Stakes Testing and Instruction." Unpublished paper, Boston College, 1989.

Madaus, G. "The Effects of Important Tests on Students: Implications for a National Examination or System of Examinations." Paper prepared for the American Educational Research Association Invitational Conference on Accountability as a State Reform Instrument: Impact on Teaching, Learning,

Minority Issues and Incentives for Improvement, Washington, D.C., June 1991.

Madaus, G., and Kellaghan, T. "America 2000's Proposal for American Achievement Tests: Unexamined Issues." Unpublished manuscript, 1991.

Markus, H., and Zajonc, R. "The Cognitive Perspective in Social Psychology." In G. Lindzey and E. Aronson (eds.), *Handbook of Social Psychology*. Hillsdale, N.J.: Erlbaum, 1985.

Meyer, J. "Centralization of Funding and Control in Educational Governance." In J. W. Meyer and W. R. Scott, *Organizational Environments: Ritual and Rationality*. Newbury Park, Calif.: Sage, 1983.

Moon, B. *The New Math Curriculum Controversy: An International Story*. Bristol, Pa.: Falmer Press, 1986.

Morone, J. *The Democratic Wish*. New York: Basic Books, 1990.

Murphy, J. *State Education Agencies and Discretionary Funds: Grease the Squeaky Wheel*. Lexington, Mass.: Heath, 1974.

Newmann, F. M. "Higher Order Thinking in the High School Curriculum." *NASSP Bulletin*, 1988, *72*(508), 58–64.

Nickerson, R. "New Directions in Educational Assessment." *Educational Researcher*, 1989, *18*(9), 3–7.

Nisbett, R., and Ross, L. *Human Inference: Strategies and Shortcomings of Social Judgment*. Englewood Cliffs, N.J.: Prentice-Hall, 1980.

Noah, H., and Eckstein, M. "Tradeoffs in Examination Policies: An International Comparative Perspective." *Oxford Review of Education*, 1989, *15*(1), 17–27.

Office of Educational Research and Improvement State Accountability Study Group. *Creating Responsible and Responsive Accountability Systems*. Washington, D.C.: U.S. Department of Education, 1988.

Ohta, T. "Problems and Perspectives in Japanese Education." *Comparative Education*, 1986, *22*(1), 27–30.

Oldham, E. "Case Studies in Geometry Education: Ireland." In H. G. Steiner, *Comparative Studies of Mathematics Curricula — Change and Stability, 1960–1980*. Haus Ohrbeck (FRG): Institut fur Didaktik der Mathematik der Universitat Bielefeld, 1980a.

Oldham, E. "Case Studies in Algebra Education: Ireland." In
  H. G. Steiner, *Comparative Studies of Mathematics Curricula —
  Change and Stability, 1960–1980.* Haus Ohrbeck (FRG): Institut
  fur Didaktik der Mathematik der Universitat Bielefeld, 1980b.
Orfield, G. *The Reconstruction of Southern Education.* New York:
  Wiley, 1969.
Organization for Economic Cooperation and Development.
  Reviews of National Policies for Education: Japan. Paris: Organi-
  zation for Economic Cooperation and Development, 1971.
Organization for Economic Cooperation and Development.
  Educational Policy and Planning: Japan. Paris: Organization for
  Economic Cooperation and Development, 1973.
Peak, L. "Learning to Become Part of the Group: The Japanese
  Child's Transition to Preschool Life." *Journal of Japanese Studies,*
  1989, *15*(1), 93–124.
Peterson, P. *City Limits.* Chicago: University of Chicago Press,
  1981.
Peterson, P., Rabe, B., and Wong, K. *When Federalism Works.*
  Washington, D.C.: Brookings Institution, 1986.
Popkewitz, T., Tabachnick, B., and Wehlage, G. *The Myth of
  Educational Reform: A Study of School Responses.* Madison: Uni-
  versity of Wisconsin Press, 1982.
Porter, A. "Assessing National Goals: Some Measurement
  Dilemmas." Paper prepared for the 1990 Educational Test-
  ing Service Invitational Conference, Assessment of National
  Education Goals, Oct. 27, 1990.
Porter, A., and others. "Content Determinants in Elementary
  School Mathematics." In D. A. Grouws, T. J. Cooney, and
  D. Jones (eds.), *Effective Mathematics Teaching.* Reston, Va.:
  National Council of Teachers of Mathematics, 1988.
Post, T., and others. "Intermediate Teachers' Knowledge of Ra-
  tional Number Concepts." Unpublished paper, University of
  Wisconsin, Madison, Aug. 1988.
Postlethwaite, T. N. (ed.). *The Encyclopedia of Comparative Edu-
  cation and National Systems of Education.* Vol. C. Oxford, En-
  gland: Pergamon Press, 1988.
Powell, A. "Private Schools." Unpublished draft essay, Cam-
  bridge, Mass., 1991.

Powell, A., Farrar, E., and Cohen, D. K. *The Shopping Mall High School.* Boston: Houghton Mifflin, 1985.

Purkey, S. C., and Smith, M. "Effective Schools: A Review." *Elementary School Journal,* 1983, *83*(4), 428–452.

Putnam, R. T., Heaton, R., Prawat, R., and Remillard, J. "Teaching Mathematics for Understanding: Discussing Case Studies of Four Fifth-Grade Teachers." *Elementary School Journal,* 1992, *93*(2).

Ramirez, F., and Boli, J. "The Political Construction of Mass Schooling: European Origins and Worldwide Institutionalization." *Sociology of Education,* 1987, *60,* 2–11.

Ramirez, F., and Rubison, R. "Creating Members: The Political Incorporation and Expansion of Public Education." In J. W. Meyer and M. Hannan (eds.), *National Development and the World System.* Chicago: University of Chicago Press, 1979.

Resnick, D. P., and Resnick, L. B. "Standards, Curriculum, and Performance: A Historical and Comparative Perspective." *Educational Researcher,* 1985, *14,* 5–20.

Resnick, L. B., and Resnick, D. P. *Assessing the Thinking Curriculum: New Tools for Educational Reform.* Pittsburgh, Pa.: Learning Research and Development Center, 1989.

Roehler, L., and Duffy, G. "Teachers' Instructional Actions." In R. Barr, M. Kamil, P. Mosenthal, and P. Pearson, *Handbook of Reading Research.* Vol. 2. New York: Longman, 1988.

Rogers, D., and Whetten, D. *Interorganizational Coordination.* Ames: Iowa State University, 1982.

Rohlen, T. "Order in Japanese Society: Attachment, Authority and Routine." *Journal of Japanese Studies,* 1989, *15*(1), 5–40.

Romberg, T. A., Zarinnia, E. A., and Williams, S. R. "The Influence of Mandated Testing on Mathematics Instruction: Grade 8 Teachers' Perceptions." Unpublished paper, University of Wisconsin, Madison, Mar. 1989.

Rosenbaum, J., and Kariya, T. "Self-Selection in Japanese Junior High Schools: A Longitudinal Study of Students' Educational Plans." *Sociology of Education,* 1987, *60,* 168–180.

Rosenbaum, J., and Kariya, T. "From High School to Work: Market and Institutional Mechanisms in Japan." *American Journal of Sociology,* 1989, *94*(6), 1334–1365.

Rowan, B. "Organizational Structure and the Institutional Environment: The Case of Public Schools." *Administrative Science Quarterly,* 1982, *27,* 259-279.

Rowan, B. "Instructional Management in Historical Perspective: Evidence on Differentiation in School Districts." *Educational Administration Quarterly,* 1983, *18,* 43-59.

Rowan, B. "Commitment and Control: Alternative Strategies for the Organizational Design of Schools." In C. Cazden (ed.), *Review of Research in Education.* Vol. 16. Washington, D.C.: American Educational Research Association, 1990.

Ruddell, R. B. "Knowledge and Attitude Toward Testing: Educators and Legislators." *The Reading Teacher,* 1985, *38,* 538-543.

Salmon-Cox, L. "Teachers and Standardized Achievement Tests: What's Really Happening?" *Phi Delta Kappan,* 1981, *62*(9), 631-633.

Sarason, S. *The Culture of the School and the Problem of Change.* Boston: Allyn & Bacon, 1977.

Scardamalia, M., Bereiter, C., and Steinbach, R. "Teachability of Reflective Processes in Written Composition." *Cognitive Science,* 1984, *8,* 173-190.

Schwille, J., and others. "Teachers as Policybrokers in the Content of Elementary School Mathematics." In L. Shulman and G. Sykes, *Handbook of Teaching and Policy.* New York: Longman, 1983.

Schwille, J., and others. *State Policy and the Control of Curriculum Decisions.* East Lansing: Institute for Research in Teaching, Michigan State University, 1986.

Scott, R., and Meyer, J. "The Organization of Societal Sectors." In J. W. Meyer and W. R. Scott, *Organizational Environments: Ritual and Rationality.* Newbury Park, Calif.: Sage, 1983.

Sedlak, M., Wheeler, C., Pullin, D., and Cusick, P. *Selling Students Short: Classroom Bargains and Academic Reform in American High Schools.* New York: Teachers College Press, 1986.

Shanker, A. *Asking the Right Questions.* Washington, D.C.: American Federation of Teachers, 1989.

Shimahara, N. "The Cultural Basis of Students' Achievement in Japan." *Comparative Education,* 1986, *22*(1), 285-303.

Sizer, T. *Horace's Compromise.* Boston: Houghton Mifflin, 1984.

Smith, M., and O'Day, J. "Systemic School Reform." In S. Fuhrman and B. Malen (eds.), *The Politics of Curriculum and Testing.* Bristol, Pa.: Falmer Press, 1991.

Sproull, L, and Zubrow, D. "Standardized Testing from the Administrative Perspective." *Phi Delta Kappan,* 1981, *62*(9), 628–630.

Stackhouse, E. *The Effects of State Centralization on Administrative Structure.* Unpublished doctoral dissertation, Stanford University, Stanford, Calif., 1982.

Stake, R., and Easley, J. *Case Studies in Science Education.* Vol. 1: *The Case Reports.* Stock no. 038-000-00377-1. Washington, D.C.: U.S. Government Printing Office, 1978.

Stevens, R. *The Questions as a Measure of Efficiency in Instruction.* New York: Teachers College Press, 1912.

Stevenson, D., and Baker, D. "State Control of the Curriculum and Classroom Instruction." *Sociology of Education,* 1991, *64*(1), 1–10.

Stevenson, H., and Lee, S. *Contexts of Achievement: A Study of American, Chinese and Japanese Children.* Monographs of the Society for Research in Child Development, no. 221, *55*(1–2), Ann Arbor, Mich., 1990.

Stevenson, H., Lee, S.-Y., and Stigler, J. "Mathematics Achievement of Chinese, Japanese, and American Children." *Science,* 1986, *231,* 693–699.

Stevenson, H., and others. "Cognitive Performance and Academic Achievement of Japanese, Chinese and American Children." *Child Development,* 1985, *56,* 718–734.

Thompson, A. "The Relationships of Teachers' Conceptions of Mathematics Teaching to Instructional Practice." *Educational Studies in Mathematics,* 1984, *15,* 105–127.

Travers, K., and Westbury, I. *The IEA Study of Mathematics I: Analysis of Mathematics Curricula.* New York: Pergamon, 1989.

Trow, M. "The Second Transformation of American Secondary Education." *International Journal of Comparative Sociology,* 1961, *2,* 144–166.

Trow, M. "American Higher Education: Past, Present, and Future." *Educational Researcher,* 1988, *17*(3), 13–23.

Tyson-Bernstein, H. "The Academy's Contribution to the Impoverishment of America's Textbooks." *Phi Delta Kappan,* 1988, *70*(3), 193–198.

U.S. Bureau of the Census. *Statistical Abstract of the United States, 1988.* Washington, D.C.: Department of Commerce, 1989.

Van der Blij, F., Hilding, S., and Weinzweig, A. "A Synthesis of National Reports on Changes in Curricula." In H. G. Steiner, *Comparative Studies of Mathematics Curricula — Change and Stability, 1960–1980.* Haus Ohrbeck (FRG): Institut fur Didaktik der Mathematik der Universitat Bielefeld, 1980.

Welch, W. W. "Twenty Years of Science Curriculum Development: A Look Back." *Review of Research in Education.* Vol. 7. Washington, D.C.: American Educational Research Association, 1979.

Westbury, I. "Conclusion to Conference Proceedings 'Reflection on Case Studies.'" In H. G. Steiner, *Comparative Studies of Mathematics Curricula — Change and Stability, 1960–1980.* Haus Ohrbeck (FRG): Institut fur Didaktik der Mathematik der Universitat Bielefeld, 1980.

White, M. *The Japanese Educational Challenge.* New York: Free Press, 1987.

Wirt, F., and Kirst, M. *The Politics of Education: Schools in Conflict.* Berkeley, Calif.: McCutchan, 1982.

Wise, A. *Legislated Learning: The Bureaucratization of the American Classroom.* Berkeley: University of California, 1979.

Witte, J. F. *Choice and Control in American Education: An Analytic Overview.* Madison: University of Wisconsin, Madison, 1989.

Witte, J. F. "Understanding High School Achievement." Paper presented at the annual meeting of the American Political Science Association, San Francisco, Aug. 30, 1990.

3

The Role of
Local School Districts in
Instructional Improvement

Richard F. Elmore

The Role of School Districts in Educational Reform

It is commonplace in America to assert that education is a state responsibility that is locally administered. Although states retain formal legal authority, this prevailing view contends, locally elected boards of education and local school administrators bear primary responsibility for most, if not all, of the decisions that have the most direct effect on teaching and learning in schools. Education reform, however, at least since the early 1980s, has been synonymous with state policymaking. States have shown an unprecedented willingness to make increasingly prescriptive policies on a broad range of subjects previously not addressed at all by state policy or left largely to the discretion of local districts: graduation standards for students, entry requirements for teachers, curriculum content, testing for students and teachers, and the like. (See Firestone and others, 1991.) The average state share of revenues for elementary and secondary education has increased steadily over the past twenty years or so from about 30 percent to over 50 percent; in many states, that share is well over 60 percent, and in those states education expenditures account for at least half of all general fund expenditures over which state governments exercise authority.

Coupled with this increase in the states' presence in education policy has been an increase in the strength of ties among policymakers across states (Fuhrman and Elmore, 1992). Policy ideas now travel fairly quickly from one state to another through established networks of state policymakers—governors, legislators, and chief state school officers, for example. Since at least the late 1970s, national policy toward education has focused primarily on reinforcing the role of states as the prime movers in educational reform. At least in terms of visible activity, then, states seem to be the primary locus for educational policymaking. Their sphere of influence seems to be steadily increasing.

Recently, policy in some states has begun to focus on systemic approaches to instructional improvement (Smith and O'Day, 1991). In this context, "systemic" means orchestrating multiple state policies—curriculum, testing, teacher education and professional development, for example—around a common set of objectives. "Instructional improvement" means that the objectives of policy focus on increasing students' access to academic learning. As the state role has developed over the past decade, state policymakers have begun to realize that past reforms have had a piecemeal and fragmentary effect on local schools. Increases in graduation requirements, for example, may result in modest increases in the number of students taking academic courses but may have little effect on the content of those courses or on students' cumulative learning in school. Increases in state testing requirements may result in better knowledge of student learning, but they also expose limits in the state's capacity to influence what students are taught and the skill and knowledge that teachers bring to the teaching of academic content. Hence, the push for systemic approaches to instructional improvement results from a desire to increase coherence among separate state policies and focus those policies on the central goal of improved student learning.

The type of policy instruments being used in systemic approaches to instructional improvement are amenable to direct administration from the state level or to administration through intermediate organizations other than local districts. New assessment techniques and standards for academic learning are costly and are more efficiently developed by states or by interstate compacts. Curriculum frameworks, which lay out the objectives for academic learning, can be made by convening panels of experts, including teachers and curriculum specialists from local school systems, at the state level, without directly relying on local districts to develop them independently. Teacher education and professional development can be more directly influenced from the state level by using contractual arrangements with third parties (higher education institutions and intermediate educational service units) rather than relying on local districts to mount their own programs.

With these new policy structures, the role of local districts arguably becomes more problematical. If states play a more aggressive role in setting goals, outlining curriculum requirements, underwriting teacher education and professional development consistent with these goals and requirements, and monitoring individual schools based on how well students are learning academic content, what role will local districts play?

This question is all the more problematical because state policies are increasingly school focused, rather than district focused. The unit of intervention for state policy has increasingly become the school, with the district treated as "context" rather than having a clearly defined role. Most state testing and indicator systems collect and report data directly on schools. A few states have designed reward systems based on student performance on statewide tests: these rewards go directly to schools, rather than to districts. A few states have launched programs designed to engender innovative practices; these programs involve grants directly to schools, rather than to districts. Indeed, a central part of the Bush administration's New American Schools program encourages private developers to design and implement new schools independently of local jurisdictions. The tendency to focus on the school as the unit of intervention, then, has led to policies that override or bypass localities.

Increases in state policy activity and in the state share of school funding have also brought increased pressures for accountability from state policymakers. In many states, an increased state presence has brought a more aggressive stance toward low-performing schools and districts. A number of states are experimenting with various strategies for putting low-performing districts into state receivership, effectively overriding local governance structures in the interest of state policy objectives (Fuhrman and Elmore, 1992).

The establishment of national goals for education has focused attention mainly on states as the locus of authority for educational policy decisions. The process of goal setting was, significantly, one in which the president and the governors of the fifty states made the key decisions. The process of monitoring national progress toward the goals mainly involves state-level actors and envisions interstate compacts to develop new assessment techniques that will be used to measure performance of individual students and schools. Furthermore, the basic idea of national standards, implemented through state policy, is inherently one that lowers the value of local diversity and, concomitantly, decreases the necessity for local districts to play an active role in determining the purposes of education.

What does this apparent expansion of the state and national presence in educational policy mean for the role of local districts? Do these changes necessarily mean a long-term diminution of local influence? Based on prior evidence of the effects of state reforms, the answer is much less clear than one might expect. Evidence from the early part of the current decade suggests that increased state policymaking does not necessarily decrease the influence of local districts, and in some cases may have increased local influence. The traditional "zero-sum" model of intergovernmental power, in which the growth of influence by one level of government results in an equal and opposite diminution of influence by another, does not seem to apply straightforwardly in education policy. In a number of states, increased state policymaking around student standards, for example, has resulted in a surge of local activity, especially in already high-performing districts, the result of which has been to raise local standards above the new state standards in an effort to maintain the district's position relative to other districts. This local response might be called a "positive-sum" result. Many localities have picked up state reform themes and built powerful local constituencies for them, pushing them much further than state policy required. This effect is far from uniform across districts, however, which raises the question of whether differential local responses to state policies designed to create greater uniformity may actually *increase* local differences rather than decrease them (Fuhrman and Elmore, 1990; Cohen, 1982).

Whatever the precise effect on localities of increased state policymaking, and increased attention to systemic approaches to instructional improvement, it is virtually certain that the conditions under which localities will operate in the future are changing. In general, the policy environment of schools is shifting toward greater attention to student learning in academic subjects, toward more ambitious goals for what all students will learn in school, and toward greater school-level accountability for results. These shifts portend significant challenges for the traditional role of local districts.

Why Local School Districts Exist

The present form of local governance of education in the United States is probably more a product of the unique historical conditions during the late nineteenth century, when the basic institutional structure of public education was formed, than it is a necessary requirement for the administration of education in the present. Early public schools were, for the most part, formed by local activists connected to national networks, explicitly designed to emulate nineteenth-century religious missionary movements. In most settings, this development literally took place on a school-by-school basis. The present form of centralized local administration of schools developed in the early twentieth century in response to reforms of the progressive period, which attempted to bring standardization, rationality, and professionalism to what had been a fairly ragged and idiosyncratic collection of schools. The progressive reformers replaced one kind of local control—control by small community groups— with another kind—control by centralized bureaucracies and community elites. During this early period, states played a very limited role, essentially enabling the creation of local administrative units. (See Tyack and Hansot, 1982.)

This form of local administration was probably well suited to a period in which neither states nor the federal government were willing to play a large fiscal role in education, but in which each had a strong incentive to encourage localities to undertake this role for themselves. Neither the federal government nor the states were eager to undertake direct responsibility for the funding and administration of local schools, since this task was well beyond their capacity, but both were eager to reap the collective public benefits that widespread education could offer. Locally centralized educational governance also allowed the nation to develop a broad-based system of universal education, without raising nationally divisive issues like race. Until the late 1950s and early 1960s, well beyond the initial phases of institutional development in public education, the issue of equal access to education was left to local convention. A system of locally centralized governance and administration of public education was well suited to the particular conditions of a developing nation.

It is much less clear that such a system is well suited, or necessary, to present conditions of increased national interdependency and state presence in both the financing and governance of education. The experience of other industrialized countries does not support the assertion that a system governed largely by locally elected boards and locally centralized administrative structures is a necessary feature of highly developed educational systems. Many industrialized European countries, for example, have far more vertically integrated systems of public education, in which many policies governing personnel, finance, and curriculum decisions are made nationally, while local administration of schools rests with units of general government — cities and municipalities — rather than separate jurisdictions. National influence on local governments is also enhanced by a vertically integrated political party structure, in which the local affiliates of governing parties at the national level are expected to follow a national program. These systems are arguably more responsive to national priorities, since local decisions are seen largely as implementation of a national program.

The scale and complexity of education in modern industrial democracies may require some form of local or regional administration, but it probably does not require one with the specific structural elements of the U.S. system. Indeed, some critics of the current structure have gone so far as to argue that local school districts are, after all, legal creatures of the states and, if they have outlived their useful functions in the present political and economic environment, they can be abolished or modified by simply changing the statutes under which they operate: they have no legal or constitutional entitlement to exist. "'Local control of public education' as traditionally conceived is in reality disappearing, even though its facade is nearly everywhere intact," argue some critics. "What appears to be happening is that local school systems are evolving in practice into something that they always were in a constitutional sense: subordinate administrative units of a state educational system, with some residual power to modify statewide regulations and procedures in order to ease their implementation within a particular community, and with the residual authority (in most states, though not all) to supplement state spending with locally raised revenues" (Doyle and Finn, 1984, p. 90).

As the objectives of state and national policy increasingly focus on what individual students learn and what schools are teaching, "the school is the vital delivery system, the state is the policy setter (and chief paymaster), and nothing in between is very important. This formulation turns on its head the traditional American assumption that every city, town, and county bears the chief responsibility for organizing and operating its own schools as a municipal function. That is what we once meant by 'local control,' but it has become an anachronism no longer justified by research, consistent with sound fiscal policy or organization theory, suited to our mobility patterns, or important to the public" (Finn, 1991, pp. 246–247).

These critics prescribe reforms that stress national standards, a common core of learning, and choice and competition among schools, among other things. Some critics have pushed this argument to its logical extension, arguing that the best system of governance for public education is one in which states license schools directly, essentially bypassing local districts, with minimal or no regulation on such matters as curriculum, entry standards for teachers, or admission and expulsion requirements for students, and then provide parents with a voucher or cash entitlement that they can redeem at any licensed school (Chubb and Moe, 1990; Doyle and Finn, 1984).

Against these rather simple, some would say simplistic, analyses, one can array a number of arguments in favor of maintaining a strong local district presence. Direct attacks on local governance structures, such as those above, underscore the question: What are the possible reasons for maintaining local governance structures in the face of an increasing state and national presence in education?

Local Democracy

One possible reason for the continued existence of local school districts is that they provide a means of mobilizing political support for public schools at a level where their impact is most immediate and a valuable buffer against precipitous shifts in state and national policy that are inconsistent with local preferences. In this view, local political institutions exist for reasons other than simply implementing state and national policy. They exist, for example, to provide opportunities for access and expression of political ideas and preferences, independently of whether those ideas are consistent with the prevailing political and economic orthodoxies at other levels of government. They exist to provide protection against the temporary ascendance of political factions, in the form of strong political interests mobilized around policies that might cause serious damage to regional or minority interests. They also exist to diffuse the exercise of political power in preventing its concentration in a few institutions. Some would argue that the very fact that educational reformers have to scratch their heads and ponder how to implement their ideas in nearly 16,000 local school districts is a valuable "reality check" on those ideas.

The conflict between viewing institutions of local government as instruments of the states or as independent political entities runs deeply in American politics. In fact, some have argued that the struggle between the instrumental and expressive views of American political institutions distinguishes American political thought from that of other countries, for better or for worse. (See, for example, Morone, 1990.) The important message of this long-running struggle is that issues such as the role of local school districts in educational governance are never definitely decided in the context of specific policy debates but rather by the flow of many smaller policy decisions around many specific questions, tailored to the pressing political demands of the moment. The fact that these institutional questions are addressed in this piecemeal fashion provides ample opportunity both for reformers to make global proposals for institutional change and for people in affected institutions to assert their own interests in preserving the existing structure. The role of local districts may change as a function of the flow of specific policy decisions, but policymakers are seldom, if ever, directly confronted with the issue of whether they should continue to exist.

Local Laboratories of Democracy

The term "laboratories of democracy" was coined by Supreme Court Justice Louis Brandeis during the New Deal to characterize the role that states play in developing and testing new policy ideas before they enter the national political agenda. (See, for example, Osborne, 1988.) It seems reasonable to ask why this role should be confined to states, when, in many instances, localities have shown an equal capacity to develop and nurture new public policy ideas. One of the most far-reaching and fundamental experiments in school reform at the moment, for example, is occurring in Chicago—a reform that spreads decision-making authority to more than 500 local school councils. This reform was the product of a state reform law, initiated by a citywide political movement formed around a broad-based constituency interested in seizing control of the schools from the existing board and administration and turning the attention of the school system to the concerns of parents and community education activists (Hess, 1991). Other similar, but less radical, decentralization reforms have been initiated in places like Rochester, New York, and Dade County, Florida. In earlier periods of history, urban school districts played the leading role in school reform: during the progressive era, for example, a number of them sponsored broadscale, ambitious, although ultimately not very effective, efforts to introduce child-centered instruction into classrooms (Cuban, 1984).

One can question at any given time how well local school districts actually function as laboratories for new educational ideas, whether they are the appropriate units of government to nurture these ideas, or whether they have sufficient incentives to develop new ideas. At the moment, school districts, as a class of governmental institutions, are not perceived to be leaders in developing new educational practices, although this may be as much a function of perception as fact.

How well local districts are performing as local laboratories of democracy at any particular moment is, however, a separate issue from whether they *should* play this role, whether playing this role serves a useful purpose in the U.S. governmental structure, or whether local districts could play this role if they were given clearer direction from the state and federal level and the resources to do it. One could make a case, for example, that local districts might be the appropriate level of government for assuring that new practices are nurtured in individual schools and for propagating those practices across schools within districts. Individual schools may have incentives to develop new practices for their own students, but they have very weak incentives to invest their own resources in the improvement of other schools. States, on the other hand, may have strong incentives to assure that the overall performance of schools meets the political and economic objectives of policymakers, but these incentives often do not translate into much concrete interest in how effective instructional practices move from one school to another, since states as governmental entities are relatively remote from schools. Local districts, on the other hand, should have incentives, at least in theory, to provide benefits to whole communities, hence to improve several schools within a community, and thus a stronger incentive than states to see that successful practices in one setting are propagated in others. As we shall see later, there is not much evidence that school districts play this role widely, systemically, or very well, but one could imagine creating an incentive structure in state and federal policy that would encourage localities to play a more prominent role as local laboratories for new instructional practices.

Balancing Interests and Incentives Across Jurisdictions

Still another reason for paying close attention to the role of local districts in education is that they may have a real comparative advantage relative to other levels of government in certain policy areas. One approach to the theory of federalism suggests that levels of government have strong incentives to emphasize some types of policy over others. (See, for example, Peterson, 1981.) Local governments, because their authority is circumscribed by state law, their revenue bases are limited by geographical constraints, and their electoral constituencies are relatively homogeneous, tend to focus on sustaining basic services within their area of jurisdiction and trying to attract economic assets that enhance their position relative to other local jurisdictions. Hence, local policy focuses on developmental purposes (increasing the economic assets of the jurisdiction) or allocative purposes (making productive use of existing assets). State governments have similar incentives, but because they have relatively diverse electoral constituencies, they face stronger pressures than localities to also pursue redistributive purposes (moving assets from one group or area to another). The federal government, because in theory at least it has relatively unconstrained access to the total economic assets of the country for revenue and its electoral constituencies are even more diverse, faces even greater pressures to pursue redistributive purposes.

Making policy in a multilevel, federated structure, then, involves, to an important degree, recognizing the comparative advantages and interdependencies of jurisdictions, in addition to their separate interests. Local jurisdictions have the strongest incentives to pursue policies that increase the value and productivity of public services but the weakest incentives to pursue policies that redistribute value among groups and areas. Local jurisdictions also have the most limited access to resources to pursue their ends. State and federal jurisdictions, on the other hand, have stronger incentives to redistribute and somewhat weaker incentives to pursue policies that increase value and productivity, but they also have access to wider revenue bases than local jurisdictions. A rational use of this structure, then, would constitute an intergovernmental bargain in which local jurisdictions were encouraged to pursue their own primary interest in the improvement of services (like instruction in education), and receive access to the redistributive power and broader sources of revenue from the state and federal level, in return for which they would agree to focus some attention on redistributive purposes within their jurisdictions, for which they have weak incentives. Under this view, then, local jurisdictions are potentially powerful partners in a strategic game of balancing interests and assets across levels of government.

Of course, as local jurisdictions expand in their geographical coverage, they begin to behave much more like higher-level jurisdictions, but some, such as large urban school systems, are often caught in a vicious version of this strategic game. Because of the diversity of their electoral constituencies, they are under unremitting pressure to focus primary attention on redistributive issues. They are, however, constrained in the extent of their capacity to do much about these issues by the legal fact that they are creatures of the states, by their limited capacity to grow and gain more economic assets, and by the limits of their existing revenue bases.

The existence of multiple levels of government is something more than a historical accident whose inconveniences we are forced to endure. Since the *Federalist Papers,* we have known that the federal structure embodies an underlying political logic, for better or for worse, in which multiple jurisdictions balance each others' interests in ways intended to disperse power and create productive tensions and dependencies among levels. The problem for policymakers, of course, is that this system requires, or invites, continued tinkering and maintenance in order to work effectively on contemporary problems. It is seldom certain what the appropriate actions are to maintain the equipoise among levels of government that allows them to work productively. The current puzzlement over the role of local school districts in educational policy is probably an example of a deeper puzzlement about relations among levels of government.

Adapting National and State Policy to Local Conditions

The previous argument assumes that important differences among levels of government are the political engine that makes federalism work. Another commonly cited reason for maintaining local school districts is more mundane: they are often seen as a key administrative link between broad policy at the national and state level and variable local conditions. This view does not assume any necessary conflict or opposition among institutions at different levels of government; in fact, it is consistent with an essentially bureaucratic model of policy and administration in which local jurisdictions are literally agents of higher-level jurisdictions, doing what such agents are supposed to do—adjusting general policy to specific local conditions. This is not so different from the role of, say, British colonial administrators in the Empire.

     The current rhetoric of educational reform often has this bureaucratic or managerial flavor to it, in part because reform has been heavily influenced by the rhetoric of recent literature on private sector management. The idea of setting national goals and relying on states and localities to adapt them and carry them out in their respective jurisdictions is essentially an administrative or managerial idea, not an especially political one. It assumes that one can get an ailing educational system going again in much the same way one might get a complex multidivision corporation going that had come upon hard times. Give the organization a sense of purpose and direction by setting corporate-level goals, hold people at the various divisional levels responsible for setting similar goals for their divisions consistently with corporate goals, hold divisional managers responsible for developing and carrying out the necessary means for implementing those goals, and use the financial resources of the parent corporation to reward and penalize various divisions and operating units in accordance with their performance on overall goals.

This metaphor has enormous persuasive power at the moment because it gives a certain order to the untidiness of American educational governance. It also provides a simple, consistent, and appealing message about the nature of responsibility at various levels of the system—at least to reformers, if not to the objects of reform. This message carries with it an implicit role for local school districts. Local administrators and school boards, under this view, would be responsible for translating the broad purposes of national and state goals into tangible practices in schools in ways that were consistent with the particular conditions of local districts. So, for example, a district with large numbers of language minority students would have to mount a different kind of instructional program than a district with all native-English-speaking students in order to achieve a stated goal that all students would achieve advanced mastery of English grammar and syntax by age sixteen. There is a certain logic to this view. Any complex, multiunit structure needs both top-down direction and bottom-up adaptation to function in a unified way around a common set of purposes.

The problems with this view become more apparent, however, the closer you get to the political and fiscal realities of the current structure of educational governance. While the state share of education funding has been steadily increasing over the past fifteen years or so, most local school systems still raise a significant amount of their basic operating revenue from local sources in ways that require them to subject themselves periodically to approval by local voters. It is difficult to sustain the notion that local districts are agents of a larger corporate structure, with its own goals and interests, when districts regularly receive strong signals from their own constituents about what the purposes of the system are. Frequently, these local signals carry a specific message—cut expenditures, for example—that makes it difficult for local districts to act consistently with higher-level goals. The resources available to local districts to carry out higher-level goals vary enormously—a three- or four-to-one ratio between per-pupil expenditures in high- and low-spending districts is not unusual. Who, then, is responsible under these circumstances for the extent of a district's success in achieving higher-level goals? Is it the local patrons of the system who provide, or do not provide, the authority and resources? Is it the local board members and administrators who are responsible for achieving results consistent with goals regardless of resource constraints? Or is it the higher-level authorities who set the goals and might therefore be expected to assume the responsibility for providing resources necessary to carry them out?

To reformers, then, it seems plausible and appealing to view local districts as agents of higher-level jurisdictions, carrying out and elaborating national and state goals at the local level. To those who are the objects of these goals, however, the picture is, to say the least, more mixed.

Against the impatience of those reformers who would do away with local districts altogether, it is possible to array a number of plausible reasons why one might want to maintain local districts even if it were possible to eliminate them. They provide a means of mobilizing political support for public schools at a level where its impacts are most immediate and a valuable buffer against precipitous shifts in state and national policy, they provide an important possible source of practical new ideas for improving education, they represent a distinctive set of political interests and incentives that complements other levels of government in a federated structure, and they provide a potentially important administrative link between higher-level goals and school-level practices.

What School Districts Do

Against the expectations of the role that local districts could play, one might ask what local districts actually do. Most people who work in local school districts, or who sit on their governing boards, would probably say that the answer is obvious: local districts run schools. But saying that local districts run schools is a bit like saying that General Motors runs automobile plants; General Motors' success as a corporation is not based on whether it runs automobile plants but whether it produces automobiles. Similarly, it seems plausible to ask not whether school districts "run" schools but how and whether they provide for the learning of students.

One would expect that if school districts were essentially in the business of providing for the learning of students, their administrative structures would reflect that purpose. One survey of local district staffing patterns in California between 1930 and 1970 sheds light on this issue (Rowan, 1982). This survey found that as district central office staff increased, job titles grew more specialized, as one would expect, but that specialization did not result in greater attention to issues of curriculum and instruction, which one would expect if school districts were primarily focused on student learning. In 1930, for example, the top ten staffing categories in local districts included at least six positions directly related to curriculum and instruction; by 1970, they included only two positions related to curriculum and instruction. Furthermore, the curriculum and instruction titles during both periods had predominantly to do with nonacademic subjects. In 1930, the highest proportion of districts had staff in physical education, vocational education, home economics, health, and music; in 1970, the highest proportions were in vocational education. Districts not only gave little attention to staffing curriculum and instruction over this period, but such attention as they did give focused primarily on subjects outside the traditional core academic subject matter areas, such as mathematics, science, language, literature, history, and the like.

Over the period 1930–1970, the largest growth in specialized positions in California school districts occurred in business management, personnel, and guidance. Positions in curriculum showed no growth over this period and were likely to be the most unstable from one year to the next.

Studies of interactions between district-level and school-level administrators confirm the relative absence of district focus on issues of curriculum and instruction. One study found, for example, that of the total amount of district-level work done during a given period of time, only about 9 percent had anything at all to do with schools directly and less than 3 percent had anything to do with curriculum. The authors of this study concluded: "The technical tasks associated with producing student learning are not supervised, managed, or coordinated in any serious sense across managerial levels within school districts.

However, our results also show . . . that there are some areas which are coordinated. These are mainly concerned with logistics and district-wide issues such as desegregation, and not with technical production tasks" (Hannaway and Sproull, 1978–1979, p. 2).

Another study, in 1982, examined district influences on curriculum and teaching in one specific subject at one grade level — fourth grade mathematics — over 100 districts in five states. The study examined a number of policies that districts could potentially use to influence curriculum and instruction, including testing, curriculum objectives and guides, textbook selection, allocation of time to subject matter, and teacher training. The study concluded that districts typically do not use a variety of policies in a concerted way to influence teaching in schools; instead, their approach tends to be scattered, piecemeal, and, for the most part, weak in influencing teaching.

> The picture that emerges is one of districts with a vague intention to direct instructional content, but without any considered stategy for doing so. Districts do not leave teachers to their devices, but neither do they make systematic use of the tools available to persuade teachers to adopt patterns of content decision making. Rather than deciding to set central instructional goals and then trying to communicate those goals through all available means, districts tend to make unconnected decisions that do not lead to any clear pattern of curriculum policies. . . . Teachers do not believe that they will be either rewarded for teaching the content indicated by district policies or punished for failing to teach that content. . . . [F]ew districts are attempting to provide leadership in content decision making. While districts are not supporting teacher autonomy in content decisions, neither are they taking seriously the job of providing clear and specific suggestions for instructional content (Floden and others, 1988, pp. 98, 108, 115).

One explanation for this relative lack of attention to issues of curriculum and instruction by school districts is that actively managing teaching and learning is a difficult enterprise. The basic work of teaching and learning is highly uncertain, the argument goes, so higher-level administrators tend to withdraw from it and focus their energies on mobilizing support in the community and actively managing the flow of people and money, rather than teaching and learning (Floden and others, 1988; Rowan, 1982; Meyer and Rowan, 1978).

Another closely related explanation focuses on the effect of intergovernmental relations and policy. Growth and specialization of administrative functions in local districts occurs, in part, because the scale of the enterprise is increasing (more students mean more schools, which in turn means more managerial oversight) and, in part, because of the increasing use of policy as an instrument for resolving issues of purpose and control. Policy was not always the main tool in American education for addressing issues of purpose and control. Well into the first few decades of the twentieth century, very little explicit policy governed schools. Most such issues were resolved by appeals to vague professional norms or community standards. As the use of policy grew, so too did the incidence of specialized titles and roles devoted to the implementation of policy. (See Cohen, 1982; Elmore and McLaughlin, 1988.) Most jobs that have to do with managing the flow of policy from one level of government to another have little or nothing to do with classroom instruction but with ensuring accountability for expenditures of money and compliance with rules and regulations. Those jobs that do focus on classroom instruction tend to be marginal in nature. It is not surprising that so many curriculum job titles in local districts in the 1930s had to do with physical education, vocational education, and home economics; this was a period in which these subjects were actively promoted by state and national policymakers. Nor is it surprising that job titles having to do with academic subject matter are among the most unstable in local districts. These jobs tend to be associated with momentary policy fads from the state or national level, many of which are unpopular with local educators; hence, their status is tenuous within local bureaucracies (Rowan, 1982).

Still another explanation for the relative lack of attention to issues of curriculum and instruction in local districts stems from the political incentives under which districts operate. (For one version of this argument, see Chubb and Moe, 1990.) Any public enterprise that is governed by an elected board is driven by necessity to reconcile divergent community interests through coalition politics. Curriculum and instruction raise difficult and volatile political questions that make broad-based coalitions difficult to form. When these issues arise — for example, in the form of debates over introducing creationist views into biology courses or multiculturalism into history and Western civilization courses — they are extremely difficult to contain and often very destructive to the careers of board members and administrators. Also, the growth of well-organized institutional political interests around local policymaking works against focusing directly on issues of curriculum and instruction. A large part of what local boards and administrators currently do is to manage labor relations with teacher unions. Neither the unions nor district management have much incentive to focus on issues of curriculum and instruction. For the unions, raising the issue works against teacher autonomy in the classroom; for management, it means risking a volatile confrontation with the union. So the institutional interests of the parties tend to push basic questions of teaching and learning to the side.

If school districts are not particularly active in their management of curriculum and instruction, this does not necessarily mean that the function is not being managed at all. It is quite possible that districts are managing curriculum and instruction effectively by delegating it to the school level, with minimal direction and control from the district. In fact, however, there is not much evidence that school-level management has much to do with curriculum and instruction either.

Studies of school principals confirm the patterns of district-school interaction found in district-level studies. School principals seem to spend large fractions of their time responding to district administrators — over 30 percent for elementary school principals and over 40 percent for secondary school principals in one study. Though principals consume large amounts of time responding to districts, district-level personnel exercise very little direct control over principals and their schools. The "bureaucratic lines of communication . . . are thin, attenuated, and seldom monitored by higher-ups" (Crowson and Morris, 1985, p. 56; see also Hannaway and Sproull, 1978–1979 and Martin and Willower, 1981). Furthermore, "such contact as there is [between district administrators and principals is] only incidentally connected to the core tasks of . . . curriculum and instruction" (Crowson and Morris, 1985, p. 57). About 80 percent of district-wide interaction focuses on such matters as budget, personnel, scheduling, pupil behavior, facilities, and parent complaints, while less than 20 percent has to do with curriculum and instruction (Crowson and Morris, 1985, p. 58).

Within that fraction of time that principals themselves control, their behavior tends to mirror that of their administrative superiors. Superintendents, for example, spend most of their time in short interactions with small numbers of people on matters largely unrelated to curriculum and instruction. Principals, likewise, spend most of the time that is not devoted to responding to district-level directives in the same way (Pitner and Ogawa, 1981; Martin and Willower, 1981).

A study of how principals affected curriculum and instruction decisions in school districts and schools found that a large proportion of teachers and principals knew little about specific district curriculum and instruction policies. Among those who manifested some knowledge, as many as two-thirds of the principals surveyed in a five-state sample of more than 100 school districts disagreed with the district curriculum coordinator on every subject of the district's curriculum policy, except testing, where the agreement was higher. Few principals saw themselves as playing an important role in mediating district curriculum and instruction policies at the school level. In those instances where principals were willing to play such a role actively, teachers appeared willing to accept guidance when it involved the addition of new content but not when it involved removing content (Floden and others, 1984).

The picture that emerges from this literature is one in which key decisions on curriculum and teaching are passed from states to districts, from districts to principals, and from principals to teachers, with little effective focus or guidance. There is little evidence that districts are staffed and organized in ways that promote attention to instructional improvement or that administrators at the district or school level spend significant amounts of time on activities that relate directly to instructional improvement. Considerable evidence exists that districts routinely overlook opportunities to influence key teacher decisions that affect instruction and pass key instructional decisions down the hierarchy until they finally come to rest in the classroom, with little or no support or reinforcement for improvement.

Although the literature on school districts' involvement in curriculum and instruction suggests a largely negative view, not all the evidence is negative. One of the earliest broad-scale studies of federal policies designed to improve curriculum and teaching found, for example, that one characteristic that distinguished successful projects — as measured by whether they reached their goals and whether they persisted over time — was whether some district-level administrator took an active interest in the project (Berman and McLaughlin, 1978). Recent studies of school restructuring reinforce the idea that when districts play an active role in promoting and organizing alternative models of school-level decision making, a significant amount of new activity occurs at the school level (David, 1990). Other reviews of school district involvement in school-based management suggest that most of what happens in district decentralization efforts is largely symbolic and short-lived and has no discernible effect on teaching and learning in schools (Malen, Ogawa, and Kranz, 1990; Hill and Bonan, 1991).

Some of the more interesting positive evidence on school district involvement in instruction comes from a study of twelve California school districts, deliberately selected because of their demonstrated capacity to produce high levels of student achievement, controlling for socioeconomic status, previous achievement, and language proficiency. This study found, among other things, that three-quarters of the districts "had a preferred approach to instruction that they expected all teachers to emphasize," introduced by the superintendent; that two-thirds of the districts had district-level textbook adoption policies and curriculum objectives; that in half the districts new principals were screened and selected based on their general knowledge of curriculum and instruction; that about 40 percent of staff development activities focused specifically on district priorities; and that in eleven of the twelve districts superintendents played a direct role in oversight of curriculum instruction (Murphy and Hallinger, 1988, pp. 177–178). The study also found: "although there was substantial evidence that the rational elements in these school systems were a product of district direction and coordination, the elements appeared to work because these systems were living, adaptive organisms rather than collections of codified procedures" (Murphy and Hallinger, 1988, p. 178).

For example, most districts used broad-based participatory processes for the development of objectives, but district-level influence and control increased as the processes moved toward implementation of objectives. Superintendents and higher-level administrators in these systems were adept at dealing on a personal level with school-level administrators and teachers and had a high level of interaction with them. And superintendents in these districts were generally viewed as decisive in their approach to management but also willing to consult widely with administrators and teachers (Murphy and Hallinger, 1988, p. 179).

Most of the research literature on the role of school districts in curriculum and instruction was done prior to the current reform period. It is possible that, with increased state-level attention to academic subject matter, increased state-mandated testing, and emerging interest in curriculum and instruction in some states, local districts in some states have shifted their organizational structures and practices to reflect greater involvement in curriculum and instruction.

It is also possible that aggregate results conceal a great deal of district-to-district variation in attention to instructional improvement. Some districts apparently have strong and visible systems for supporting curriculum and instruction in schools. These systems do not always show up in large-scale studies.

Alternatively, the seemingly low priority that most districts give to curriculum and instruction matters in their management, organization, and staffing arrangements may conceal other activities within districts that are related to curriculum and instruction. These exceptions are well worth exploring.

Overall, though, if one were basing current policy on existing research about the district role in instructional improvement, one would have to be skeptical about the readiness of school districts to be active participants in some broad-scale effort to improve teaching and learning. This skepticism might lead in any number of directions. One might simply conclude, for example, that the reformers who would like to eliminate school districts are probably right; the value added by school districts to the instruction actually received by students seems to be considerably less than the resources they consume. One might alternatively conclude, based on the reasons outlined in the previous section, that whether school districts are effective in their role of improving teaching and learning, there are a number of important reasons for continuing to treat them as important actors. Or one might conclude, also for reasons outlined in the previous section, that the district role in instructional improvement is a worthy object of policy in itself. That is, state and federal policy should focus attention and resources on deliberately improving the capacity of districts to manage instructional improvement because the success of higher-level policy depends, in some respect, on that capacity.

A Framework and Some Research Issues on the District Role in Instructional Improvement

One might think about explaining district involvement in instructional improvement as a two-step problem. First, if our earlier analysis of districts as units of government is true, then districts must find some niche in the intergovernmental system, or arrive at some resolution of their competing responsibilities as units of local government in a federal system of governance. Four such responsibilities were outlined earlier: (1) mobilizing support and buffering policies from other levels of government;

(2) developing and testing new policy ideas; (3) balancing developmental, allocative, and redistributive functions across levels of government; and (4) adapting policies from other levels of government to local needs and circumstances. Districts focus these responsibilities in different ways, depending on the local problems they face and the external pressures exerted on them from other levels of government. A district with weak or volatile community support and a diverse student body, for example, might focus on policies and administrative practices that strengthen local alliances and show responsiveness to diverse student backgrounds. A district with strong community support and a homogeneous student population might focus on buffering external influences and making the system work more efficiently. These resolutions are likely to differ according to the particular circumstances of a given district, and it is worth some sustained attention to how particular districts go about finding a niche in the intergovernmental system.

This level of analysis can be captured in questions like the following:

- What are the important political divisions around educational issues within the community, how are they articulated in district policy, and how are they expressed in relations with other levels of government?
- From where do district personnel see solutions to local problems emanating? From within? From outside?
- How does the district view its role in allocating resources internally? As assuring adequate resources for everyone? As compensating for inequities among neighborhoods and schools? As improving the performance of all schools?
- Does the district see itself as an initiator of policy or as a receiver of policies from other levels of government?

The second step is that, after establishing this niche, district involvement in instructional improvement is likely to be a function of five main factors: (1) internal pressures and incentives from the community for attention to instruction; (2) external pressures and incentives from other levels of government for attention to instruction; (3) district capacity to provide useful assistance to schools on matters of instruction, in the form of staffing and discretionary money; (4) district structures and processes for reaching schools on some regular basis; and (5) district policies for fixing responsibilities in attending to instructional matters.

One imagines a district that has established a niche in the intergovernmental system that puts it in the role of passive mediator of community interests and passive receiver of external mandates, which also takes a passive role toward instructional improvement, and in which little pressure from the community has come to bear on issues of instruction. Consequently, little pressure has emanated from the state or federal government. The district provides a low level of internal staffing for instruction and no explicit guidance on how responsibilities will be allocated around instructional issues.

One also imagines a district that has established a niche in the intergovernmental system that casts it in an activist role toward both internal and external sources of authority, in which strong pressure emanates from the community for attention to instructional issues, and in which the district focuses resources and policies on responsibilities for instructional improvement. Schools resolve these various factors associated with instructional improvement in various ways, and their general approach to resolving them varies with the prior step of finding a niche in the intergovernmental structure.

This level of analysis can be captured by questions like the following:

- What pressures and incentives exist in the community for attention to matters of instruction? How do district administrators read and interpret these pressures?
- What pressures and incentives exist in external policies for attention to matters of instruction? How do district administrators read and interpret these pressures?
- What resources exist within the district for assistance to schools and teachers in matters of instruction?
- How are district resources for instructional assistance and

improvement organized? How are they connected to schools organizationally?

- What policies or practices exist at the district level for defining responsibilities, within the central office and in schools, for instructional improvement?

Studying the forms of attention that school districts pay to instructional improvement can be seen as a process. First, one observes generally how a given district perceives its niche in the intergovernmental system, and second, how it resolves the various factors that influence attention to instructional improvement within that niche.

Studying how districts define their role vis-à-vis their own clients and other levels of government, and then studying how they deal with internal and external pressures, or their absence, for instructional improvement, may help in explaining why districts overall seem to pay so little attention to instructional improvement. Such a study would also suggest the sources of attention and approaches when districts *do* attend closely to this. This kind of study has not yet been done.

This line of research could also lead to a more direct focus on state and local policies that influence instructional improvement. For example, if these policies generally encourage school districts to take a passive role toward their constituents and toward other levels of government, then it is possible to design state policies that raise the visibility of instructional issues and focus more responsibility on local districts as agents of improvement. One can view some recent state reform policies as moving in this direction. Likewise, if research shows that some localities respond positively to external pressures and incentives to focus on instructional improvement but lack the capacity or the organizational structures and processes to engage schools in any kind of constructive approach, then state policy needs to focus on the internal problems.

Overall, evidence of school district involvement in instructional improvement does not paint an optimistic picture. Given what we know about the complexities of the intergovernmental roles that local school districts play and the problems associated with constructive involvement in instructional improvement, though, it does seem worthwhile to look more closely at how districts define their niche in the intergovernmental system and how, within the various niches they occupy, districts develop a focus that includes instructional improvement.

References

Berman, P., and McLaughlin, M. *Federal Programs Supporting Educational Change.* Vol. VIII: *Implementing and Sustaining Innovations.* Santa Monica, Calif.: RAND Corporation, 1978.

Chubb, J. E., and Moe, T. M. *Politics, Markets, and America's Schools.* Washington, D.C.: Brookings Institution, 1990.

Cohen, D. K. "Policy and Organization: The Impact of State and Federal Educational Policy on School Governance." *Harvard Educational Review,* 1982, *52*(4), 474–499.

Crowson, R., and Morris, V. C. "Administrative Control in Large-City School Systems: An Investigation of Chicago." *Educational Administration Quarterly,* 1985, *21,* 51–70.

Cuban, L. *How Teachers Taught: Constancy and Change in American Classrooms, 1890–1980.* New York: Longman, 1984.

David, J. "Restructuring in Progress: Lessons from Pioneering Districts." In R. Elmore and Associates, *Restructuring Schools: The Next Generation of Educational Reform.* San Francisco: Jossey-Bass, 1990.

Doyle, D., and Finn, C. "American Schools and the Future of Local Control." *Public Interest,* 1984, *77,* 77–95.

Elmore, R., and McLaughlin, M. *Steady Work: Policy, Practice, and the Reform of American Education.* Santa Monica, Calif.: RAND Corporation, 1988.

Finn, C. *We Must Take Charge: Our Schools and Our Future.* New York: Free Press, 1991.

Firestone, W., and others. *Educational Reform from 1983 to 1990: State Action and District Response.* Report of the Center for Policy Research in Education, Eagleton Institute of Politics, Rutgers University, New Brunswick, N.J., 1991.

Floden, R., and others. "Elementary School Principals' Role in District and School Curriculum Change." Paper presented at the annual meeting of the American Educational Research Association, New Orleans, La., 1984.

Floden, R., and others. "Instructional Leadership at the District Level: A Closer Look at Autonomy and Control." *Educational Administration Quarterly,* 1988, *24*(2), 96–124.

Fuhrman, S., and Elmore, R. "Understanding Local Control in the Wake of State Educational Reform." *Educational Evaluation and Policy Analysis,* 1990, *12*(1), 82–96.

Fuhrman, S., and Elmore, R. "Governors and Education Policy in the 1990s." Paper presented to the annual research conference of the Association for Public Policy and Management, San Francisco, Oct. 20, 1992.

Fuhrman, S. H., and Elmore, R. F. *Takeover and Deregulation: Working Models of New State and Local Regulatory Relationships.* New Brunswick, N.J.: Consortium for Policy Research in Education, 1992.

Hannaway, J., and Sproull, L. "Who's Running the Show? Coordination and Control in Educational Organizations." *Administrator's Notebook,* 1978–1979, *27,* 1–4.

Hess, G. A. *School Restructuring, Chicago Style.* Newbury Park, Calif.: Corwin, 1991.

Hill, P., and Bonan, J. *Decentralization and Accountability in Public Education.* Santa Monica, Calif.: RAND Corporation, 1991.

Malen, B., Ogawa, R., and Kranz, J. "What Do We Know About School-Based Management? A Case Study of the Literature—A Call for Research." In W. H. Clune and J. F. Witte (eds.), *Choice and Control in American Education.* Vol. 2: The Practice of Choice, Decentralization and School Restructuring. Bristol, Pa.: Falmer Press, 1990.

Martin, W., and Willower, D. "The Managerial Behavior of High School Principals. " *Educational Administration Quarterly,* 1981, *17,* 69–90.

Meyer, J., and Rowan, B. "The Structure of Educational Organizations." In M. Meyer (ed.), *Environments and Organizations.* San Francisco: Jossey-Bass, 1978.

Morone, J. *The Democratic Wish.* New York: Basic Books, 1990.

Murphy, J., and Hallinger, P. "Characteristics of Instructionally Effective School Districts." *Journal of Educational Research,* 1988, *81,* 175–181.

Osborne, D. *Laboratories of Democracy.* Boston: Harvard Business School Press, 1988.

Peterson, P. *City Limits.* Chicago: University of Chicago Press, 1981.

Pitner, N., and Ogawa, R. "Organizational Leadership: The Case of the Superintendent." *Educational Administration Quarterly,* 1981, *17,* 45–65.

Rowan, B. "Instructional Management in Historical Perspective." *Educational Administration Quarterly,* 1982, *18*(1), 43–59.

Smith, M., and O'Day, J. "Systemic School Reform." In S. Fuhrman and B. Malen (eds.), *The Politics of Curriculum and Testing.* Bristol, Pa.: Falmer Press, 1991.

Tyack, D., and Hansot, E. *Managers of Virtue: Public School Leadership in America, 1820–1980.* New York: Basic Books, 1982.

4

Systemic Educational Policy: A Conceptual Framework

William H. Clune

The idea behind systemic educational policy is that the current policy goal of substantial increases in student achievement will require a major shift in a large number of educational policies. The term *systemic* suggests "many policies pointed toward student achievement."

Historically, educational policies have not been effectively aimed at achievement and have not been coordinated (pointed in the same direction). On the other hand, educational policy is beginning to respond to the pressure for increased student achievement with a variety of more systemic approaches. The purpose of this chapter is to describe the historical problems with educational policy, propose a conceptual framework for describing systemic policy (which will allow us to recognize it when we see it), discuss the advantages and disadvantages of centralized instructional guidance, give examples of systemic educational policy from several states and Chicago, discuss the role of decentralization and choice within systemic policy, and conclude with some thoughts about the interplay of centralized policy and school-level innovation in a systemic reform strategy.

This chapter is reprinted with permission of the original publisher, Robert M. La Follette Institute of Public Affairs, University of Wisconsin — Madison. © 1991 Board of Regents of the University of Wisconsin System.

Limits of Current Educational Policy as a
Means of Increasing Student Achievement

Traditional educational policy is incapable of producing major gains in student achievement. This is the fundamental reason for all the contemporary interest in educational reform. Consider these problems:

- Educational reform and rhetoric have been more or less continuous for some time, but student test scores have remained relatively stable (Linn and Dunbar, 1990). On the other hand, some favorable developments in achievement (for example, the recent narrowing of the black/white gap in mathematics and reading achievement) may be due to isolated examples of a systemic approach (O'Day and Smith, 1990).
- Twenty-five years of research have shown that many educational practices are unrelated to achievement. For example, research suggests that the factors that absorb most increases in educational funding — slight increases in teacher salaries and small decreases in class size — are not likely to increase student achievement (Odden and Picus, 1992). But more targeted approaches may be effective (for example, salary increases for beginning teachers plus effective recruitment programs in schools with high teacher turnover and carefully designed tutorial remediation in third grade reading) (Murnane and others, 1991; Madden and others, 1991).
- Many of today's goals for education will require massive, coordinated change in educational practice and delivery systems. For example, new approaches in mathematics and science will require changes in teachers' knowledge, attitudes, and training, as well as in teaching method, student testing, and parents' attitudes (Fennema, Carpenter, and Peterson, 1989; Guthrie, 1990; National Council of Teachers of Mathematics, 1989).
- Educational policy is typically extremely fragmented and ineffective, producing a great volume of uncoordinated mandates, programs, and projects that provide no coherent direction, increase the complexity of educational governance and

practice, and consume a lot of resources. The United States produces the largest quantity of educational policy in the world, and the least effective (Cohen, 1990).

• Education for the urban poor has reached such a state of crisis that well-designed and coordinated supplementary educational and social services will be required as the foundation for the regular academic program. Yet social and educational policies aimed at poor school-age children are presently fragmented and poorly coordinated (Kirst, 1991).

A Conceptual Framework for Systemic Educational Policy

A conceptual framework for systemic educational policy is given in Figure 4.1. Systemic policy has five characteristics:

1. *Research-based goals for changes in educational practice and organization.* The importance of educational research is underestimated because much research is not useful, and much of the research that is useful shows that many educational practices are ineffective. But research findings about effective practices are gradually accumulating, and these tend to be quickly seized upon by a policy system that is hungry for solutions. Finding out how to increase educational achievement is a difficult task for everyone, including policymakers and practitioners; good research is needed to establish new directions.

Summarizing the useful findings of educational research is difficult. Some types of influence are very deep and pervasive; for example, decades of research by cognitive scientists on the nature of reading and mathematical reasoning (which then work their way into curriculum and student testing).

Specific practices identified by research as promising include higher curriculum content, targeted tutorials or accelerated remediation in elementary school, upgraded and supplemental instruction in high school academics, new vocational courses with high academic content, school/business partnerships, easier transition from secondary to postsecondary school, meaningful report cards, schools in the effective schools model (for example, with active instructional leadership), and preschool and children's services, such as nutrition and health care.

Figure 4.1. A Schematic Representation of Systemic Educational Policy.

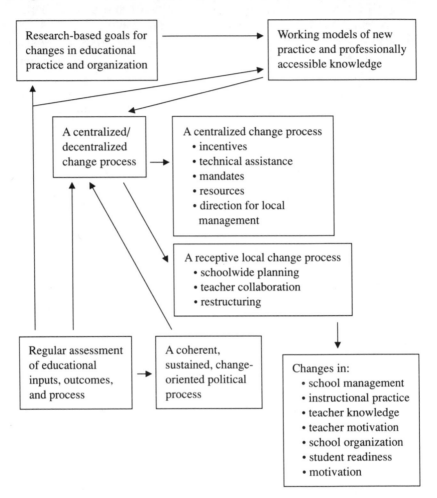

One could characterize the items on this list as embodying one of four kinds of coherence: coherence of the curriculum, coherence of the eduational experience and its consequences for the individual child, coherence between the entire life of the child and the school experience, and coherence in school organization. A fifth might be added: Japanese teachers create a coherent educational experience within the classroom (Stigler and

Stevenson, 1991); as we will see, producing this kind of coherence then requires coherent — or systematic — educational policy.

2. *Working models of new practice and professionally accessible knowledge.* Change requires more than good ideas for new directions: it requires a real understanding on the part of teachers and other people in schools about how to implement the change. In the case of new mathematics, for example, curriculum frameworks might be supplemented with new instructional materials, new forms of student testing, and groups of teachers who can teach other teachers how to engage in active teaching of the new material.

3. *A centralized/decentralized change process.* Systemic change requires a change delivery system that usually includes both centralized and decentralized aspects. A centralized dimension is needed because schools and teachers often lack the capacity to conceive and implement innovations on their own. Even the centralized process must acquire decentralized aspects, however. The state government may set goals centrally (as with curriculum frameworks) but an effective delivery system is likely also to require something like a network of consultants — teachers trained in the new curriculum content, effective schools management teams, and so on. This central system plus outreach then must be matched by some kind of active change process within schools and among teachers. A teacher who attends a workshop on a new approach to mathematics will not change math instruction in the school unless the workshop process is replicated among the rest of the math teachers in the school (Clune, 1990).

4. *Regular assessment of educational inputs, outcomes, and process.* Methodologically valid and reliable measures of student achievement and other educational outcomes (for example, graduation, college entrance, job skills, and placement) are the cornerstone of systemic educational policy. The most important reason for indicators of educational outcomes is our substantial and continuing ignorance about the determinants of student achievement (Clune, 1991). If we knew exactly what to do to increase achievement, we might dispense with student assessments and concentrate on educational practice, but the exact effectiveness

of most proposed reforms and the best way to implement them are uncertain. The effectiveness of reform in different states, school districts, and schools is also very hard to judge. For example, when school report cards are implemented, a common experience is that some schools with previously top-notch reputations do not look very good on "value-added" criteria across grades.

The design of a first-class system of student assessments is extremely important and should be given careful attention, with input from experts and teachers. Student assessments used for educational planning should have five basic characteristics: representativeness (achieved through a census approach of testing every child, or random sampling); measurement of periodic gain (comparisons of different schools are otherwise ambiguous); correspondence to ambitious curriculum goals (corresponding to what is taught in schools but also pushing the curriculum higher); availability of data by administrative unit (ability to measure gains by the whole state, district, and school); and some measures of corresponding educational inputs and process related to achievement (for example, student characteristics and course offerings).

Contrary to some recommendation, the indicator system probably should not be high stakes (including strong rewards and punishments). Because of uncertainty about desirable educational practice, and the enormous diversity of the system, responses to problems identified by the indicators should be open-ended and flexible.

5. *A coherent, sustained, change-oriented political process.* The analysis of systemic change to this point paints a picture of a change process working over a period of time to produce new practices among teachers and within schools. But the political process creating and supporting this type of change must have qualities of coherence and durability not usually found in American educational policy. At least three dangers must be avoided: (1) discontinuing change efforts during periods of budgetary difficulty; (2) dissipating and fragmenting coherent change through a continuing stream of disjointed reforms, programs, and projects; and (3) loss of momentum through inertia and

lack of leadership. Avoiding these dangers requires a political process with at least two attributes: public consensus and a powerful, supportive political coalition; and a set of legislative and executive institutions for maintaining the reforms and preventing policy disruptions.

The Logic of Systemic Instructional Guidance

Many of the changes in educational practice needed to improve student achievement do not directly involve curriculum and instruction. For example, achievement gains can be expected from better social services, safer schools, a heightened sense of community, greater parental involvement, a reduction in absenteeism and the dropout rate, and stronger external incentives for high achievement, such as links to college and employment opportunities.

Nevertheless, there is a strong push in systemic educational policy toward what can be called "systemic instructional guidance"—an effort by the state to coordinate curriculum frameworks, student assessments, teacher training, and school change around a powerful, coherent vision of curriculum content (Smith and O'Day, 1991). There are several reasons for this effort.

First, curriculum in the United States is quite weak; upgrading curriculum content has a powerful influence on student achievement; curriculum reform does not require massive new resources, since the instructional time is already available; and spontaneous, widespread curriculum reform at the school level is unlikely.

Second, in theory, upgrading the curriculum allows the system to achieve a higher degree of coherence and a lower level of fragmentation because of the focus on the entire educational experience of students. The authors of the Science Project 2061, for example, decided that science instruction in the United States could not be saved by tinkering and adding new material but could be greatly improved and focused through the substitution of an entirely new curriculum (Rutherford and Ahlgren, 1990).

Third, the coordination of curriculum standards, student

assessments, and teacher preparation requirements provides an opportunity, not otherwise readily available, for policymakers to send a clear, consistent message to schools about the nature of their educational mission. Such a strong message from the policy environment encourages schools to develop a corresponding, clear educational mission of their own. Clear goals and high academic expectations are two characteristics of effective schools. Since the elements of instructional guidance usually exist for independent reasons (for example, student testing for accountability), coordinating them reduces policy dissonance and provides a potentially powerful tool for upgrading curriculum.

Whatever the justifications for systemic instructional guidance, to be effective it must conform to the basic structure outlined in Figure 4.1, including a centralized/decentralized change process. Curriculum frameworks will have little effect in the absence of a process to push new forms of practice into the schools.

Potential problems with instructional guidance also should be recognized. The two most commonly discussed problems are the stifling of ambitions and innovative curricula in local schools and the stifling of teacher initiative and responsibility through excessive prescriptiveness and control. Solving these problems is not necessarily easy. For example, many Ivy League-oriented fast-track private schools in New York do not participate in the justly acclaimed New York State Regents examinations, because they believe that their own curricula are much better than the Regents'. Perhaps even a high-end standard curriculum is a resource mainly for weaker schools; clearly, special attention should be given in such a standardized system to the curriculum for lower-achieving students (for example, building a high-quality entry-level math course for high schools, rather than emphasizing college prep, as does the Regents examination).

The solutions usually recommended to avoid problems with instructional guidance are to adopt instructional guidance only when there is a consensus or common core of learning goals and to use long-range learning goals rather than detailed regulation of the scope and sequence of each course. The recent trend toward performance assessment (for example, math problem solving and written essays versus multiple choice) may help solve the problems of instructional guidance by requiring a high degree of activity and autonomy on the part of both teachers and students, by adapting easily to ambitious curriculum goals, and by corresponding closely to the actual learning goals of most teachers.

State and Local Models of Systemic Educational Policy

My purpose in this section is to indicate, very briefly, how the policies of a number of "lead" states and Chicago fit the model of systemic instructional policy described here, and also how the model helps identify gaps and flaws in those policies.

South Carolina has a simple and effective design for systemic educational policy (Peterson, 1991). A strong political movement at both the grass-roots and elite levels created a reform bill and corresponding joint legislative committee. Various common educational goals were adopted: gains in standardized achievement tests, more coursetaking in academic subjects, higher graduation and college entrance rates, lower teacher absenteeism, higher teacher satisfaction, and so on. Progress on the goals is reported for the state, districts, and schools. Limited incentives and regulatory waivers are offered for progress at the school level. Consulting teams from the state assist schools needing improvement. Coherence in the whole effort is provided by public adoption and reporting on a variety of educational goals, which are adjusted over time. Political institutions protect funding for the reforms, and the public remains supportive of improvement (as opposed to maintenance of the status quo). To this point, South Carolina has not adopted instructional guidance at the state level and thus implicitly promotes the goals embedded in standardized achievement tests, which perhaps can be best characterized as "the basics" (except for the emphasis also given to higher enrollments in advanced academic courses).

Historically, California's reforms have been coordinated by powerful legislative leadership and the state superintendent of schools (recently, Bill Honig). Curriculum frameworks and statewide student assessment provide educational goals. Change is encouraged through a complex state management system, including networks of and workshops for teachers, state-sponsored school improvement related to the goals, and training for district superintendents and principals. California has adopted instructional guidance at the state level, but adoption of the state goals is technically voluntary. Publication of student gains provides some pressure, but the enthusiasm of people in the management system probably is at least an equal force for change. The political base for reform in California is not nearly as strong as South Carolina's, with the result that the reforms have been more disrupted by political and budgetary difficulty (for example, disputes between the superintendent and governor and funding gaps for the statewide assessment).

Connecticut is a state that uses student testing to lead reform. Statewide mastery tests of basic skills have been gradually introduced and upgraded (Connecticut State Board of Education, 1987). Scores are reported by school. A well-publicized set of teacher entrance exams is not coordinated with content of the student assessments. The most recent and highly publicized wave of performance testing is still in the pilot stage but also marks a move toward a state role in choosing instructional materials. So-called prompts (standardized, open-ended problems) are being developed in math and science, in a highly decentralized process. Teachers and state government workers design prompts, which are then evaluated on the basis of pilots in the classroom. Thus, Connecticut is moving from a system of statewide assessments with little additional incentives for instructional change toward a more complete system of instructional guidance that includes, in addition to the prompts, a system for gradual training of teachers. Politically, Connecticut gets leadership from the superintendent's office but, in some ways, operates on a political shoestring, with public support for current activities used as the political capital for continued reform. Thus, as with California, the political durability of the reforms during budgetary difficulties is questionable.

New York is the one state in the country where systemic instructional guidance is fully institutionalized (Tyree, 1991). New York has been doing things for decades that some other states are just now trying to begin from scratch, but New York gets less attention because it has an old system. At the high school level, New York has a complete system of instructional materials and student examinations (the Regents exams and Regents competency exams). In a position exactly opposite from its neighbor, Connecticut, New York exercises extensive control over curriculum but does not publish test scores by school. New York also attaches high student stakes to some of its tests (for example, course credit and the Regents diploma) and has been gradually introducing mastery exams at the lower grade levels. Centralized and decentralized change are provided in New York in at least two ways: a so-called turnkey system for gradually training teachers in the new curriculum materials once they are officially adopted and decentralized piloting of new curriculum materials and test items. Politically, New York relies, for stability, on the highly autonomous Board of Regents, with its independent constitutional powers, as well as the set of institutions within the department of education built around the state curriculum and testing enterprise. For example, since the state is always developing and piloting new materials for tests, it can rely on this established role and need not compete for new resources.

Chicago approached systemic reform from the bottom up. Many people equate the Chicago reform with the well-publicized school councils. These school councils are important elements of decentralization, as discussed below, but Chicago actually has a complete centralized/decentralized change process (Moore, 1990). A central agency keeps track of indicators of student performance, and the reform coalition that sponsored the reform remains extremely active in evaluating its success, making adjustments, and protecting the reforms from political and legal disruption.

Questions About Decentralization in a Systemic Framework

Decentralization of authority is a necessary part of a systemic approach to educational policy, but fundamental questions remain to be answered before we understand how decentralization can improve student achievement. Policymakers should be aware of the primitive state of our understanding of this topic and avoid rushing toward solutions based on ill-defined philosophies or fuzzy analogies to decentralization in business organizations. I will address two important questions here.

One question is how to structure effective minimum control, or how to achieve what has been described as the goal of "simultaneous loose/tight coupling" (Peters and Waterman, 1982). Principals and teachers doing complex tasks have a lot of information that is unavailable to their supervisors. One goal is to give them the freedom to use this information productively; another is to prevent them from concealing information and diverting organizational effort from its proper goals. For example, on the side of the need for greater discretion, only teachers are in a position to understand the complexities of the learning process in each child and classroom. On the side of the need for greater supervision, newly elected school councils in Chicago discovered large amounts of instructional downtime in many schools (for example, the whole month of September in homerooms and many classrooms without any teachers for substantial lengths of time). Apparently, in the absence of parental control, principals had the incentive to conceal educational problems from their supervisors in the bureaucracy rather than ask for help in solving them. A second kind of control that is probably necessary is regular monitoring of student achievement, because parents are not in a good position to observe progress relative to social norms, and school personnel may not want to admit they lack the means or the will to produce rapid gains in achievement.

The second question is how to structure teacher discretion. A common dream has been completely individualized education regardless of age or grade chronology, yielding the most rapid possible gains for each student, but this imposes too much complexity; the economics of age-graded classrooms are very powerful. Rapid achievement gains in age-graded classrooms require at least two things currently lacking in American education. First, curriculum must be structured to expect significant new learning each year; for example, new material currently accounts, on average, for only about 10 percent of the material presented in elementary school mathematics each year (Porter, 1989). Second, teachers must know how to get rapid gains from age groups. Japanese teachers, for example, keep the level of mathematics instruction high, focused, and accessible for heterogeneous groups of students; the Japanese model also involves effective teacher training and collaboration.

In other words, the issue of decentralization appears to be simpler than we sometimes picture it. On the one hand, we need selective, targeted organizational watchdogs, such as statewide student assessments and carefully designed parental control. On the other hand, instead of the unstructured free-for-all in local planning and discretion often associated with school-based management, we need exactly the opposite: a strong structure that allows exercise of teacher discretion in the most productive manner. Systemic instructional guidance offers a possible vehicle for this kind of structure.

School Choice: Useful Component or Complete Alternative?

Some proponents of choice in education believe that parental choice, by itself, would improve student achievement by producing coherence of mission and a sense of community at the school level (Chubb and Moe, 1990). Choice might well create some benefits from increased parental involvement, but unregulated choice seems to lack a mechanism to change practice and seems to lack nearly all the elements of systemic change. Missing elements include (1) a set of ambitious common learning objectives, (2) mechanisms to evaluate innovations and ratify those that are successful, (3) a means of training teachers and disseminating successful practices, and (4) a political process and coalition that would protect the change effort over time.

Furthermore, perhaps the easiest way politically to implement choice on a large scale — the political path of least resistance — would be to let people choose their schoolmates, thereby encouraging severe stratification of enrollments by race and class and ultimately reducing political and financial support for public education (as wealthier parents resort to supplementary contributions). Thus, a logical approach to choice is to encourage experimentation targeted specifically to low-income students and to locate choice within a larger context of systemic educational reform.

Conclusion: Policy Coherence and Exemplary School-Level Success

Many aspects of systemic educational policy described in this chapter might not seem to be very coherent — for example, the complexities of a centralized/decentralized change process adjusting to variations in local school context. But coherence in the change process is required to keep innovation on track, while coherence in the political process is required to protect the reforms over time. Coherence of educational objectives would be useful as a way to develop common indicators of success, realize time savings from streamlined curriculum objectives, and provide a metric for coordinating otherwise independent elements of the system (for example, teacher training).

But the success of systemic educational policy also depends on demonstrable success at the school level with, for example, a few urban schools demonstrating large achievement gains for typical urban students (see, for example, the results reported for a Houston elementary school in the Accelerated Schools Project (1991). President Bush's America 2000 strategy (U.S. Department of Education, 1991) has the advantage of trying to encourage school innovations but the apparent disadvantage that few institutions support systemic change.

What is the ultimate potential of systemic educational policy? Given inevitable variability in the change process and local school capacity, the most that can be expected from well-designed systemic educational policy is modest annual gains in average achievement, with rapid gains in especially successful schools. Though they are less than an immediate educational revolution, these are goals well worth pursuing.

References

Accelerated Schools Project. *Accelerated Schools*, 1991, *1*(2) (available from Stanford University, Stanford, Calif.).

Chubb, J. E., and Moe, T. M. *Politics, Markets, and America's Schools.* Washington, D.C.: Brookings Institution, 1990.

Clune, W. H. "Educational Governance and Student Achievement." In W. H. Clune and J. F. Witte (eds.), *Choice and Control in American Education.* Vol. 2. Bristol, Pa.: Falmer Press, 1990.

Clune, W. H. "Educational Policy in a Situation of Uncertainty; or, How to Put Eggs in Different Baskets." In S. H. Fuhrman and B. Malen (eds.), *The Politics of Curriculum and Testing.* Bristol, Pa.: Falmer Press, 1991.

Cohen, D. K. "Governance and Instruction: The Promise of Decentralization and Choice." In W. H. Clune and J. F. Witte (eds.), *Choice and Control in American Education,* Vol. 1. Bristol, Pa.: Falmer Press, 1990.

Connecticut State Board of Education. *Connecticut's Common Core of Learning.* Hartford: Connecticut State Board of Education, 1987.

Fennema, E., Carpenter, T. P., and Peterson, P. L. "Teachers' Decision Making and Cognitively Guided Instruction: A New Paradigm for Curriculum Development." In N. F. Ellerton and M. A. Clements (eds.), *School Mathematics: The Challenge to Change.* Geelong, Victoria, Australia: Deakin University Press, 1989.

Guthrie, J. W. (ed.). *Educational Evaluation and Policy Analysis,* 1990, *12*(3), 233–353 (entire issue).

Kirst, M. W. "Improving Children's Services: Overcoming Barriers, Creating New Opportunities." *Phi Delta Kappan,* 1991, *72*(8), 615–618.

Linn, R. L., and Dunbar, S. B. "The Nation's Report Card Goes Home: Good News and Bad About Trends in Achievement." *Phi Delta Kappan,* 1990, *72*(2), 127–133.

Madden, N. A., and others. "Success for All." *Phi Delta Kappan,* 1991, *72*(8), 593–599.

Moore, D. "Voice and Choice in Chicago." In W. H. Clune and J. F. Witte (eds.), *Choice and Control in American Education.* Vol. 2. Bristol, Pa.: Falmer Press, 1990.

Murnane, R. J., and others. *Who Will Teach: Policies That Matter.* Cambridge, Mass.: Harvard University Press, 1991.

National Council of Teachers of Mathematics (NCTM). *Curriculum and Evaluation Standards for School Mathematics.* Reston, Va.: National Council of Teachers of Mathematics, 1989.

O'Day, J., and Smith, M. S. "Retention Policies in U.S. Schools." Paper presented at the Consortium for Policy Research in Education, Rutgers University, New Brunswick, N.J., 1990.

Odden, A. R., and Picus, L. O. *School Finance: A Policy Perspective.* New York: McGraw-Hill, 1992.

Peters, T. J., and Waterman, R. H., Jr. *In Search of Excellence: Lessons from America's Best-Run Companies.* New York: Harper-Collins, 1982.

Peterson, T. "School Reform in South Carolina: Implications for Wisconsin's Reform Efforts." Paper prepared for the Wisconsin Center for Educational Policy, Robert M. La Follette Institute of Public Affairs, University of Wisconsin, Madison, 1991.

Porter, A. "A Curriculum Out of Balance: The Case of Elementary School Mathematics." *Educational Researcher,* 1989, *18*(5), 9–15.

Rutherford, F. J., and Ahlgren, A. *Science for All Americans.* New York: Oxford University Press, 1990.

Smith, M. S., and O'Day, J. "Systemic School Reform." In S. H. Fuhrman and B. Malen (eds.), *The Politics of Curriculum and Testing.* Bristol, Pa.: Falmer Press, 1991.

Stigler, J. W., and Stevenson, H. W. "How Asian Teachers Polish Each Lesson to Perfection." *American Educator,* 1991, *12*(20), 13–47.

Tyree, A. K., Jr. "The Potential Strength of State Curriculum Control Systems: Four Case Studies." Paper prepared for the Consortium for Policy Research in Education, University of Wisconsin, Madison, 1991.

U.S. Department of Education. *America 2000: An Education Strategy.* Washington, D.C.: U.S. Department of Education, 1991.

5

Student Incentives and Academic Standards: Independent Schools as a Coherent System

Arthur G. Powell

The Problem of Student Incentives

Lord Bryce, perhaps the most astute commentator on the American scene aside from de Tocqueville and Riesman, once observed: "To the vast majority of mankind nothing is more agreeable than to escape the need for mental exertion" (Osgood, 1952). His late nineteenth-century comment still retains a quality of universal truth — teachers and parents today will nod their heads in assent. This is doubtless why the indefatigible administrator of a major private school association, Miss Esther Osgood (1952, pp. 10–12), once used Bryce to make a point about the need for student incentives to work hard. The modern, post-World War II age had created more enticing "avenues of escape" from mental exertion than ever before, she said in a 1952 speech: comic books, television, pop culture generally. Bryce could not be ignored.

Miss Osgood's adult life was spent promoting her one sure way to prevent youths' escape from mental effort, in order to speed their transformation into "adults of culture and intelli-

Research support for this chapter was provided in part by the Esther A. and Joseph Klingenstein Fund, Inc., the Geraldine R. Dodge Foundation, the Edward E. Ford Foundation, Gates Foundation, the Rockefeller Brothers Foundation, and the New York Community Trust.

gence." That strategy was quality education. "The little boy buy-ing a comic book and the children watching Milton Berle are not monsters," she assured her audience (in the exact year this writer was avidly consuming both). "They are the reasons schools exist. They are the reasons teachers exist."

Forty years later, vastly more enticing and more danger-ous avenues of escape from mental exertion are readily avail-able to American youth. They make the threats Miss Osgood observed seem innocent and charming. In fact, many schools now incorporate both comic books and commercial TV as regu-lar parts of instruction to lure youth away from more danger-ous preoccupations.

And forty years later the society also values mental exer-tion. Although most educators gag at the vaguely un-American notion of "cultured" adults (and would have when Miss Osgood confidently used the word), there is no mistaking the contem-porary educational commitment to produce intelligent adults. Much more than in the early 1950s, when notions of life ad-justment education still commanded professional respect and mass postsecondary education had not yet fully happened, most educators in the 1990s accept the development of intelligence as the central task of schooling.

In the 1990s we believe Americans should acquire think-ing or higher-order skills, develop cognitively, learn to think for a living, use our minds well, appreciate that intelligences are multiple, and finish first in world-class end-of-season academic polls. The issue is not whether these objectives are important but how they can be achieved by a society also concerned with equality and genuine opportunity. How, in short, can intelli-gence be developed in all youth?

Lord Bryce wisely reminded us that hard mental work is not a natural preference of humankind. It is certainly not a natural preference of youth, especially American youth whose options for pleasure are perhaps unrivaled in the history of the world. Thus one significant piece of the broader educational puzzle — how to develop intelligence in all youth — is the prob-lem of student incentives or motivation to work seriously on ac-quiring broadly "intellectual" skills, knowledge, and dispositions. Why *should* students work hard to acquire these things? What desirable, perhaps even pleasurable consequences might flow from hard work at school and academic achievement? What undesirable consequences might flow from little work and academic mediocrity?

For most of the century desirable personal consequences did not normally depend on superior school achievement. Highly undesirable personal consequences were rarely associated with the absence of achievement. The egalitarian public policies that produced universal secondary education and aspired to near-universal postsecondary education, even when most sensitive to equity, mandated only the most general kind of access to education. They did not mandate much in the way of achievement, unless achievement was imagined in the most minimalist ways. A high school diploma could be obtained largely by persisting in school courses — attending them regularly, behaving decently. The courses continually expanded in number in response to student and teacher interests and those of outside interest groups. Students had great choice about what to study as well as how hard to study.

Persistence was nothing to be sneezed at. To most Americans it represented responsible behavior with clear workplace and civic implications. It was and is better to persist from a vocational standpoint than to drop out — especially since high school graduation has been the usual prerequisite for postsecondary continuation. One important incentive for large numbers of Americans to finish high school is the vocational impact of that choice. The other clear incentive is the central role of high schools in teenagers' social lives.

Real academic achievement in school, as distinct from persistence in winning a diploma, is supported by a much weaker foundation of incentives operating on large numbers of students. Increased aspirations for college have admittedly pushed increased numbers of teenagers to undertake college preparatory programs since the 1950s. It is also true that in the fifteen years after 1945 the growth of teenagers who wished to go to college outpaced the growth of postsecondary education places. In those years considerable academic pressure existed for a wide range of students to work hard and do well in high school.

But higher education did expand, backed by tremendous

federal and state financial resources, and by the 1960s a more familiar American situation was restored. Higher education had always been expansionist and entrepreneurial, driven in the nineteenth century by religious zeal and local boosterism. Supply traditionally exceeded demand — except for the postwar years. When supply once again exceeded demand in the late 1960s, the historical reluctance of higher education to make serious academic demands on prospective students and schools reemerged.

A few colleges provided the exception to the rule. Between 100 and 200 public and private colleges and universities could afford to be somewhat selective in admissions at various times after the war because they had more qualified applicants than places — an unprecedented situation that existed virtually nowhere in 1941.

But higher education in general had no reason to erect barriers to discourage prospective enrollees. There was always a college somewhere for almost anybody — regardless of attainment, interest, or financial circumstance. For the last generation the name of the game in most of higher education has been recruitment and marketing, not selection and imposing requirements, with astonishing success. In the early 1990s about 60 percent of high school graduates went to some postsecondary education immediately after high school, and about two-thirds were so enrolled within two or three years of graduation. Nearly half of the entire age cohort of eighteen- to nineteen-year-olds was in college.

If neither public policies nor college admissions requirements (except for a small number of institutions) provided clear incentives for students to exert much mental effort in schools, what other incentives existed for students to engage in academic learning? Employers of college graduates or graduate school admissions offices never thought to look at high school performance — subsequent college graduation rendered all high school work permanently invisible. Employers of high school graduates, more surprisingly, rarely examined what students did in high school. Persistence to the diploma was enough, and perhaps for most of the century was a better proxy for workplace performance in the jobs high school graduates filled than would have been high attainment in academic studies.

Nor did America as a civilization value learning for its own sake. The cultural incentives in support of mental exertion werē remarkably weak compared with many other societies. Richard Hofstadter (1963) authoritatively described the pervasiveness of anti-intellectualism in American life a generation ago. This has not changed: in our ism-obsessed society, this is the forgotten ism. It is not just that pop culture celebrates that we do not know much about "his-tor-ee" but that within schools teachers seriously committed to academic learning — be they traditionalists or progressives — are often but one of many faculty interest groups present.

Many teachers instruct in fields that have little to do with the development of intelligence but have strong advocates for continued inclusion in the curriculum. Imagine the enormous stake in preserving jobs concerning "remediation" at all levels of the educational system. If incentives supporting academic learning reduced the need for remediation, the potential effect on these jobs would rival the potential effect of the end of the Cold War on the military-industrial complex. And it would be equally resisted. Schoolpeople also understand very well how little effect actual achievement in school (as distinct from persistence) has except on a tiny student group of the already annointed. For students not bound for one of *U.S. News*'s top-rated colleges, what justifies the struggle of student or of teacher with Advanced Placement history over "regular" history?

In this near vacuum of social incentives for intellectual exertion, Americans have characteristically placed the greatest burden for generating such incentives on individual teachers and individual students. Perhaps the main job of the American teacher, a job that distinguishes him or her from teachers in many other countries, is the job not of teaching but of motivating students to want to learn (at best) or to tolerate schooling without revolt (at worst). It is an enormous job to be asked to motivate as well as to teach (as if the surgeon not only operated but had to persuade patients not to walk out of the operating room), especially in a society that gives teachers so little support. American pedagogy, in both its public and private school manifestations, has overemphasized the unique motivational power of the individual teacher. We hope teachers can motivate either by means of trained professional technique or by their charismatic personalities. But one way or the other, we expect them to do it.

Motivation is a crucial field within the history of American psychology and pedagogy. It is hardly surprising that the many versions of progressive education, with their fundamental appeal to existing student interests as the starting point in instructional and curriculum design, have had such a lasting (if infinitely varied) impact on schooling. Without many external incentives to provoke mental exertion, the work of teaching is helped enormously if students want to learn because they are interested in learning. Unfortunately, efforts to make school fun, interesting, and entertaining—to appeal to a presumed natural curiosity—has a long practical history of disappointment. These efforts have often had the unintended effect of removing complexity and the need for any mental effort. This is the on-site trade-off: emphasizing "interest" often seems to require deemphasizing the active use of mind. A second problem is that successful progressive education has often been achieved with bright, curious students from educated families who in fact have some developed intellectual interests. The pedagogical intervention has not created the interest but built on one already present.

A third problem is the technical one of producing teachers with the skills to motivate youth to work hard voluntarily. Almost all schools have at least one or two heroic, charismatic individuals with ability to command the attention and interest of large numbers of students. These teachers are often remembered as quirky and idiosyncratic "personalities." All schools and parents know and covet them, but they are unfortunately rare. We do not know how to reproduce them in great numbers, although the effort to learn how goes on and has become increasingly sophisticated as it has attracted more imaginative researchers.

Just as American teachers are expected to motivate students, so students are expected to motivate themselves. The school's job, if it attends seriously to equity, is mainly seen as providing rich and varied opportunities for learning with minimal barriers to participation. This is our version of the level playing field: opportunities must exist and be genuinely open to all, but students still choose whether or not to seize these opportunities. Opportunity is voluntary and choice based, which places an enormous burden on students and their families, in the absence of strong cultural supports for academic learning, to seek out opportunity alone and unaided.

Some groups provide these incentives regularly to most of their members. Some parents exemplify for their children the pleasurable effects of sustained academic work by the satisfaction they demonstrate from vocations in which the active use of intelligence is demanded (for example, scientists, good elementary school teachers), or by reading, participating in the arts, or talking politics at suppertime. Students from such groups or families are lucky: interests and motivations to work hard and to learn rub gently off on them, tastes acquired in the course of growing up, tastes that are ordinary to them although strange and sometimes threatening to students less fortunate.

Regardless of family or group background, of course, some students seem internally motivated to study and learn and others do not. Teachers covet the self-starters who are genuinely interested in the material. They exist, as Bryce recognized, but like brilliant teachers they are rare and, unsurprisingly, are usually quite proficient at the academic studies that command their interest.

We greatly admire such teachers and students, but we should not be ashamed to admit they are not typical. It seems foolish to place so many of our incentive eggs in these two baskets. Most American youth do not find demanding academic study pleasurable, something they would happily pursue on their own. Most American teachers have their hands full with problems of instruction without in addition solving problems of basic motivation. Serious academic work, at least at first, is often hard work and not much fun.

So it is no surprise that Americans have rediscovered the problem of incentives at a time when social imperatives to focus seriously on both intelligence and equity are very strong. We want to get the incentives right to support the development of intelligence. But what are those incentives — in addition to the ones already mentioned? How extensive, for example, should local, state, or national mandates be? Should they affect only course selection or testing (if even these), or should they extend further into curriculum and teacher education? Should more colleges tighten admissions requirements and should employers of high school graduates pay greater attention to high school achievement? Will radical decentralization of educational authority to school sites — in what already may be the most decentralized educational system in the industrialized world — create professional communities with a collective power to engage students more potent than that of today's isolated individual teacher?

If all youth should learn to use their minds well, then they must have clear reasons for changing behavior to achieve that end. Equally important, the change must be seen to be in the immediate self-interest of agencies whose opinions youth cannot afford to ignore (colleges, employers). And schools themselves must have incentives to carry out with passion and focus the task of developing student intelligence. They too must win something for doing a good job. The problem of incentives is a cultural and "systemic" problem that needs to be addressed in a coherent, systemic way.

The Relevance of Prep Schools

Many of the problems of persuading students to work hard at demanding academic subjects find illumination from an unlikely source: the experience of private independent schools over the last century. Independent schools form a distinct subset of incorporated private nonprofit schools governed by individual boards of trustees. Their mission almost always is academic and college preparatory. They charge higher tuitions than any other type of private school except those which cater to special needs populations of various sorts. (When an agency was established in the 1950s to measure the financial needs of candidates for these schools, an analyst working on the parent form argued seriously that a question on airplane ownership might help reveal the financial backgrounds of scholarship applicants.)

Independent schools are thus the sort of private schools

most Americans mean when they say "private" or "prep" school. They are the privileged private schools, resembling affluent suburban public schools much more than the main body of low-tuition, religiously affiliated private schools. Independent schools can and often do have religious associations, but they are governed by their own boards and the dominant religions represented — Episcopal, Catholic Order (such as Jesuit), and Quaker — mirror the generally upscale characteristics of the student population. In 1990 about 369,000 students attended about 1,000 members of the National Association of Independent Schools.

These schools began to emerge as a recognizable American type only as recently as the 1880s. Their entire history is essentially modern — we have photographs, not paintings, in which people wear clothing, not costumes. As junior partners with a small group of aspiring universities, they mobilized a somewhat different type of student incentive to pursue demanding academic work than existed in most other schools at the time and for many decades afterward. Incentives to exert mental effort did not depend only on happy occasions where selected, motivated students eagerly and spontaneously engaged in academic study. Nor did they depend only on the ability of wonderful teachers to stimulate interest in the life of the mind. The independent schools had their share of such students and teachers, of course, and always wished for more.

What was unique about their situation, especially during the first four decades of the twentieth century, was the addition of other powerful incentives for all students to work hard on their studies: incentives that were mobilized in a coherent, systemic way. What parents and students wished to happen to students' lives after school graduation — acceptance to certain colleges — became specifically contingent on the level of academic work students achieved while in school. Schools and colleges had to want this achievement as much as did students — want it enough to cooperate and compromise with one another in a way they had never done before.

It took an entirely new voluntary organization, the College Entrance Examination Board, to give shape and bite to this simple-sounding incentive for students to work hard. The board's main function between 1900 and 1941 was to create a linked system of procedures that would tightly bind the decision to admit to college with the character of academic work done in school. (After 1941, crucial elements in that system collapsed. They were restored in a somewhat different form during the 1950s.)

All this happened because of overlapping developments within certain families, colleges, and schools near the end of the nineteenth century. One crucial event was the creation of a post–Civil War monied class who believed that their children — usually but not always male — should go to college. Privileged Americans also believed, with greater frequency than earlier in the century, that their children should be educated in schools rather than by private tutors and, further, in schools somewhat removed from the urban centers where they lived. The most popular independent school models were boarding schools and country day schools.

Aside from college preparation, which they frequently regarded as necessary but uninteresting, these parents wanted a healthy, safe, religious, and socially appropriate environment for their children. The teeming city was to be avoided for practical health reasons. In an era before wonder drugs, when many privileged children died of diseases, the idea of a healthy and safe environment had enormous appeal. The city was also suspect because it was morally corrupt — a place for dissipation of all sorts. Independent school parents often wanted their offspring protected from the social temptations of arrogance and conspicuous consumption. The most socially elite private schools usually avoided conventional ostentation — they emphasized simplicity within a religious atmosphere.

Parents also wanted their children to associate with their own kind, to become friends with and marry people like themselves. They wanted them to develop social skill and confidence by participating in respected activities such as sports, drama, choral music, and writing. All these wishes created a new and important market for a certain type of school where college preparation was an important but not a decisive purpose.[1]

At the same time that a student market was emerging for

a new type of school, many of the colleges these students wished to attend were stiffening entrance requirements. The pace and character of the changes differed according to what each institution aspired to become. But in most of the better known private northeastern colleges, the trend was not only to demand more of students in traditional subjects but to add requirements in the "modern" subjects that began penetrating college curricula in the 1870s.

For the colleges the task was a difficult balancing act. Tuition dependent and desirous of more students, they wished to broaden their appeal to a larger student market. At the same time their own faculties and curriculums were being transformed from traditional institutions stressing religion and the classics into modern colleges or universities. Professors of the newer subjects wanted to push down into the schools elementary instruction in many emerging academic disciplines. How to get schools to supply not only more but better prepared college freshmen was a vexing problem with several possible answers.

The bulk of colleges needed live bodies to survive and had virtually no admission requirements. For those with requirements, the most popular mechanism was admission by certificate, a plan in which schools were approved or certified by some external body (a state, or state university, or consortium of colleges). Cooperating colleges then agreed to admit any graduate recommended by the school.

Those favoring greater control of schools by colleges sometimes established preparatory schools with the specialized function of meeting the requirements of a particular college (for example, Hotchkiss for Yale and Lawrenceville for Princeton). But the usual approach was to admit candidates by individual examinations, rather than by certifying the schools they attended. This seemed a surer way to produce better trained freshmen and force schools to teach what colleges wanted. The most vigorous defender of the examination system was Harvard president Charles W. Eliot. He and professor (later president) Nicholas Murray Butler of Columbia were the moving forces behind creating the College Board in 1900.[2]

The emerging preparatory schools were strongly influenced

both by the preferences of their well-off constituency and the colleges their graduates wished to attend. In curriculum matters they were clearly dominated by higher education. Eliot liked to say that "schools follow universities, and will be what universities make them" ([1885] 1898, p. 131). But college domination per se was not a major prep school worry. They really were, after all, "preparatory" to college, and without that function a major reason for their existence would collapse.

In fact, the increasing complexity of college entrance examination requirements gave a tremendous boost to those few institutions (including certain public high schools) who specialized in preparing students to take them. Porter Sargent, a former prep school teacher who created the first private school consumer guide, wrote in its first 1915 edition that "the private school is still almost essential . . . for the special training that has been necessary to enter the older universities, . . . so that we find today at Princeton eighty percent, at Yale seventy percent, and at Harvard fifty percent of the students prepared at private schools" (1915, p. xx). The good part of college domination was a near prep school monopoly over elite college preparation.

Further, most of the qualities that gave each school a distinct personality — its religious character, the ideals of its head, the role of sports, and so on — were not controlled by the colleges. The schools had enormous freedom to do their own thing in precisely the areas of greatest importance to them. "Learning from books is but one small part in the educational process," said Frank Hackett (1924, p. 15), a pioneer founding head of the first country day school near New York (Riverdale). Most school heads agreed with him.

Moreover, many teachers and heads did not resent the close ties that entrance examinations and student attendance provided to well-known older colleges. They enjoyed the sense that in some respects they were all part of the same cause, profession, system — that the boundaries between good secondary schools and good colleges were permeable. This gave them a sense of membership in a large and respected professional community — a sense often denied other American teachers.

Finally, the matter of college domination was not exacerbated by the problem of selective admission. Acceptance in the college of one's choice—until after World War II—was mainly a matter of fulfilling entrance requirements. Almost everyone who did, and could pay, was accepted (except where discrimination against groups, usually against Jews, reared its head) (Wechsler, 1977; Synnott, 1979). Even those who did not meet the requirements in this or that subject were often admitted conditionally. There was no surplus of qualified candidates over places, no unhappy rejection letters to good but not good-enough applicants.

The major strain in school-college relations was not domination but the chaos caused by the incredible diversity in what individual colleges required for admission and the often idiosyncratic way that examination questions were asked. Even the head of a large school, Phillips Academy, which prepared students for many colleges, complained in 1885 that "out of over forty boys preparing for college next year we have more than twenty Senior classes" (Fuess, 1950, p. 7). Since unreasonable diversity in admissions requirements inconvenienced not just the schools but powerful university figures wishing to increase enrollments and raise entrance standards, it was no surprise that an agency created by the universities, with representation from the schools, the College Board, eventually produced a single annual examination in each of the major subjects.

Independent Schools and the College Board System

The College Board was essentially a treaty among colleges and between colleges and schools. By 1920, most of the important eastern colleges used the board's exams for admissions and abolished their own separate examinations. Sixty percent of the small group of 973 candidates who sat for the first examinations in 1901 were from private schools. By 1925, when the number of candidates approached 19,000, the fraction from private schools had risen to 70 percent.[3]

During four decades after 1900, the College Board organized the intricate links between what students wanted (admission to the college of choice) and what they had to do to get it ("passing" board examinations). The board also organized what colleges had to do to sustain student incentives to perform in the manner colleges wished, as well as school practice so that students performed well enough to demonstrate that their schools were effective. The board not only pushed students to work hard but pushed colleges and schools to do the same.

The board thus presided over a fully developed, coherent system[4] of academic incentives: one of the best examples of educational coherence in American history. Independent schools were an essential part of this system, as many relied on it for their very survival. Their proclaimed identity as "independent" disguised their profound *dependence* on the larger system, a system that few other Americans knew about because few used it.

Years later a veteran schoolman summarized its workings. "Parents . . . were obliged to seek some independent preparatory school to do a specific and limited job — the necessary intensive preparation of the student for the rigorous college board examinations. . . . The preparatory schools were thus in a peculiar middle-man position in a process that was generally binding as long as the colleges and universities kept to their high academic standards and required for entrance success in these college boards. . . . New independent schools came into being whose selling point to the parent was a virtual guarantee to place the young student in any college or university, however difficult the requirements" (Craig, 1946, p. 5).

The College Board system has been largely forgotten or stereotyped, but it contained many educational characteristics of great interest to 1990s reformers concerned with student assessment, student incentives, and academic standards. Four linked elements in this system account for its relative success in promoting hard academic work among often reluctant youth: the necessity to deal with students of diverse academic capacities; the ability to sustain a rough consensus about the content of academic standards; the capacity to convert standards into credible examinations with predictable consequences; and the ways its examinations directly influenced school curriculum, teaching, and professional development.

Although most prep school students were economically

privileged in the 1900–1940 period, in other respects they were a fairly random sample of their social class. They did not gain admission to the schools on grounds of academic promise or aptitude; some were enrolled literally at birth, when gender was the only selective factor. (The story was that St. Paul's fathers enrolled their male newborns by regular letter, whereas Groton fathers sent telegrams. Lacking amniocentesis, it was impractical to enroll candidates for single-sex schools while *in utero*.)

Before World War II independent schools paid little attention to academic capacity. Committed to prepare most of their students for colleges like Harvard, Yale, and Princeton, these schools contained the academically gifted, the average, and the truly unintelligent. They surely enrolled far more "diversity" (as defined by scholastic aptitude) in the first part of the century than they do today. McGeorge Bundy recalled his school days at Groton in the 1930s: "If you weren't a notorious and incorrigibly stupid or lazy person you could go to any college you wanted, you really could" (Bundy, 1988).

All this was accepted at the time as the way things were. The prep schools catered to an economic rather than to an academic class. They routinely assumed that public high school graduates who attended prestigious colleges were, on the whole, more able and motivated — a more academically select group — than their own students (Davis, 1930).

Frederick Winsor, for example, had been founding head of the first country day school (Gilman, in Baltimore) and subsequently founding head of a nonsectarian boarding school near Boston (Middlesex). He told a 1930 Harvard alumni meeting that the job of private schools was to "give an education to all the sons of such men as you if you want to send them to us, not to a selected few of your sons." It was not the "bright boy who specially needs the best and wisest of handling," Winsor went on, "but the boys below the average in intelligence." He assured the sympathetic crowd that true leadership in later life depended less on brainpower than on "determination and fight and character" (1930, p. 5).

Most independent school commentators followed Winsor's reasoning: their institutions should be broadly accessible to those who could pay. Some independent school leaders trumpeted the "true talent of the slow, cautious, and searching mind" (Smith, 1948, p. 4) and unfavorably compared the "facile, lazy students as against the hard-working slower student" (Bragdon, 1947, p. 19). The latter might not excel at studies or care much about them but often would exert considerable leadership in extracurricular and social activities in school and college. The prep schools could be undefensive about the academic quality of their student bodies because they did not regard this as highly as would their successors following World War II.

Nor was there any reason for schools or students to fear that College Board examinations would be impossibly difficult. It was not their intention to keep students out of college but to ensure that students did the necessary work to get in. These examinations, though generally judged more rigorous than the written ones of individual colleges that had preceded them, were designed with a broad student ability range in mind. Their purpose was to bring everyone up to a minimum standard in the possession of knowledge and the ability to use it, in order for them to pursue successfully the work offered in major colleges.

The board had no interest in winnowing the best and the brightest from the merely proficient because, until the late 1930s, few influential educators cared much about such high-end individual distinctions. Board tests, in more recent terminology, were criterion referenced rather than norm referenced. Schools and students knew what "passing" a board examination meant and that large numbers—theoretically, everyone—could pass if they worked hard enough. The examination process could be for "high stakes" without seeming to be beyond the power of diligent students to control.

There were obviously limits to what could be accomplished when academic raw material was extremely weak. The secretary of the College Board lamented in 1919 that many students with abominable board scores aspired to college only for "social advantages" and should not be encouraged to advance beyond high school (Fiske, 1919, p. 7). The most thorough survey of boarding schools of its generation (Cole, 1928, pp. 131–133) found large differences in the average age of 1921 graduating seniors at certain boarding schools compared with the Cleveland, Ohio, public high schools. There was little doubt that the reason for so many "overage" private school seniors (Cleveland's average graduating age of 17.1 years contrasted with Lawrenceville School's average of 18.7!) was their limited academic capacity combined with parental desire that they attempt the boards just one more time. A private school research group politely concluded in 1933 that the "nonacademic pupil" had been a priority for years, but research had been deferred because "just now many schools are engaged in laboratory experience with that very problem, after which a thorough study will have a better point of departure" (Smith, 1933, p. 42).

Despite these concerns about the limits of educability, what is most significant about the relation between the College Board system and student aptitude was the expectation that a wide variety of aptitudes could succeed on a serious academic examination if the stakes were high, the preparation specific, and the work thorough and demanding.

What, then, were the concrete standards the board sought to uphold? Professor Carl Brigham of Princeton, a wise observer of the College Board through the 1920s and 1930s and principal architect of the Scholastic Aptitude Test, emphasized (1933, p. 8) that the board's "entire intangible assets, including goodwill," were not its annual examinations but the academic standards on which the examinations were based: written syllabi or descriptions of the essential concepts and themes in each of the fields where the board examined. Called *Definition of the Requirements* for most of the 1900–1941 period, these annual publications spelled out in greater or lesser detail, according to the subject or moment in time, what students should be prepared to know and be able to do. Brigham described the *Definitions* in 1934 as a "framework" that distinguished broad domains of knowledge from specific examination topics (Valentine, 1987, p. 48).

The *Definitions* made concrete what the board — or rather its various responsible subject committees — believed "academic standards" to be. A half century after the last version appeared in 1941, one is struck by the large areas of fundamental agreement they represented. The board's long-term executive, mathematics professor, Thomas S. Fiske of Columbia, attributed its successful first twenty-seven years to the "voluntary cooperation of the institutions and the associations whose interests are most vitally concerned" (1927, p. 1). Behind Fiske's bland language was the crucial point that the board exerted a clear and consistent influence year after year because it was run by people with roughly similar views and interests. There was consensus behind many *Definitions* because the individuals who established them — primarily drawn from higher education and within higher education from various commissions of national discipline-based associations — shared many values about the primacy of academic education organized by the disciplines.

The College Board was and is a voluntary and privately chartered organization, not a government agency. Its system was a voluntary one in which schools and colleges could freely choose an association or choose to stay away. Most chose to stay away, their decision, not the result of board exclusivity. (The board would have loved more schools and colleges to accept its examination program in the twenties and thirties, because student registration fees provided most of its income.) Its voluntary, nongovernmental nature gave it real power over the limited number of families, schools, and colleges who basically concurred with the values of the *Definitions*.

The overall consensus produced by voluntarism allowed the board to concentrate on what proper school standards should be within each of the modern academic disciplines. The board did not have to consider whether those disciplines should be the centerpiece of preparatory education or whether a unitary conception of standards was the best way to think about cognitive development — matters that then dominated discussion in the rapidly expanding public schools.

Clearly influenced by a few universities after 1910, especially by Harvard, Yale, and Princeton, the board allowed furious battles about standards and the precise content of the *Definitions* to rage because they were the serious intellectual battles the board *wanted* fought. It was easier to get disagreeing parties to compromise — say, about the English or history *Definitions* —

when the disputants all agreed that demanding instruction in English or history was obviously to be mandated for all high school students who aspired to attend college.

Such battles were waged within virtually all the disciplines. They ranged from the importance to be given this or that topic to the balance between mandated coverage of content and teacher freedom. (Other battles, especially over whether high standards meant quality past performance or proficiency to perform in the future, were usually fought not within the content of the *Definitions* but within the content of the actual examinations.)

In English, for example, the *Definitions* gradually reflected a move toward less content prescription. The early English *Definition* had specified a list of books about which students were to know "the most important parts" (for example, *The Merchant of Venice* and *The Last of the Mohicans*) and another list of books they had to know in very minute detail (for example, *Macbeth* and Burke's speech on *Conciliation with America*) (Valentine, 1987). But by the end of the 1920s an elaborate Board Commission on English — its final report was published as a book by Harvard University Press — pressed for and won a less restrictive conception. The English *Definition* for 1934 had no required books and a simplified overview: "The requirement in English is designed to develop in the student (1) the ability to read with understanding, (2) knowledge and judgment of literature, and (3) accurate thinking and power in oral and written expression."

At the time those involved furiously debated whether or not the changes had lowered or raised standards. From a more distant perspective, the process seems to have mainly changed standards within a context of basic agreement. The new, merely suggested six-page reading list contained fourteen Shakespeare and eight Shaw plays as examples of appropriate literature. Teachers were assured (*Definition*, 1934, pp. 7–14) that the composition test would "assume continuous and thorough training in mechanics." The *Definition* then specified that this training implied "mastery" in such matters as grammar, punctuation, spelling, vocabulary, and "a command of varied and flexible sentence forms." The instruction required to produce such mastery, teachers were told, "necessitates constant and painstaking practice by the candidate in criticism and revision of his own written work." In such ways as this, subject by subject, the board defined and refined what it meant by academic standards.

Sadly, the rather lively and imaginative battles over the *Definitions* were increasingly perceived by outside critics of the board as well as by those intimately involved as concerned with "maintaining" or "keeping up" academic standards rather than *inventing* or *rethinking* them. Because the thrust of public school curriculum expansion in the 1900–1940 period was largely hostile to academic schooling, the work of the board seemed in contrast to be conservative and even snobbishly exclusionary — despite the remarkably broad band of student abilities presumed by participating schools to be able to succeed on board examinations.

To both private schools and to the country at large, academic standards took on an "undemocratic" tinge when the very opposite idea — holding a widely varying group of youth accountable to serious demands — prevailed. The tone of the private school discussion of standards increasingly seemed a *defense* of something under siege, something in danger of being lost. This did not help correct the misapprehension. Examples are: "We hold that every idea must be made as interesting as possible; but we refuse to water down its essence . . . [for] the pseudo-democracy of leveling and mediocrity" (Gummere, 1941, pp. 6, 12; or "We set high standards and owe it to the nation not to supply watered stock" (Roberts, 1947, p. 6); or "The independent schools, although serving a minority, have helped to protect us from the menace of mediocrity and the domination of the average" (Fuess, 1952, p. 9).

Finger-in-the-dike images like these permitted many to forget that the standards represented by the *Definitions* were a triumphant victory of the modern subjects — history, English, science, modern languages — over the curriculum domination of the classics and formal mathematics. They were a victory for progressive and democratic forces, not for forces of reaction and exclusivity. The creators of the College Board system, men like President Eliot, saw their work as expanding the curriculum to keep pace with the growth of modern knowledge. They also saw their work as expanding opportunities for individual students of all backgrounds by creating standards that all could aspire to — *if* their schools also aspired to them in their instructional program. The private schools' defense of standards was not articulate enough to keep alive Eliot's uncompromising amalgam of academic quality and individual opportunity.

Schools and students experienced the *Definitions* directly when they became actual College Board examinations. Created by committees of examiners with substantial private school representation, the College Boards were largely of the essay variety and usually three hours in length, administered in nationwide test centers during one hectic week each June. By 1940, for example, over 37,000 examinations were taken in 36 subjects at 318 test centers. The examinations were then scored during an equally hectic week at Columbia University by hundreds of readers. The familiar 0–100 scale was adopted, with 60 initially defined as a passing grade. In 1901, the first year of the examinations, only 59 percent received scores of 60 or higher. Nicholas Murray Butler, the board's first secretary, was highly satisfied that "the one criticism that the board could not afford to face, namely, that the questions set were too easy, has not been made" (1901, p. 20).

This astonishingly un-American system of annual academic essay examinations externally set and externally assessed profoundly affected schools that participated in the program. It was, as Carl Brigham said, a direct form of "institutional control" (1933, p. 8), once colleges gradually abandoned their own examinations and accepted only the board's. For many schools the gains won by simplification of college preparation offset any losses attributable to college domination — especially since the schools had been dominated academically by the colleges prior to the board and continued to retain nonacademic freedom after the board.[5] Other influential private schoolpeople welcomed college domination because they believed, as did Wilson Farrand, a longtime board leader and headmaster of Newark Academy in New Jersey, that "the great need of secondary schools of today is the establishment of adequate standards of attainment. Their great weakness is sloppiness and superficiality; their great need is thoroughness and genuine mastery of the subjects taught" (Fuess, 1950, p. 68). Lawrenceville's Frederick J. V. Hancox (1936, p. 15) praised the board for its "guiding and standardizing and controlling effect on school curricula and teaching."

One of Frederick Winsor's successors at Gilman School in Baltimore, for example, regarded the board as a "measuring stick against which he could raise the educational standards of the school." It was now possible to "use continuing poor averages in any particular subject as a whip on masters who taught the subject." Teachers predictably responded by developing extensive practice or coaching sessions to review examinations from previous years. (The board published its examinations.) Despite the "almost airtight system" developed to make Gilman boys study and pass the exams, the school's historian concluded that the system "served its purpose . . . by raising the educational standards from the level of average good schools to the level of the highest in the country" (Jacobs, 1947, pp. 59–61).

The ambivalence in this position — the exams led to some rigidity and cramming but got students to work and raised standards of achievement — was shared among private schoolpeople of the time, who needed a practical incentive for a differently abled population to work hard. The direct link between the examinations and college admission provided that incentive. Further, given the fact that the examinations could in fact be studied for in advance, they could be attempted by students whose academic skills were not extensive.

In short, the examinations often enabled "hard and specific work" (Roberts, 1947, p. 28) to pay off, and the private schools resolutely insisted that for many students "uphill thinking is the best way to think" (Gummere, 1941, p. 12). One schoolman's educational credo was "a tradition of thoroughness of instruction, of mastery of skills, and of insistence on the carrying through to completion of tasks undertaken" (Litterick, 1947, p. 22). The hard work needed to succeed on the College Board exams was thus a good thing in itself — an outcome the schools often valued as a worthwhile lifetime habit quite aside from the academic achievement it produced in the short run. The headmaster of St. Paul Academy in Minnesota believed examinations made lazy privileged boys work hard perhaps for the first time because they had to and academically slow privileged boys work hard because they would gain confidence that they could pass (Briggs, 1932).

Other private school defenders of the examinations, such as Winsor, emphasized how they had changed with the times just as had the *Definitions*. He denied in 1932 (p. 619) that the exams could be passed by candidates who had "only facts in their possession and no knowledge of their meaning nor power to think." The examinations above all else were "tests of power which require a knowledge of facts." The head of the Detroit Country Day School agreed that the English examination, for example, had become "a test of creativeness and appreciation" (Shaw, 1932, p. 620).

The last three-hour English essay examination ever given by the Board (English Examination, 1941, pp. 29-30)—one based on the *Definition* discussed earlier—backs this assertion. In June 1941, one of the four questions asked students to read Yeats's poem "An Irish Airman Foresees His Death." They had to respond to eight different assertions about the poem and were graded on understanding the poem, accuracy in writing, and clarity in writing. The question combined a concern for standards, for differences among the answering students, and for sensitivity to the times in which they lived.

In a general way, teachers began to teach to these tests or at least to their predictions and hopes about how the examinations might resemble those of prior years. More specifically, the tests clearly reined in teachers' freedom to define subjects as they personally wished. One private school historian of the College Board, who remembered how liberating it had been for him as an English teacher finally to be able to teach Frost and Sandburg and not just Milton and Whittier, also admitted that "individualism in American schools in the 1900's had so far run riot that the establishment of a uniform standard of excellence had become not only desirable but even obligatory" (Fuess, 1950, pp. 85, 63).

The examinations pressed teachers to perform to an outside common standard, clearly opposed the idea that individual teachers could and should define their fields as they wished, and established at least part of what accountable teaching meant. One teacher complained: "Slight chance for continued professional service has that teacher who fails to 'get results' in the 'College Boards,' valuable and inspiring as his instruction may otherwise be" (Valentine, 1987, p. 29).

But there were compensations for teachers who saw some classroom freedom eroded. One was that the external examinations tended to make students and teachers allies rather than adversaries. The objective was to move all students forward, not to emphasize differences in their attainments. Gilman's historian nicely said, "If everyone passed . . . the master was considered to have done a fine job" (Jacobs, 1947, p. 60).

Another compensation was that thousands of the small cohort of private school teachers were not just passive recipients of College Board commands but active participants in the grand enterprise of creating and grading the examinations. This was surely one of the most powerful professional development experiences in American educational history: it was task oriented, deadly serious, and enormous fun.

Most of the examiners, the small committees which actually created the examinations, were always drawn from the colleges. Yet in 1941, the final year of the program, the private schools provided more than a fourth — nineteen examiners, compared with forty-two for higher education and thirteen for public schools. Much more impressive was the distribution of readers of the June examinations. These were the teachers who descended on Columbia dorms and Barnard dining halls to confront thousands of blue books. In 1932 alone 313 private school teachers participated in this experience, along with 112 public school teachers and 216 college professors.

This huge gathering resembled an "educational congress" (Fiske, 1927, p. 10). It was, in the 1920s and 1930s, the one place where high school and college teachers struggled with a common task and where teachers brought back to their schools helpful criticisms and broader points of view. The annual reading session, the board concluded the year after it had been abolished, had "helped immeasurably in upholding standards" (College Entrance Examination Board, 1942, pp. 5–6; College Entrance Examination Board, 1944, p. 8). Perhaps even more important was the colleagueship, stimulation, and prestige it gave to participating teachers. Readership was a professional plum, readers hated to rotate off, and public school teachers began to resent private school dominance. Their protests led to a 1934 College Board decision that the future reader target ratio should be 4:3:2 among colleges, private schools, and public schools (College Entrance Examination Board, 1935, pp. 35–36). Yet in June 1941 over 42 percent of the readers were still drawn from independent schools: reading the examinations remained to the end a largely private school privilege.

The large fraction of private school candidates and large number of private school teachers who served as readers solidified the loyalty of most independent schools to the College Board and the system it embodied. The system seemed to work for the schools. Their students decisively outperformed public school students on these examinations over the 1901–1941 period, and most graduates went on to the colleges of their choice.

Perhaps the most dramatic example of private school commitment to the system was a remarkably ambitious effort by some to create an examining board of their own in 1924. They would apply the College Board model of transition from school to college to the transition from elementary to secondary schools. The Secondary School Examination Board, soon renamed the Secondary Education Board (SEB), attracted private secondary schools who sought the same influence over elementary instruction and the same uniformity in student preparation as had the colleges (Osgood, 1925). The cooperating elementary schools wanted a standard from outside to improve their instruction and also wanted guaranteed access to high schools of choice.

The parallels with the College Board were striking, although the new board had no money or ambition for external assessment. Its examinations would be graded by the high schools children wanted to attend, not by external examiners. This nontrivial difference created curious logistical problems. In 1928, for instance, a New York City boy took the SEB entrance exam for St. Paul's School in New Hampshire, given at

St. Bernard's School in Manhattan. After completing the exam, he took a taxi over to the Buckley School, also in Manhattan, where exactly the same examination was given for admission to the Hill School in Pennsylvania. The two New York schools that administered the examinations then sent them off to the appropriate boarding schools. When the Secondary Education Board learned of this strange affair, its solution was not to suggest a process of uniform external assessment. It recommended instead that candidates in the future be sure to bring carbon paper (Hancox, 1930, p. 13).

Such events quickly revealed that the SEB perhaps might not become as efficient an examining agency as the College Board. But there was no denying that its existence indicated that many important private schools wanted, somehow, to insert the College Board system of coherent instruction inside K-12 education itself. The ultimate dream of SEB founders was for their examinations to connect directly with the College Boards. Frederick H. Osgood of Milton Academy, the SEB's first chair (and also father of Esther Osgood) claimed: "This would tend to insure sequence in our work, progress in our classes, and success in our results" (1925, p. 9). This nicely summed up the goals of a coherent system.

Monopoly, Meritocracy, and the Fate of Standards

On Sunday, December 7, 1941, the "Three Musketeers"—the affectionate nickname for the admissions directors of Harvard, Yale, and Princeton—were meeting informally at the New Jersey home of the Princeton director. When the news from Pearl Harbor arrived after lunch, the men decided that the sudden war emergency might permit them to achieve instantaneously what one admitted might have been "a long hard fight" otherwise: the complete abandonment of the College Board's program of three-hour June essay examinations. In effect, they proposed to destroy the central element in the coherent system that had prevailed for four decades (Fuess, 1950, pp. 154–158).

Days later the three universities announced that all candidates for admission would not take the June series but instead a series of short-answer, machine-gradable tests given on a single Saturday in April. Later, when other colleges announced their intention to follow the lead of the Big Three, the College Board decided to cancel the June 1942 examinations. They were never given again. The decision marked an era: the system that had governed college admissions and student incentives since 1900 was no more.

The April tests had been instituted by the board four years earlier for the convenience of colleges wanting earlier data on scholarship applicants. They included several subject-specific short-answer tests, originally called scholarship tests but now relabeled achievement tests, and the short-answer multiple-choice Scholastic Aptitude Test. The latter, previously given in June as a supplement to the essay examinations, had been created in 1926 by psychological consultants to the board, notably Carl Brigham. The SAT had grown rapidly in student registrations and in popularity with college admissions officers in the 1930s.

The admissions officer perspective differed from that of the presidents, academicians, and schoolpeople who organized and managed the College Board in its early years. The Eliots and Butlers saw the board's program as bringing order from the chaos of divergent admission requirements and also upgrading standards of training in the preparatory schools. The admissions officers saw the board's program as a strategy to enlarge the number of college applicants and also to enlarge the number of those who would perform well after enrollment.

These were different, equally legitimate purposes. But their gradual adoption by the board changed the old system profoundly and reduced its impact on independent school curriculum and student incentives to work hard. The older goals meshed nicely with the goals of most independent schools. The new ones did not. When the old essay examinations were abolished, recalled Millicent C. McIntosh, head of the Brearley School in New York, "at one stroke the special privileges of the private school student disappeared" (1946, p. 31).

Two powerful converging forces in the 1930s — the psychological testing movement and the Depression — pushed prestigious colleges to rethink their attitudes about the uses of examinations. The board exams were originally intended to show levels of previous school achievement and training; they were demonstrations of past performance, about what individuals in fact had learned and how hard they had worked. They also were assessments of how well schools taught the curriculum and how hard they pressed students. If this was what colleges wanted examinations to measure — if this was what their statistical "validity" depended on — then the tests could be very valid indeed. But if colleges defined examination validity differently, as predicting how students would perform later on in the colleges, the Scholastic Aptitude Test provided a far more valid measure.

The latter was increasingly what the colleges wanted to know. The psychological testing movement, even in the twenties, had convinced most psychologists and many admissions officers that intelligence was, if not wholly innate, then at least mainly so. "Training" dull but decent students might give schools some satisfaction; such training was what the board essay exams were designed to measure. But the training that schools provided caused colleges increasingly to yawn and look away. Statistical studies from the Big Three and similar institutions indicated that private school students with higher board scores than public school students were soon surpassed academically in college by the public school graduates. Other studies used the new intelligence tests to demonstrate that public school graduates in the prestigious colleges, on average, were indeed brighter (Spencer, 1927; Leighton, 1935).

None of this was news. The private schools were proud of their success in training a diverse academic population. They were not embarrassed or apologetic: it was in part the service they sought to provide. What was new — besides concrete data and quantitative research reports — was the gradual realization by colleges that the old examinations gave an unfair advantage, almost a monopoly, to schools that had the resources to prepare for them. Able boys who did not attend such schools (almost all of the discussion concerned boys) were at a major disadvantage.

It finally dawned on the colleges that things did not have to be that way — they could be changed. Soon after 1910 Harvard had created "comprehensive" examinations deliberately designed *not* to be curriculum driven. One purpose was to appeal to a larger applicant pool. By 1916 the board had adapted some of the Harvard examinations as an option to its standard essay program. The Scholastic Aptitude Test promised to do an even better job of identifying raw talent regardless of the quality of education it had received. It was no accident that SAT enrollments grew mainly through public school students and that the brief April scholarship tests proved immensely popular with the gigantic but still slumbering public school market.

The Depression added urgency to developing strategies for increasing educational opportunity and limiting monied privilege. Many educational leaders were frightened by the prospect of class war. No one better amalgamated all these tendencies — love of able students, infatuation with the SAT as a test of inborn ability, deep suspicion of the social impact of the private school monopoly, fear of class war — than Harvard's president James B. Conant (Conant, 1970; Powell, 1980). And no important university's actions better clarified how these beliefs would affect private schools than did Harvard's.

In 1943 Harvard's Richard M. Gummere, one of the Three Musketeers and a former private school headmaster, summarized with notable brevity the long-run meaning of the shift from essay examinations to the SAT and the achievement tests. "Learning in itself has ceased to be the main factor [in college admissions]," he told a private school audience. "The aptitude of the pupil is now the leading consideration" (1943, p. 5).

After the war, the reliance upon promise rather than training had the hoped-for effect at institutions like Harvard. In combination with the tremendous and unexpected American surge toward college, stimulated by the GI Bill but not explained by it, college applications shot up. Of the 1,181 final applicants to Harvard for the fall of 1941, 1,092 were accepted and 1,004 enrolled. But by 1952, the new dean of admissions, W. J. Bender, could report a revolution: for the first time in its history Harvard could "consciously shape the make-up of our student body" because it had a real surplus of qualified applicants over places. Bender said, "In effect we now admit students on the basis of ability and promise and a secondary school diploma. Little attention is paid to the content of their secondary school programs" (1953, pp. 104–106).

While private school enrollment percentages plummeted at Harvard, from 57 percent in 1941 to 32 percent in 1980, Bender reported that the percentage of all freshmen who had met official entrance requirements at the time of enrollment had also dropped. But admissions authorities believed that any reemphasis on the content of secondary education would only "reverse the general trend of recent years towards an abler and more nationally representative student body" (1954, p. 239). This was unacceptable. McGeorge Bundy, now dean of the faculty of arts and sciences after his Groton days, fittingly proclaimed meritocracy triumphant in 1956: "The really bright boy is desirable in the college, even if the schools have hopelessly mismanaged his educational training up to the age of seventeen or eighteen. The untrained boy of real brilliance is more valuable to us than the dull boy who has been intensely trained. Therefore, we are committed to the notion of a talent search" (1956, p. 510).

Such candor revealed the widening gap between elite colleges and elite private schools at the dawn of meritocratic admissions in the early 1950s. Many in the private school fraternity felt betrayed by their own kind. Conant's Jeffersonian search for the best and brightest, for example, made him an outspoken national advocate of public schools (preferably large ones with facilities to detect talent) and a public enemy of independent schools as divisive institutions (Conant, 1970).

The essence of the Gummere-Bender-Bundy-Conant point was that hard work was no longer important. It did not get you anywhere, certainly not to Harvard. There were no longer subjects to study that, if mastered to specified levels as evinced through examinations based on them, would lead to good things. Instead, only very smart students could win in the now deadly serious contest of college admission.

How did the prep schools respond to this meritocratic assault on a central *raison d'être*? Although they responded in many ways to the postwar end of their old quasi-monopoly (usually quite successfully), their most poignant response—and their most coherent and energetic — was to accept the tide of the times. Instead of defending the tradition of common standards applied to a diverse student group, the leading private schools decided to emulate the colleges. They would recruit and educate exactly the academically gifted students so coveted by the leading colleges. They would play the same game of admissions as the colleges, but they would play to win.

They too would define prior preparation as less important than individual aptitude. So, for example, the SEB exams attracted fewer and fewer candidates while the private schools took steps to create admissions tests for secondary school based on the SAT. By 1957 a Secondary School Admissions Test was in place (Whitman, 1991). The prep schools would attempt to reshape their own student bodies — to conduct their own "talent search" — in order to preserve their admissions track records at the better colleges. Additional organizations were developed to coordinate, for example, need-based financial aid to able youngsters, and schools spent more time recruiting not just paying customers but academically strong customers.

Perhaps the most important symbol of the new private school initiative was the prominent involvement of several of their number in the creation of the Advanced Placement Program in 1956. AP was not a project of the College Board, since at its inception it represented much of what the board had explicitly rejected (although the board did agree to administer the program once established). AP was an attempt to offer college-level courses in high schools in many academic subjects. Its key elements were remarkably reminiscent of the old College Boards (Allis, 1979; Valentine, 1987).

Advanced Placement course syllabi and examinations were created by teams of professors, teachers, and test specialists. The examinations, strongly biased toward essay or "free-response" questions, were read externally in June by teachers and professors. Scoring was criterion referenced, based on a simple 1–5 scale with 3 being the de facto passing grade. Students and teachers were on the same side: high AP scores — the more the better — enhanced teachers' reputations. AP was driven by student incentives although, especially in the early years, the incentives were somewhat different from those behind the old College Boards. The main incentive was not college admission but the avoidance in college of repetitive introductory courses and the possibility of some financial savings if formal academic college credit was given for courses taken in high school. In later years, a powerful additional incentive to enroll in AP courses was to boost chances for admission to selective colleges (Dillon, 1988).

The most significant difference between AP and the old College Boards was their student constituency. AP was unabashedly for the gifted and talented, for smart and ambitious adolescents who wanted to get a head start on college. AP brought back the past, after a fifteen-year absence, with better developed ideas about what students should know and be able to do. But it did not bring back the idea that average college-bound students could profit from a similar model. AP was a way for privileged schools who could offer the courses — and independent schools in particular — to market themselves as secondary school analogues to Dean Bundy's notion of elite colleges: places where talented students could find an appropriate and challenging curriculum just for them (Davies, 1962).

As the better independent schools coped with the deck American democracy had dealt them, their first response was to attempt to abandon — as if it were some sort of embarrassment — their long-standing commitment to work hard at educating not just the gifted but everyone with some promise, some commitment, and the wherewithal to pay. Of course, the prep schools were unevenly successful at converting to teen meritocracies. Some found the idea distasteful from the start and preferred less intellectually homogeneous student bodies. Others lacked the money or geographic location crucial for success.

But the lure to make the attempt was very strong. Schools realized that "prestige" in the new age of near-universal secondary and postsecondary education would be based on which institutions students attended, not on whether they did so. There was also evidence that the labeling of independent schools as exclusive or elitist — a label the schools typically loathed but could not shake off — was at least partially softened if they enrolled not merely privileged students but talented students. Francis

Parkman, a private school leader very much concerned with public image, shrewdly observed that nearly half the initial schools offering AP courses were independent schools and that "the fast section has never been considered undemocratic in these schools" (1958, p. 55).

It is fascinating but disgraceful that since 1956 the powerful incentives contained in the old College Board system have been available only to that tiny fraction of students who typically are the most committed and successful to begin with. At the beginning of the 1990s there was nothing remotely comparable to AP for any other group in the population (although the Advanced Placement program had plans to develop a more broad-based version). Neither the model of AP nor of the old College Boards was examined much by educational reformers, despite the enormous number of overlapping points of interest: AP seemed irrelevant because of its association with only top-track students; the old College Boards seemed irrelevant (to those who remembered them at all) because of their association with old-fashioned academics and old-fashioned privilege.

Some recovery from this educational amnesia is needed. Why should we lack any voluntary, incentive-based, externally and authentically assessed, curriculum-driven, teacher-produced system of syllabi and examinations designed for a large fraction of teenagers? It is important not to assess blame casually. It would surely be simplistic to blame only the meritocratic impulse itself, or American egalitarianism and anti-intellectualism, or the overconfidence of the objective testers, or other cosmic forces.

A more practical clue comes from Carl Brigham himself, the founder of the SAT yet also a thoughtful defender of the idea of clear academic standards, "Definitions of Requirements," and essay examinations. In a wise and candid report to the College Board in 1933, Brigham (pp. 12–13) observed that "the Board has developed as an organization of *Readers* and is not a body of *Examiners*." There was no organized body of knowledge — technical knowledge about reliability and validity — on curriculum-driven essay examinations. The board had made all its bets on the expensive annual process of reading examinations and had ignored all the questions about how such examinations might assess individual potential that the colleges were just beginning to ask. The creation of the SAT and other objective tests was a serious research and development task, but the board seemed to care nothing about research and development on its own essay examinations. Brigham argued for a major financial commitment to experimental research on such examinations to save them from the psychometricians, but nothing was ever done.

There was a stubborn, irreconcilable gap between the defenders of the old system — who did not care for research — and the psychologists about to overthrow it — who had little interest in the quality of schools. One of the achievements of AP has been to bridge that gap somewhat. The *Technical Manual* (College Entrance Examination Board, 1988) devoted to free-response AP questions is amazingly more sophisticated than anything imagined by the defenders of the old system. The gap needs further closing, and a new coherent system (or systems) must be devised to embrace far more youth. Then some of the advantages of the old system can finally be reclaimed, to serve not just top-track students but the great majority. They need all the incentives that can be mustered to develop intelligence in a society filled with doubters and outright enemies.

Notes

1.   There is no general account of the origins of the American prep school. The closest approximation is the standard study of boarding schools (McLachlan, 1970). The new country day schools, new urban day schools, and transformation of old private schools and academies into prep schools are best explored through school histories (for example, Hackett, 1957; Jacobs, 1947; Eliot, 1982; Waterbury, 1965). McLachlan is especially interesting in exploring the transformation of old boarding academies into new boarding schools, especially Lawrenceville and Exeter.
2.   The standard history of college admission requirements is Wechsler, 1977. See also Hawkins, 1972, and Powell, 1980.

Two complementary histories of the College Board are of value, especially for the prewar period. The first is a memoir by a long-time private school headmaster who knew most of the important figures in the period under discussion. The other is a recent scholarly account by a long-term board staff member (Fuess, 1950; Valentine, 1987).

3.   Quantitative data on the number of board candidates, the number of examinations taken, scores received, and type of school attended are drawn from the various College Entrance Examination Board (CEEB) *Annual Reports of the Secretary,* printed by the board and consulted at the board's archives in New York.

4.   The idea of "system" is not contemporary social science jargon projected back onto the past. It was used at the time to describe the interconnected processes that made the board work, notably by Carl Brigham in 1934 (Valentine, 1987).

5.   Independent schools were never members of the board. Any school or student could participate in the board's examination program. Thus the board exerted no influence on schools other than on their curricula, had no policies on nonprofit status or discrimination, for example, and had no means to enforce such policies.

References

Allis, F. S. *Youth from Every Quarter. A Bicentennial History of Phillips Academy, Andover.* Andover, Mass.: Phillips Academy, 1979.

Bender, W. J. "Committees on Admission." In *Harvard Annual Reports 1952–53.* Cambridge, Mass.: Harvard University, 1953.

Bender, W. J. "Committees on Admission." In *Harvard Annual Reports 1953–54.* Cambridge, Mass.: Harvard University, 1954.

Bragdon, H. W. "The College Entrance Examination Board Test in Social Studies." *Independent School Bulletin,* Jan. 1947, pp. 19–20.

Briggs, J. D. "Letter to Editor." *Harvard Alumni Bulletin,* Feb. 19, 1932, *34*(20), 620.

Brigham, C. C. "Views of the Associate Secretary." In College Entrance Examination Board, *Thirty-Third Annual Report of the Secretary*. New York: College Entrance Examination Board, 1933.

Bundy, M. "Who's Going to Get to College?" *Harvard Alumni Bulletin*, Apr. 7, 1956, *58*(12), 509–511.

Bundy, M. "The American Dream at Groton." Public television documentary, televised in Boston, Oct. 28, 1988.

Butler, N. M. *First Annual Report of the Secretary, College Entrance Examination Board of the Middle States and Maryland.* New York: College Entrance Examination Board, 1901.

Cole, R. D. *Private Secondary Education for Boys in the United States.* Philadelphia: Westbrook, 1928.

College Entrance Examination Board. *Definition of the Requirements. Edition of December 1934.* New York: College Entrance Examination Board, 1934.

College Entrance Examination Board. *Thirty-Fifth Annual Report of the Secretary.* New York: College Entrance Examination Board, 1935.

College Entrance Examination Board. *English Examination. June 16, 1941.* New York: College Entrance Examination Board, 1941.

College Entrance Examination Board. *Forty-Second Annual Report of the Secretary.* New York: College Entrance Examination Board, 1942.

College Entrance Examination Board. *Forty-Fourth Annual Report of the Secretary.* New York: College Entrance Examination Board, 1944.

College Entrance Examination Board. *Technical Manual for the Advanced Placement Program.* New York: College Entrance Examination Board, 1988.

Conant, J. B. *My Several Lives. Memoirs of a Social Inventor.* New York: HarperCollins, 1970.

Craig, A. W. "Why Independent Schools Need to Have a Well-Planned and Well-Executed Program of Religious Instruction." *Independent School Bulletin*, Feb. 1946, pp. 5–8.

Davies, J. D. "But, Mr. Bender—." *Harvard Alumni Bulletin*, Mar. 17, 1962, pp. 464–466.

Davis, W. E. "Editorial." *Private School News,* June 1930, *6*(8), 4.

Dillon, D. H. "The AP Effect." *Independent School,* Spring 1988, *47*(3), 35–45.

Eliot, C. W. "Liberty in Education." In C. W. Eliot (ed.), *Educational Reform.* New York: The Century Company, 1898. (Transcript of speech presented in 1885.)

Eliot, T. H. *Two Schools in Cambridge. The Story of Browne and Nichols and Buckingham.* Cambridge, Mass.: Windflower Press, 1982.

Fiske, T. S. *Nineteenth Annual Report of the Secretary, College Entrance Examination Board.* New York: College Entrance Examination Board, 1919.

Fiske, T. S. *Twenty-Seventh Annual Report of the Secretary, College Entrance Examination Board.* New York: College Entrance Examination Board, 1927.

Fuess, C. M. *The College Board. Its First Fifty Years.* New York: Columbia University Press, 1950.

Fuess, C. M. "Free Enterprise in Education." Speech given Oct. 21, 1952. In National Council of Independent Schools, *Report.* Boston: National Council of Independent Schools, 1952.

Gummere, R. M. "Twenty Years Onward, or the Next Two Decades in Secondary Education." Speech given Mar. 1, 1941. In Secondary Education Board, *Annual Report for 1940.* Milton, Mass.: Secondary Education Board, 1941.

Gummere, R. M. "The Independent School and the Post-War World." *Independent School Bulletin,* Apr. 1943, pp. 5–10.

Hackett, A. *Quickened Spirit. A Biography of Frank S. Hackett.* New York: Riverdale Country School, 1957.

Hackett, F. S. "The Country Day School Movement." In P. Sargent (ed.), *A Handbook of American Private Schools 1924–25.* Boston: Porter Sargent, 1924.

Hancox, F. J. V. "Report of the Chairman of the Executive Committee, Feb. 15, 1930." In Secondary Education Board, *Annual Report for 1929.* Milton, Mass.: Secondary Education Board, 1930.

Hancox, F. J. V. "Report of the Chairman of the Executive Committee, Feb. 15, 1936." In Secondary Education Board, *Annual Report for 1935.* Milton, Mass.: Secondary Education Board, 1936.

Hawkins, H. *Between Harvard and America: The Educational Leadership of Charles W. Eliot.* New York: Oxford University Press, 1972.

Hofstadter, R. *Anti-Intellectualism in American Life.* New York: Vintage Books, 1963.

Jacobs, B. M. *Gilman Walls Will Echo. The Story of the Gilman Country School 1897–1947.* Baltimore, Md.: Gilman Country School, 1947.

Leighton, D. "The College." In *Harvard Annual Reports 1934–35.* Cambridge, Mass. Harvard University, 1935.

Litterick, W. S. "The Faith We Live By." *Independent School Bulletin,* May 1947, pp. 22–23.

McIntosh, M. C. "The Girls' Schools and College Entrance." *Independent School Bulletin,* Nov. 1946, pp. 31–32.

McLachlan, J. *American Boarding Schools.* New York: Scribner's, 1970.

Osgood, E. "Report of the Executive Secretary." In Secondary Education Board, *Annual Report for 1951–52.* Milton, Mass.: Secondary Education Board, 1952.

Osgood, F. *Report of the Annual Conference of the Secondary School Examination Board, Oct. 31, 1925.* Boston: Secondary School Examination Board, 1925.

Parkman, F. *The Problems and Future of the Independent Schools.* In American Council on Education, *Long-Range Planning for Education.* Washington, D.C.: American Council on Education, 1958.

Powell, A. G. *The Uncertain Profession: Harvard and the Search for Educational Authority.* Cambridge, Mass.: Harvard University Press, 1980.

Roberts, A. S. "Report of the Chairman of the Executive Committee, Mar. 8, 1947." In Secondary Education Board, *Annual Report for 1946.* Milton, Mass.: Secondary Education Board, 1947.

Sargent, P. *A Handbook of the Best Private Schools.* Boston: Porter Sargent, 1915.

Shaw, F. A. Letter to the Editor. *Harvard Alumni Bulletin,* Feb. 19, 1932, *34*(20), 620.

Smith, H. T. "Report upon the Curriculum Study, Feb. 25,

1933." In Secondary Education Board, *Annual Report for 1932*. Milton, Mass.: Secondary Education Board, 1933.

Smith, H. T. *Commission on Relations with Higher Education, April 21, 1948*. Report to the National Council of Independent Schools. Boston, Mass.: National Association of Independent School Archives, 1948.

Spencer, L. T. "College Achievement of Private and Public School Entrants." *School and Society,* Oct. 1, 1927, *26*(660), 436–438.

Synnott, M. G. *The Half-Opened Door. Discrimination and Admissions at Harvard, Yale, and Princeton, 1910–1970*. Westport, Conn.: Greenwood Press, 1979.

Valentine, J. A. *The College Board and the School Curriculum*. New York: College Entrance Examination Board, 1987.

Waterbury, J. P. *A History of Collegiate School 1638–1963*. New York: Clarkson N. Potter, 1965.

Wechsler, H. S. *The Qualified Student. A History of Selective College Admissions in America*. New York: Wiley, 1977.

Whitman, B. T. "The Evolution of the Secondary School Admission Test Board (1957–1983)." Unpublished doctoral dissertation, Department of Educational Administration, Teachers College, Columbia University, 1991.

Winsor, F. "Is Harvard Too Hard on the Undergraduates?" *Private School News,* Nov. 25, 1930, *7*(3), 5.

Winsor, F. Letter to the Editor. *Harvard Alumni Bulletin,* Feb. 19, 1932, *34*(20), 619.

6

New Directions for Early Childhood Care and Education Policy

W. Steven Barnett

It is widely recognized that public policy regarding early childhood care and education (ECCE) is fragmented and inconsistent (Grubb, 1987; Kagan, 1990; Robbins, 1990). Concern with these coherence problems arises from the substantial costs that they impose on society. Their extent and importance can be assessed through an analysis of what will be called internal and external consistency. Internal consistency is a problem when there are interprogram inconsistencies with respect to (1) rules for program eligibility and participation and (2) characteristics of the services provided. External consistency is a problem when there are inconsistencies between (1) the magnitude of resources required to achieve policy goals and the resources committed and (2) the types of activities required to achieve policy goals and the activities promoted by policy. Early childhood policy has serious problems of both internal and external consistency. The purposes of this chapter are to identify the origins and extent of these problems with coherence, weigh their costs, and consider the merits of proposed remedies.

Framework for Analysis

A basic premise of this chapter is that public policy in the United States tends to be made as a series of responses to social problems and the constituencies that develop around them. In the case of the care and education of young children, the legitimate scope for government intervention was extremely limited for most of our history (O'Connor, 1990). The social problems addressed were highly specific and the target populations tightly restricted, serving only a small portion of those nominally eligible. Thus, policy became defined by a conglomerate of small, highly particularistic programs. Organized interests around these problems were weak. Political support increased for one early childhood program or another due to immediate pressures (labor force needs during World War II or the anger and frustration of blacks in the mid 1960s), but it receded when pressures eased (Grubb and Lazerson, 1982).

In the context of narrow policy goals, tightly limited program target populations, and most Early Childhood Care and Education (ECCE) occurring in the home, coherence was not much of an issue for many years, although the kind of programmatic approach to policy described above tends to produce highly differentiated and largely unconnected programs. After all, public programs designed to address different problems and serve different children are expected to vary in their rules, regulations, practices, and outcomes. Moreover, any agency seeking to expand a program tries to differentiate that program as much as possible from others that might compete for the same resources. This changed when a historic transformation in ECCE arrangements created circumstances in which the traditional approaches to ECCE policy produced serious problems of coherence.

A Historic Transformation

For most of our nation's history, families have provided the education and care of young children in the home. Prior to 1960, it was rare for young children to attend formal educational programs and uncommon for them to be cared for outside the home for a few hours per day. By 1990, this had changed dramatically. A national survey of households with young children found that 71 percent of all first and second graders had attended either a day care center or nursery school prior to entering kindergarten (West, Hausken, Chandler, and Collins, 1991). More than one in four children ages three and four were reported to be in nonparental care and education for more than twenty hours per week (Hofferth, Brayfield, Deich, and Holcomb, 1991).

A number of demographic and economic changes contributed to the dramatic change in ECCE. The most important change may be the increased labor force participation of mothers of young children. As late as 1965, only 23 percent of the mothers of children under six were in the labor force and many of these had only part-time employment outside the home (U.S. Bureau of the Census, 1980). By 1990, 58 percent of the mothers of children ages three and four were in the labor force, and two-thirds worked full time (Hofferth, Brayfield, Deich, and Holcomb, 1991). Other factors contributing to the increased demand by families for nonparental care and education of young children include (1) increased demand for investment in the education of each child due to increased family income and a decreased family size (Becker, 1981), (2) increased need for peer experiences and socialization outside the home as children have fewer siblings and fewer opportunities for interaction in the neighborhood than in the past, and (3) changing public opinion regarding the value of group ECCE experiences. What was once considered a sometimes necessary evil has come to be viewed as an opportunity that is beneficial for children's healthy development.

A Changing Public Interest

The revolution in ECCE arrangements and attitudes described above fundamentally altered the possibilities and demands for public policy. In this radically new social context, four basic goals for ECCE policy have emerged, attempting to improve the welfare of society as a whole rather than merely promoting special interests. An argument can be made for each goal that the benefits to society as a whole exceed the costs (Barnett, 1991). The first goal is to provide intensive early intervention services to children who live in poverty or have disabilities. The second is to subsidize the costs of child care to lower-income families at risk of welfare dependency. The third is to subsidize child care for working women in such a way as to contribute to women's workforce entry and advancement. The fourth is to increase the well-being of children in nonparental ECCE by reducing the cost and increasing the quality of ECCE purchased by parents of all children.

The Evolution of ECCE Policy

The revolutionary changes in ECCE arrangements and attitudes and the public interest in a greater government role in ECCE have had important impacts on public policy. In particular, because the political system responded to these changes by expanding government activities in the context of the existing programmatic structure, the potential for severe problems of coherence developed. Although the highly particularistic programmatic structure of ECCE policy may have worked tolerably well through the 1970s, by the 1980s the social problems public policy addressed were defined at more general levels and encompassed larger populations than the old program structures were intended to deal with.

  This section tracks the evolution of policy primarily by describing the patterns of change in program funding (or, more generally, cost) over time. When policy is embodied in programs, program funding is a critical measure of its importance and direction. The amount of funding a program receives indicates the political commitment behind its policies. Funding is also a fairly accurate indicator of the impact of programs that purchase goods and services or transfer income. It is less satisfactory for tax expenditures (credits, deductions, and exemptions) and regulations, because most of their costs are "off-budget." However, reasonable estimates are available for the costs of most important tax expenditures, and the available evidence indicates that the impacts of government regulations have been extremely small relative to the impacts of spending (Gormley, 1991).

Federal Policy

Only a few years ago the consensus among policy analysts was that the important policy action in ECCE was at the state level

(Grubb, 1987; Schweinhart, 1985). Now it appears that the federal government has been the dominant policymaker and will continue to be so for some time. The sheer number of federal programs is impressive. Even before the most recent outbreak of policymaking, the U.S. General Accounting Office (1989) had identified forty-five federal programs affecting nonparental care of young children, administered by seven departments and agencies. Even this was an undercount of programs, as it focused on child care and omitted a number of relevant education department programs.

For many years, the four largest federal programs relating to early childhood care and education have been the Child and Dependent Care Tax Credit (CCTC), Head Start, Title XX, and the Child Care Food Program (CCFP). Although all of these programs are sometimes thought of as early childhood programs, only Head Start focuses on children ages three and four and also is the only program that directly provides services. The other programs provide funds that are used to purchase services for child care and education received by children from birth to adolescence. It is noteworthy that Head Start is the only program in which the federal government sets standards for service quality. Title XX and the CCFP require only that programs meet state licensing regulations, and there is no attempt to regulate quality through the CCTC.

Funding figures indicate a steady increase in federal support for ECCE programs from 1972 through 1988 (Besharov and Tramontozzi, 1989). These data contradict the widely held view (noted by Zigler and Lang, 1991) that President Nixon's veto of the 1971 Child Development Act marked the beginning of a period of stagnation in federal support for child care. However, the distribution of growth across programs was quite uneven after 1976. Table 6.1 shows the estimated amounts of funding spent on three- and four-year-olds from each major program in 1977 and 1988.[1] A small amount of additional funding supports five-year-olds whose entry to kindergarten is delayed a year (even though they are age-eligible), but estimation of this amount is beyond the scope of this chapter.

Table 6.1. Estimated Funding for Federal Programs Supporting ECCE in 1977, 1988, and 1992 (in Millions of 1992 Constant Dollars).[a]

Program	1977	1988	1992
Child and Dependent Care Tax Credit	$ 377	$1,357	$ 891
Head Start	$1,041	$1,291	$2,202
Title XX (SSBG)	$ 626	$ 262	$ 224
Child Care Food Program	$ 93	$ 232	$ 391
JOBS	----	----	$ 116
At-Risk Child Care Entitlement	----	----	$ 100
Child Care and Development Block Grant	----	----	$ 275
Earned Income Tax Credit	----	----	$ 50
IDEA	----	----	$ 155
Even Start	---	----	$ 70
Chapter 1	----	----	$ 536
Others	$ 163	$ 298	$ 350
Total	$2,300	$3,440	$5,360

Source: 1977 and 1988 figures: U.S. General Accounting Office (1989); 1992 figures: Dervarics (1992).

[a]The amount of support for threes and fours was determined for each program as follows. Based on 1990 data, 90 percent of the children served in Head Start are ages three and four, 7 percent are age five, and 3 percent are age two. All of the other programs serve children from birth to age twelve. Based on data from the National Child Care Survey (Willer and others, 1991), it is estimated that the distribution of costs for other programs by age is one-third for children under three, one-third for children three and four, and one-third for children five to twelve. The tax credit estimates are based on payments for claims made for the previous tax year. The amount of the SSBG spent on child care is at each state's discretion and so is difficult to estimate; Besharov and Tramontozzi (1989) recommend a slightly higher estimate for 1988. The estimate for "Others" is limited to twenty-six programs for which comparable data were available for 1977 and 1988. As no figure for "Others" was available for 1992, it was projected from 1988 by assuming the same annual increase from 1988 to 1992 as occurred from 1977 to 1988.

The fastest growing of the large federal programs from 1977 to 1988 was the CCTC, which was created as a deduction in 1954 and changed to a credit in 1976. The credit was expanded in 1982 and in 1981 Congress enacted a similar tax credit for employer-provided programs.

Head Start was launched in 1965 as part of the war on poverty. A primary goal was to improve the lives and development of young children from low-income families by providing health, nutrition, and education services. Up to 10 percent of those served may be children with disabilities who need not be low income. For most of its history, Head Start funding has been sufficient to serve less than 25 percent of the eligible children. When Head Start has been pressed to serve more children, it has responded by decreasing the intensity or quality of service in order to reach more children with the same amount of money. Never conceived of as a child care program, Head Start is usually provided for two to three hours a day in a center, though in some cases services consist entirely of home visits. Head Start centers usually operate on the same calendar as schools and are closed for the summer.

Head Start's organizational structure is the source of some of its unique characteristics. It provides no official role for states — the federal government makes grants directly to local agencies and administers the grants through regional offices. Head Start's structure is an attempt to avoid traditional state and local political power structures and create new ones that are more receptive to participation by poor and minority parents. Also, Head Start has a uniform set of national standards, although there is considerable program variation in practice. As Head Start emphasizes the need to provide services designed to match the unique characteristics of each community, much of the variation across sites may be desirable. However, it is fair to say that service quality varies significantly within Head Start, which is not always to the good (McKey and others, 1985).

The Title XX program was started in 1976. Although its funding levels declined over the years, especially when it was incorporated into the Social Services Block Grant (SSBG), it has continued to be a source of substantial funding. This program was never thought of as educational at the national level but as assisting poor families with child care in order to facilitate work and reduce welfare dependency. Many of the smaller federal programs that provide funds for child care (see U.S. Government Accounting Office, 1989) are similar in intent, and some are specifically part of efforts to enable women to leave welfare for work. States use the funds to purchase child care services for families and in many instances operate the program as a de facto voucher system in which parents choose care from among licensed or registered providers. As it is a block grant, states have complete discretion over how much if any to spend on ECCE (though the grant may indirectly contribute to ECCE if spending it on other services allows more state funds to be spent on ECCE). Thus, the amount of the SSBG allocated to child care depends on state policies as well as on federal policy regarding the total size of the SSBG.

The Child Care Food Program subsidizes meals and snacks for lower-income children up to age twelve in child care centers, Head Start, and licensed (or registered, where there is no state licensing requirement) family home day care. This program has grown substantially, with real expenditures doubling in the last decade.

The year 1988 was an important turning point in federal policy regarding early care and education: over 100 bills concerning child care and early education were introduced in Congress (Zigler and Lang, 1991). The number of bills suggests that some threshold had been reached in terms of attitudes toward nonparental care of young children and that the grounds for government intervention in this area had been substantially enlarged. Major new legislation was introduced and eventually passed that resulted in the provision of substantially increased funding for ECCE. Several entirely new programs were created to subsidize child care, tax credits were expanded for lower-income families with children, and a commitment was made to greatly expand Head Start. Even the SSBG saw its declining funding rebound.

The passage of PL 101-508 in 1990 created a new subsidy for child care in the form of the Child Care and Development Block Grant (CCDBG). Three-quarters of the CCDBG funding is earmarked to provide child care vouchers for families with incomes below 75 percent of the state median income level who have children under age thirteen. One quarter of the grant is to be spent on specific programs. Some of the funds may be used to increase staff wages and program quality (for example, raising a state's payment rates per child rather than increasing the number of children served).

PL 101-508 provided two other measures that increase funding for ECCE of children in lower-income families under Title IV-A of the Social Security Act. The law authorized funding to provide child care when parents are at risk of becoming Aid to Families with Dependent Children (AFDC) recipients, and to help improve the quality of programs funded by AFDC. Under the JOBS program of the Family Support Act of 1988, welfare recipients required to enroll in work or training programs must be provided with child care services including as much as a year of child care services after leaving AFDC to facilitate the transition to work, but the cost of this is borne by the states (Robbins, 1990).

Other provisions of PL 101-508 increased and expanded the Earned Income Tax Credit (EITC) for low-income working parents with children. The credit increases the disposable income of families with children under age nineteen (twenty-four if the child attends school) and is not directly linked to the purchase of child care. PL 101-508 also provides another new tax credit for family expenditures on health insurance for children. Whether the EITC (and the smaller health insurance credit) can be considered an important policy tool in supporting ECCE is unclear; exactly how much the quantity and quality of early childhood services purchased will increase as a result of the tax credits is unknown.

The other major spending initiative in this period was the expansion of Head Start. Congress authorized "full funding" for Head Start by 1994. Substantial increases in Head Start funding were subsequently appropriated but full funding was not. In 1991, a Senate bill was introduced to make Head Start an entitlement for three- and four-year-olds by 1997, but it seems unlikely that Congress will approve a new entitlement when existing ones are difficult to finance.

At the same time funding was expanded for programs for lower-income families, general support in the form of the CCTC was reduced. Beginning with 1989, Congress added a requirement that claimants identify the provider's Social Security number or tax code and reduced the eligible age range for children from fifteen to thirteen. The result was a drop in total credits claimed. Most of the drop in the credit's cost can be attributed to fewer false claims and a decline in claims by families whose care providers do not want their Social Security number reported. Although this may be viewed as a tax compliance measure, it substantially reduced federal financing of ECCE.

None of the major changes in policy involve the Department of Education (ED), but gradual increases in funding have given ED a significant, if minor, role in ECCE policy. The largest ED effort for young children was launched by 1986 legislation that increased financial incentives for states to provide early childhood programs for children with disabilities. Other ED programs include small programs to serve bilingual and migrant preschoolers and Even Start for preschoolers and parents in poverty. In addition, ED allows schools to use federal compensatory education funds (Chapter 1) for three- and four-year-olds.

Overall, two major changes have taken place in federal policy. First, the size of federal involvement in ECCE has increased substantially, as shown in Table 6.1. Federal support for the care and education of three- and four-year-olds reached $5.4 billion for 1992. Even measured in constant 1992 dollars, support increased more in the four years after 1988 than in the prior ten. Proposals for future program funding suggest that more rapid growth will continue in the near term. Second, policy has focused more clearly on two of the public interest policy goals identified earlier: early intervention and increased returns to employment for lower-income families. Nearly half of all federal support for ECCE now goes to Head Start; more than 80 percent targets young children facing problems of poverty or disability.

State and Local Policy

If financial support is used as the measure, state and local governments appear to be of secondary, but still substantial, importance in ECCE policy. State and local funding for the ECCE of children ages three and four is estimated at about $2 billion in 1990. Inclusion of federal funds over which states exercised control adds another $200 million. Local additions to state funding include funds for regular and special preschool education. The 20 percent matching requirement that grantees must meet to obtain federal Head Start programs amounted to another $440 million (much of it in-kind rather than cash) for 1990, not included above. These totals are rough approximations that depend on uncertain estimates for some of the components of state and local spending, such as the proportion of child care funds spent on three- and four-year-olds. However, the 1990 estimates benefit from data collected from the states by the Children's Defense Fund (Sandfort, 1992) on spending for child care and preschool education by program. These data are otherwise unavailable, as few programs have federal reporting requirements.

State and local ECCE funding can be grouped into three major categories: payments for federally sponsored programs, payments for state and locally sponsored programs, and tax breaks. These categories represent different approaches to support for ECCE and the degree of primacy of state policy varies across them. In particular, federal policy may play a leading role in the first category by offering strong incentives for state spending on ECCE. Funding in each category is discussed in detail below as a basis for constructing estimates of total funding and for assessing the allocation of resources to different kinds of programs meeting different kinds of needs. Due to the lack of information, most of the discussion focuses on estimates of funding for 1990 and other recent years, but change over time is discussed where information is available.

State and Local Funding of Programs

Three types of circumstances lead state and local governments to pay for federal programs. The first occurs when federal law mandates a service but requires that state or local governments pay much or all of the cost, for example, the Family Support Act of 1988 (FSA). This law requires states to provide child care for AFDC mothers whose oldest child is age three or older who participate in job training. It has been estimated that the FSA accounts for 10 percent of all nonparental child care, but estimates of the potential impact of this relatively new program should be employed with considerable caution. The second situation arises when a certain percentage match is required to receive federal funds for a program, for example, preschool special education and Head Start. In the case of preschool special education, the federal government pays a fixed amount per child — about $1,150 per child in 1990. State and local governments are left with the rest of the estimated $6,800 cost per child if they want to participate (Moore, Strang, Schwartz, and Braddock, 1988). Head Start requires a 20 percent match for federal funds that can be met by state and local government funds or by community contributions. The third occurs when state or local officials conclude that expansion of an existing federal program is more efficient than creating a separate program to provide the same service. State and local governments supplement federally sponsored preschool education programs (Chapter 1 and bilingual education) and Head Start to increase the numbers served and the duration, intensity, or quality of service. The total amount of funding that is added in this way is difficult to ascertain since these state expenditures are not monitored by the federal government.

All three of these reasons are important in early childhood care and education policy. The first two are so important that it can be argued that most state spending on ECCE is in response to federal policy. Together the three types of supplementation of federal programs are estimated to provide nearly $1.5 billion in resources for preschool services, with an estimated half of this going to special education.

State and Locally Sponsored Programs

Another growing source of funds for ECCE has been new state and local programs, especially half-day preschools in the public schools. Almost all of these programs target children from low-income families. Prior to 1980 only seven states and the District of Columbia funded preschool education, but by 1988, sixteen more states and some large cities (most notably, New York) had such programs. However, the number and prominence of these initiatives can be a misleading indicator of policy change. Several of these are quite small and many are limited to four-year-olds. Total state funding was $200 million per year in 1988 (Marx and Seligson, 1988) and about $350 million in 1990 (Sandfort, 1992). Local spending is unknown, but a survey of twenty-eight large city school districts (Schweinhart and Mazur, 1987) found that on average local districts paid about 30 percent of the cost of the preschool education programs they operated while state and federal governments paid about 35 percent each. Thus, local funding might have provided as much as $300 million more for preschool in 1990.

States operate a variety of child care programs, with and without federal funding, that serve children ages three and four, though usually not exclusively. Until recently the largest source of federal funding for these programs was Title XX child care money. Although Title XX child care traditionally has been regarded as a federal program that states supplement, it can be treated as a state-sponsored program after its incorporation into the SSBG. When these funds were combined with other program funds into the SSBG, states were no longer required to spend any of the funds for child care, though this is one of the permitted purposes. Thus, the SSBG's impact on ECCE is jointly determined by federal and state policy, and the size of that impact is difficult to assess.

Federal policy determines the overall amount of the SSBG, but state policy determines how much impact that amount has on ECCE spending. The SSBG increases the money available to states for spending of all kinds, and how much SSBG money the state spends on ECCE is not strictly related to the impact on ECCE. For example, a state that spends $30 million on services for the elderly and $20 million on child care without an SSBG might spend all of a $10 million SSBG on the elderly and shift $5 million of its own funds from services for the elderly to child care. Alternately, it might spend all of the $10 million SSBG on child care and shift $5 million of its own funds from child care to services for the elderly. In both cases child care spending increases by $5 million in response to the SSBG, but in one case no SSBG funds are spent on child care and in the other child care receives $10 million SSBG funds.[2] Obviously, the division of state ECCE spending into federal and state shares based on fund origins is risky and should be considered a first approximation.

The CDF figures for 1990 state spending on child care (all ages) and preschool (excluding preschool special education) totaled approximately $2 billion, of which about $1.4 billion was state money and $560 million (all for child care) was federal money (Sandfort, 1992). Total state funds for child care alone were about $1.05 billion. Again, it is assumed that one-third of child care funds are spent on children ages three and four as there are no data on expenditure by age across all the states. With the difficulties presented by the SSBG in mind, state funding for three- and four-year-olds in child care programs in 1990 is estimated at $350 million with an upper bound of $550 (one-third of the total of state and SSBG funds spent on child care).

California provides an interesting example of diversity in state-sponsored ECCE programs because it has had a unique history of sponsoring a broad array of programs for many years (Grubb, 1987; Grubb and Lazerson, 1977).[3] This array includes the Children's Centers, all-day programs operated by the public schools for children ages two to five; community-based child care centers originally funded by Title XX but now receiving only state funds; half-day preschool programs in the public schools; a voucher program that allows parents to select providers; and a number of smaller, highly specialized programs (Grubb, 1987; Sandfort, 1992). California also funds a statewide resource and referral network, as well as programs for facilities development, professional development, and recruitment of new service providers. Families with incomes under 85 percent of the state median are eligible for subsidized services and can continue to receive subsidies until they reach 100 percent of the median. This does not mean that all families eligible for subsidies are fully served, of course.

Tax Expenditures

State tax expenditures for child care subsidize early childhood services in the District of Columbia and twenty-eight states through tax deductions or credits (Robbins, 1990). Most of these state tax subsidies are tied to the federal CCTC and so have had a similar pattern of growth. Robbins (1990) estimated the cost of state tax expenditures to be 5 to 10 percent of the federal CCTC. That would have been $120 to $240 million in 1989, of which $40 to $80 million can be attributed to children ages three and four. Another state tax expenditure that is less recognized is the cost of the exemption of nonprofit organizations from state and local taxes. However, no estimate of the value of this to ECCE is available.

Licensing and Regulation

One of the more important state and local policy dimensions not captured by funding measures is the impact of state regulatory and administrative activities. Licensing and regulation of child care and education are primarily state responsibilities, and states can exercise substantial discretion in the administration of many federal programs as well. The federal government acted to limit such state discretion in some PL 101-508 programs by restricting the percentage of funds to be spent on various types of activities and age groups, emphasizing the use of voucher-type mechanisms, and requiring states to avoid regulations that would tend to limit parental choice. Skirmishes can be expected over state licensing standards and their effects on choice in these programs. Information on the impacts of state licensing standards is limited, but theory and the available evidence suggest that state standards may limit the supply of licensed services and produce higher prices (Gormley, 1991; Nelson, 1988; Rose-Ackerman, 1983). Whether standards have the desired impact of increasing quality is more difficult to assess, because of uncertain links between standards and quality and because some families shift from licensed to unlicensed ECCE.

More serious problems may result from the structure of state oversight than from state standards per se. Typically, separate sets of agencies and regulations cover services classified as education and those classified as child care. Most "education" programs are under public education agencies, and most "child care" programs are under human services agencies, but there are exceptions. State Head Start or Head Start-like efforts tend to be under human service agencies. Many other agencies are involved in providing and regulating ECCE as a relatively minor part of their responsibilities, including those in charge of community development, recreation, job training, treatment of disabilities, public safety, health, and mental health. Further fragmentation occurs within agencies. For example, within education agencies, programs for preschool children with and without disabilities tend to be in separate divisions. The classification of a program as education or child care usually is based on length of day, but public school programs tend to be exempt from child care regulations regardless of length of day, and private schools may be exempt, as well. Marx and Seligson (1988) provide a state-by-state description of the administrative and regulatory situation.

Extent and Costs of Incoherence

Description of federal, state, and local policy on funding provides one basis for evaluating coherence in terms of external and internal consistency and indicating the nature of the costs imposed. With respect to external consistency, the magnitude of funding committed to ECCE is far too limited to effectively address the national interests. This continues to be true despite a substantial increase in the rate of growth for ECCE funding in recent years. Increased funding has concentrated on expanding early intervention and, to a lesser extent, increasing the employment and earnings of mothers in low-income families. Financial support for the goals relating to maternal employment and the quality of ECCE for the general population has actually declined. It can be argued that this reallocation of resources is desirable, as the goals receiving the most financial support concentrate on poor families and have the strongest evidence of important public benefits. However, at present none of the four policy goals are fully funded, and the full funding of all of them does not appear likely in the foreseeable future. The costs of this inconsistency between funding and the public interest are continued inequity and a substantial loss of economic benefits, though data allow a dollar cost to be estimated only for the policy gap in early intervention.

The funding committed to ECCE thus remains insufficient to adequately address even the early intervention goal. While preschoolers with disabilities are guaranteed access to relatively well-funded services, funding of early intervention for the much larger population of disadvantaged preschoolers is still only at about half the level required to provide the current services to all eligible children. Based on benefit estimates in the Perry Preschool study (Berrueta-Clement and others, 1984), the cost to society of *not* providing quality early intervention services to half the eligible population is over $35 billion annually. If funding continues to grow at the rate of the last several years, complete coverage of the target population might be reached by the end of the decade. Even then there remains a serious question about whether the level of funding per child will be adequate to provide the quality of services needed to produce the desired benefits (Barnett, 1990).

It is difficult to identify clear problems of consistency between the national interest (policy goals) and the types of programs and activities promoted by policy. For the mid 1980s, the share of resources devoted to tax credits was unduly large. Of course, this requires a judgment that greater benefits are likely from programs targeting lower-income families. By 1990, the distribution of spending across programs had shifted strongly in favor of lower-income families. Whether this should be seen as a realignment of spending with national interests or a reassessment of national interests may be debated. A more recent example of a gap between interest and action is represented by the EITC. As noted earlier, views on the likely impact of the EITC reasonably differ; some may not consider the EITC an ECCE program at all. Others may see income support for lower-income families with employed parents as a key element in early intervention and increased equity for women in the labor force. Overall, this aspect of external consistency appears to be much less important than issues about total funding for ECCE policies.

The internal consistency problems of ECCE policy are to a considerable extent problems of suboptimization resulting from the programmatic structure of policy. Changes in ECCE and national goals for ECCE policy vastly enlarged the target populations and scope of public policy, but policy continues to be made in the context of existing agencies and through narrowly defined programs. This approach to policy fails to recognize that to a considerable extent the same children are targeted by Head Start, state and local compensatory preschool education, preschool special education, and child care programs. The dimensions of the internal consistency problem are to some extent apparent from the description of the agencies and programs involved in ECCE, but further discussion should help clarify the nature and extent of its costs.

At present there is little or no coordination of services across programs to best meet the needs of children and families. Participation in one can mean that a child is de facto excluded from another. On the other hand, some children may receive multiple services while similarly eligible children receive no services. Families are bounced from one program to another by changes in eligibility. Differences in eligibility criteria and other program characteristics produce segregation of services by income, ability, class, and race and ethnicity (Rose-Ackerman, 1983; Wrigley, 1991). Integration is desirable for a variety of reasons, only some of which are pedagogical (Turnbull, 1982; Wrigley, 1991). Inconsistencies across programs produce duplication of effort, competition for resources, conflicting participation and eligibility requirements that burden and confuse service providers and clients, competition for some potential clients and neglect of others, and discontinuities and inconsistencies in services that create uncertainty and disrupt the lives of children and their parents. Fairness suffers as well as efficacy and efficiency.

A few concrete examples may be helpful. The short hours of most Head Start and state preschool programs may close out many children from low-income families because their parents have to arrange for all-day care. The provision of free child care through AFDC and the JOBS program may draw children out of Head Start and preschools. A child with a disability may be eligible for free transportation and other support services if she attends the segregated half-day preschool special education program but not if she attends a mainstream full-day preschool program operated by the same school district. Head Start and public school preschools compete for the same children in one area of a state, while neither operates in another area. Children whose parents piece together arrangements from various public and private sources may find that the expectations of the adults in their lives change dramatically by time of day and day of the week.

Though some of the costs of incoherence described above result from the sheer number of agencies promulgating rules and regulations, determining eligibility, monitoring compliance, and providing money and services in ECCE, the greatest costs stem from the strong differences among agencies. The most salient of these is the divide between child care and education programs and their agencies. Child care agencies view their central mission as enabling parents to work; education agencies view their central mission as enhancing development or schooling the child. Both types of agencies stubbornly ignore the joint nature of the production of child care and education in setting eligibility criteria and determining the characteristics of services. Both operate programs with the potential to contribute to learning and development and facilitate parental employment by providing a safe, healthy, and happy environment for the child. Nevertheless, each type of agency neglects the aspect of this activity not considered central to its mission and vigorously resists pressures to expand its mission. At the same time, each views the services provided by the other type of agency as sadly deficient.

Other divides also present significant problems for the consistency of services. These include the divisions between preschool and elementary school agencies, administrations, and professionals; regular and special preschool education; Head Start and state agencies, particularly the public schools and state departments of instruction; classroom-type services and family home day care; for-profit and not-for-profit providers; and religious and nonreligious service sponsors. To a large extent these divides are internal to ECCE, but the split between ECCE and elementary education represents differences between all of those involved with children under five and the public school programs that take over at kindergarten. The conflict between ECCE and elementary school forces is long standing and well known; it has been described in detail by Grubb (1987). As will be seen, a common characteristic of proposals seeking to increase the coherence of ECCE policy is an effort to eliminate the effects of these divisions on policy.

Solutions to the Coherence Problem

The search for ways to promote more coherence in early childhood policy is motivated by a desire to avoid the costs of incoherence. A variety of alternative approaches have been proposed. All of the proposals recognize the need for large increases in the total public resources devoted to ECCE if public interests are to be adequately met, though the mechanisms proposed do not explicitly require large increases in total funding. All address the internal consistency problems created by the programmatic and other divisions in ECCE and between ECCE and other services and professions. Professionalization strikes at the root of the internal consistency problem by seeking to eliminate differences in interests and beliefs among professionals designing, administering, and implementing policy. The other approaches seek to limit the effects of these differences on ECCE service eligibility and characteristics.

Professionalization

An important concomitant of the large increase in nonparental care and education has been the development and organization of a professional class with an interest in increased funding for early childhood programs and other measures to improve their working conditions and salaries. Membership in the National Association for the Education of Young Children (NAEYC) rose from less than 1,500 in 1964 to more than 80,000 in 1992, and NAEYC became a strong public voice for ECCE professionals (National Association for the Education of Young Children, 1992). Although NAEYC's membership remains small relative to the total number of providers, its efforts to professionalize the field tend to increase the coherence of policy, in part by shaping the views of the general public and the professionals who develop, administer, and implement policy. In addition, it works through the political process to press the profession's interests with respect to legislation and rulemaking relating to ECCE.

During the 1980s NAEYC established a set of standards for "developmentally appropriate practice" (Bredekamp, 1987a) and developed a voluntary national accreditation system based on those standards (Bredekamp, 1987b) as well as on a national network of validators based in the ECCE teaching profession who visit centers to conduct observations of practice. Potentially, this system could evolve into a national curriculum and inspectorate for ECCE. However, even in their present form, NAEYC's standards for practice and accreditation system could result in substantial national standardization and promotion of ECCE, with public policy playing an important role. Government agencies could adopt NAEYC standards (saving the effort and risks of developing and defending their own) and require accreditation. For example, the Department of Defense requires all of its ECCE programs to obtain accreditation. States could require accreditation for licensing or incorporate NAEYC standards into licensing standards or public school curriculum guidelines.

In 1990, NAEYC launched a "full cost of quality" campaign that supports its efforts to promote its standards. This campaign seeks to strengthen public support for the substantially increased funding, staff qualifications, and compensation that would facilitate widespread attainment of NAEYC standards and accreditation. The success of the campaign would greatly improve the fit between the magnitude of public financial support and the requirements of all four policy goals representing public interest in ECCE. At the same time it would substantially increase the consistency of services received by children across different types of programs. It is notable that NAEYC has been at the forefront of the movement to recognize the inseparability of child care and education for young children.

NAEYC efforts to influence professional development also have important implications for coherence. NAEYC is seeking to develop "an articulated professional development *system*" (Brede-kamp and Willer, 1992). First steps include a 1991 joint state-ment on teacher certification with the Association of Teacher Educators (ATE) and the establishment of the National Institute for Early Childhood Professional Development under NAEYC auspices. The institute proposes to construct a "career lattice" that sets out staff hierarchies with qualifications and responsi-bilities for each position in all types of programs. The institute will attempt to specify a common core of knowledge that defines the profession and the levels of preparation and specialization required of each position. Goals of the system include improv-ing and standardizing service quality, staff qualifications and responsibilities, and compensation (Bredekamp and Willer, 1992).

If NAEYC succeeds in its aims, early childhood care and education will vary considerably less from program to program and from the public sector to the private than it does today, there will be more comparability across ECCE classrooms than there is across elementary classrooms, and public subsidization will be considerably higher than today. However, it is by no means obvious that NAEYC can succeed. Much of the profes-sion is unorganized, and there is competition from other orga-nizations. In 1992, the American Academy of Pediatrics (AAP) and the American Public Health Association (APHA) put for-ward their own standards for ECCE (American Public Health Association and American Academy of Pediatrics, 1992), and the National Child Care Association launched an accreditation system for private providers. A proliferation of standards could reinforce policy incoherence. Thus, governmental support for one organization's standards may be required if standards are to increase coherence.[4]

Intergovernmental Collaboration

Of the alternative approaches to increasing the coherence of policy, the most common is the creation of coordinating or col-laborative bodies (Kagan, 1991). These may be formed at any level of government, but current attention is focused at the state and local levels. At the state level, coordinating councils or committees typically consist of representatives from all of the state agencies supporting early childhood services. Head Start and private organizations may be invited to participate. These committees try to increase coherence by reaching agreements that minimize overlaps and gaps in services, standardize rules and regulations, and facilitate collaborative service provision. Their greatest success is in clarifying agency responsibilities to eliminate relatively small overlaps or gaps in service. At the local level, resource and referral agencies are the most common coordinating agencies, though proposals have been made to create local coordinating councils or ECCE service districts (Sugarman and Sullivan, 1992). Resource and referral agencies help consumers navigate through fragmented systems to bring coherence to the actual pattern of services received by families rather than attempt to negotiate agreements among providers.

Sugarman and Sullivan (1992) have proposed the creation of community-based (local) voluntary child care coordinating councils. These voluntary councils would be initiated by private or public sector leaders concerned with improving services for young children and their families. Although the ultimate goal is the development of a coherent system for planning, supporting, and delivering services, Sugarman and Sullivan (1992) recommend that the councils begin with a small set of collaborative projects. Work on these projects would shape agency roles and responsibilities gradually and produce high payoffs for the participating agencies that would encourage them to continue and expand collaboration. Suggestions for initial projects include collaborative efforts in rate and standard setting; staff preparation and development; provision of transportation; facility expansion and improvement; or the negotiation of uniform agreements with agencies providing health, mental health, nutrition, and social services.

The coordinating body approach has several advantages. It does not threaten the existence of any organization or alter the distribution of resources. It provides a means for organizations supporting ECCE to combine their political power in support of common interests. At the local level, it may substantially lower the costs to small providers of negotiating relationships and formal agreements with agencies funding and regulating ECCE as well as those providing other services to children and families. The diversity of the present system of services is preserved. Federal ECCE policies have encouraged this approach by requiring and encouraging agencies to coordinate and collaborate. For example, the Family Support Act requires that the AFDC program include representatives of most organizations providing childcare in its child care planning. The federal government has funded research and demonstration programs on fostering cooperation at state and local levels between Head Start and other agencies serving young children, particularly the public schools.

Among the major limitations of state coordinating bodies are that they add another layer of bureaucratic activity and they have little formal power. Additional resources are required for the organizations that coordinate planning and policymaking whether they direct traffic from the top or bottom. In addition, success depends on political leadership, good will, and flexibility. To this point, state and federal governments have declined to designate a lead agency for coordination. A governor may require agency cooperation, but some state agencies are independent, and others can be expected to resist. Head Start presents a special problem: it is not operated through state government, has no state administrative structure, and may be politically aligned against state officials. Also, the narrow problem definitions of most federal programs and restrictions imposed by Congress and federal agencies impede collaboration. State and local agencies are understandably wary of the charge of inappropriate use of federal funds. If collaborative approaches such as voluntary coordinating councils are to work, local agencies and providers must be granted substantially more flexibility by federal and state agencies.

Public Schools

Another approach to the development of coherent policy is to build a system based on the public schools. This approach has been developed in detail by Edward Zigler as the "School of the

Twenty-First Century" (Zigler, 1989; Zigler and Lang, 1991). Zigler's proposal provides universal access to comprehensive care and education services for children of all ages under the auspices of the public schools. All-day year-round programs would be offered to children from age three to kindergarten entry. Older children would be provided with before- and after-school care and all-day care during school vacations. Children under the age of three would be served by a network of family home day care providers trained, supported, and administered by the school's child care center. A resource and referral network and a home-based family support and education program would be linked with the school's child care center, as well. The ECCE staff would be separate from regular school staff and would have different training; the ECCE curriculum would not consist of formal schooling but would emphasize play and socialization.

In Zigler's formulation, ECCE could at first be funded by parent fees on a sliding scale (varying with income) or by combining funds from available public and private sources. Participation would be voluntary, and parents could choose other ECCE providers if they preferred (at their own cost, of course). However, if the School of the Twenty-First Century is to be an important source of coherence, it will have to dominate ECCE much as public schools dominate the education of older children. This would require that early childhood services in the public schools be heavily subsidized, that all ECCE be regulated by the state department of instruction, and that other ECCE be minimally subsidized. With these provisions, this public school model could increase the consistency of regulation, eligibility criteria, and characteristics of services while providing a single point of contact for parents in each school district.

Zigler and Lang suggest a number of advantages for the twenty-first century school: convenient location, higher standards of service and staff qualifications, universal early screening and diagnosis services, ongoing staff training, and linkage of family home day care providers to a professional organization. Although many of these advantages would require an increase in funds over the present system, they argue that the elimination of administrative duplication and use of slack school resources might produce offsetting cost savings. It may be added that most preschoolers already attend classroom programs and the majority of four-year-olds attend one in a school building. If one agency is to take charge, it makes some sense for it to be the agency that presently houses most programs. Also, operation by the schools increases the potential for greater continuity between prekindergarten and the early elementary grades.

The disadvantages of the public schools as a locus for early childhood education are largely the problems identified by the critics of public schools as providers of elementary and secondary education: mediocre quality and results, high cost, a lack of parent involvement and choice, and persistent inequalities in services and outcomes. There is little reason to believe that the public schools would work better with younger children. Moreover, placing early childhood programs in the public schools is likely to make them much more expensive. Raising ECCE salaries to public school levels would nearly double cost, while the lack of ties between performance and salary in public schools suggests that corresponding increases in quality are unlikely. A substantial literature indicates that public schools are inefficient (Hanushek, 1989). Hopes for large cost savings from the use of slack resources are at odds with the growing school-age population, and the difficulty of curtailing existing bureaucracies while limiting the growth of the new one should not be underestimated.

Preservation of the diversity of approaches to ECCE in the present system poses a difficult problem for the public school approach. Although there is a great deal of variation in public schools, it does not, for the most part, reflect a response to the diversity of parental wishes. Most problematic is the continuation of a strong role for religious sponsors of ECCE. Historically, the public schools and public child care agencies have had quite different relationships with religious organizations. In general, the law regarding separation of church and state has not been interpreted as prohibiting religious organizations from receiving public child care funds for ECCE. Unless church provision of ECCE can be accommodated, many of the religious organizations now providing child care can be expected to strenuously oppose any attempt to place ECCE under the control of the public schools. Others can be expected to oppose any such accommodation between religious organizations and public schools.

Although the public schools might bring uniformity at some levels, it is important to recognize that the quality of public school services is not uniform and that their services remain substantially segregated and unequal by income, race, and disability. This is only partly a matter of the dependence of school finance on local property taxes, as differences in spending do not explain much of the variation in quality (Chubb and Moe, 1990), which varies substantially across regions, states, districts, and schools within districts. Even schools that appear to be quite integrated from the outside may be segregated on the inside by tracking and special education. The ideal public school system might reduce the segregation and disparities in the current mix of ECCE services, but the actual public school system might exacerbate them. It is because of the negative experiences of African-American children and their parents with the public schools that the National Black Child Development Institute (1985) has strongly questioned the wisdom of moving early childhood programs into the public schools and has committed its support to a diverse delivery system not limited to the public schools (Moore, 1987).

One of the strongest fears of early childhood professionals is that the public schools would make ECCE more like elementary education (which is widely considered developmentally inappropriate for the early grades as well as preschool) rather than vice versa (Grubb, 1987). Zigler and Lang (1991) propose strong boundaries between the preschool and elementary programs with respect to staffing and curriculum, but, if successful, this would inhibit the development of more desirable continuity, as well. However, the likelihood that the public schools will not produce curricular continuity of any kind should not be exaggerated. A recent study in Massachusetts found large differences between kindergarten and first-grade classrooms with respect to developmentally appropriate practice, with kindergartens much more similar to preschool classrooms than to first grades (Frede, Baron, and Lee, 1992). In addition, teacher practices in the public schools may be more strongly influenced by teacher preparation and culture than by administrative guidance and policy (Cohen, 1990). In this case, the administration and location of ECCE may be less important for practices than who teaches and how they are trained.

Federal Alternatives and Parent Choice

As the federal government provides most of the public funding for ECCE and is responsible for much of the coherence problem, it seems reasonable to consider the possibility of a federal solution. One alternative would be the creation of federal standards for all ECCE programs. The closest approximation to this has been the Federal Interagency Day Care Requirements (FIDCR) created in 1968 and revised in 1972 and 1980 (Phillips and Zigler, 1987). The most noteworthy facts about the FIDCR are that they were never fully enforced and were eliminated in 1981. Subsequent efforts to include comprehensive standards in child care legislation have failed, and Zigler, who worked toward that goal for decades, recently concluded that "it is unlikely that national standards will ever be enacted and enforced" (Zigler and Lang, 1991, p. 73).

Another federal alternative would be to create a comprehensive system based on Head Start. Zigler's twenty-first century school model provides a ready plan. Like the schools, Head Start is an established, trusted, and respected community-based institution. Moreover, Head Start has had greater success with low-income and minority families, more parent involvement, a broader approach to education and development, and lower costs than the public schools. On the other hand, Head Start does not serve every community, and questions can be raised about the quality of Head Start compared to public school programs. The primary reason Head Start's costs are low is that staff are paid much less than public school personnel, in part because they have lower formal qualifications. Whether or not lower pay and formal qualifications result in lower quality is difficult to determine. Should this be a key disadvantage, Head Start salaries and qualifications could be upgraded, but this would reduce Head Start's cost advantage.

A third federal alternative would be to allow parents to choose providers and to distribute all federal funding for ECCE through direct payments to providers. State funding could be pulled into such a system by requirements for matching funds. Funds could be allocated based on a formula that recognizes all major policy goals and determines the amount of public subsidy for each child received based on (1) family income, (2) maternal employment, and (3) disability. An example of how this might work in practice is presented in Table 6.2. For families

Table 6.2. Example of Public ECCE Payments
per Child under a Parent Choice Approach.

Income Group	Payment		
	Baseline	Mother Works	Disability
Poverty (25 percent)	$6,000	$2,000	$1,000+
Next 25 percent	$3,000 (average)	$1,000 (average)	$1,000+
Top 50 percent	$0	$0	$1,000+

below the poverty line, there is a baseline payment for each preschool child of $6,000. Between the poverty line and the median income, the baseline credit falls to zero. For families in poverty where the mother works full time, there is a further payment of $2,000 per preschool child. Between poverty and the median income this falls to zero, as well. This "working mother" payment would be prorated for hours worked, where the mother works part time. For every child diagnosed as disabled, an additional payment based on the child's needs would assure that children with disabilities would experience no decline in special services but would be able to receive them in settings chosen by the parent.

The payment figures in Table 6.2 are based on data on the costs of quality ECCE services and judgments about the impacts of payments on net maternal earnings and family budgets (Escobar and Barnett, forthcoming; Barnett, 1988; U.S. General Accounting Office, 1990; Clifford and Russell, 1989; Willer, 1990; Willer and others, 1991). Payments would be $6,000 to $8,000 per child in poverty and $3,000 to $4,000 for a child in a family midway between poverty and the median income. Head Start and state preschool programs spend only about $3,000 per child, an indication of how poorly funded they are compared to what is required to have a significant impact on the development of children in poverty. Nonpoor children require less extensive and intensive services, and $4,000 would cover roughly 85 percent of the cash cost of a year in the average all-day, NAEYC accredited center.

The administrative distribution of funds in a parent choice system can be accomplished through (1) state government payments to providers on a fee-for-service basis, (2) vouchers, or (3) government-managed credit accounts. With credit accounts, parents would be given charge cards that they present to providers to pay for monthly services (in full or part). To protect the public and children, only "approved" providers would be eligible for public payments. State approval might require NAEYC accreditation and compliance with health and safety regulations. IRS tapes could be used to verify the income and employment information provided by parents. Eligibility might be determined annually or at the request of parents who believed their eligibility had changed substantially.

The estimated total cost of the parent choice system proposed in Table 6.2 is $20 billion annually, but the actual cost would vary from year to year depending on the number of children ages three and four and their poverty rates.[5] This assumes full participation. Some parents might choose not to send their child to out-of-home ECCE despite eligibility for subsidies. If 90 percent of eligible families participated, the cost would fall to $18 billion. Administrative costs using credit accounts would be negligible, less than 2 percent of the payment amounts (Goodman and Musgrave, 1992). Thus, the proposed parent choice system would require about $10 billion in funding beyond existing federal, state, and local resources, which would more than double public spending on ECCE.

Ten billion dollars is a minimum estimate of the new public funds required to secure the public interest in ECCE. Other policy approaches would have higher administrative costs, and this example provides no funds to families with incomes above the median (either to assure quality ECCE or increase equity for women). For comparison purposes, the cost of providing all three- and four-year-olds with high-quality services through the public schools could exceed $45 billion annually, even assuming no increase in the administrative bureaucracy.[6]

Chief among the advantages of a parent choice system is that it abolishes existing programs and their distinctions while preserving the diversity of the existing services and stimulating competition. The array of services children receive would be determined by parents and a funding formula tied to policy goals. Programmatic boundaries would no longer segregate children or determine the characteristics of services. Public schools, Head Start grantees, private nonprofits, and for-profit providers would compete to satisfy parents that they provide the best service for the money relative to the individual needs of each child and family. Concern that some parents might slight their children's needs, suffer from a lack of information, or be deceived by unscrupulous providers is met by restricting choice to approved programs. As another supportive measure, payments might be made available for resource and referral services that would advise parents regarding the best available services for their child. Alternatively, local government units could be set up to advise parents and administer payments.

An additional advantage of the parent choice approach is its political transparency. Its payment allocation formula makes it obvious to every voter how much is committed to preschoolers as a whole, how much is committed to each policy goal (antipoverty, proemployment, antidisability), and how many children benefit from each level of payment. It makes the rationing of subsidies explicit rather than implicit, which tends to increase the equity of distribution. For example, current funding limits for Head Start mean that some poor children receive comprehensive services entirely free of charge while others receive nothing at all. With a pooled payment system, the public would be unlikely to tolerate large government subsidies to only 25 percent of those eligible, even though this is what has happened for years under Head Start.

The most commonly suggested disadvantage of parent

choice approaches that rely on market interactions to produce and allocate services is that parents cannot be relied upon to choose as well as the government. The fear is that some parents are not sufficiently interested in their children's welfare and some, perhaps many, are not well enough informed to choose wisely. This fear is compounded by the difficulty of observing ECCE services as they are provided in the parent's absence and providers may cut corners in ways that are difficult for parents to discover. It is difficult to know how much of a problem with quality of service would arise even when providers must be state approved. Under a parent choice system, every effort should be made to allow parents to choose relatives, religiously sponsored providers, parent cooperatives, local government, and other nonprofit forms that may increase trustworthiness. However, the public interest must be preserved: only high-quality professional services would qualify for payments.

It is not always recognized that information and trust problems in ECCE are not peculiar to parent choice approaches or that the market may be stimulated to create remedies. Government and nonprofit failure pose as many potential problems as market failure (Wolf, 1991; Zimmerman, 1991). Although government and other nonprofit providers have no profit motive to do so, the administration and staff may increase their own salaries, benefits, and leisure by cutting corners and shirking their responsibilities. Moreover, public sector managers have no profit motive and limited means to prevent shirking by rewarding highly productive workers and penalizing unproductive ones. Finally, it is equally difficult for guardians of the public interest to monitor and assess the quality of services offered by public and private sectors.

Concluding Thoughts

Any proposal that seeks to improve the coherence of ECCE policy faces serious problems of practical politics. In order to improve the consistency between the national interest and policy, a great deal more public money must be put into ECCE, which will require a tax increase, a greater deficit, or reduced public expenditures in another area. In order to improve the internal consistency of ECCE policy, it will be necessary to restructure government's involvement. Much of the inconsistency in ECCE policy results from the development and implementation of new policies in an anachronistic programmatic structure antiquated by historic changes in family, work, and child rearing. All of the proposed policy alternatives considered above threaten existing interests and require reconceptualization of social problems, agency missions, and responsibilities. Legislative committees, executive agencies, their clients, and other beneficiaries of the existing distribution of power and spending can be expected to resist these changes.

It is easy to become discouraged about the potential to obtain substantial increases in public funding for ECCE policy and to dislodge or reorient the existing bureaucratic structure, but there are reasons to be hopeful. Families with preschoolers are a relatively high percentage of the population at present. The evidence substantiating important national interest in ECCE is growing and widely disseminated. Attitudes toward maternal employment and nonmaternal ECCE have changed tremendously and are much more favorable than in the past. These circumstances increase the political leverage of advocates for increased resources and changes in the structure of early childhood policy.

At the federal level, it may be wise to seek added resources without any proposal regarding how those resources are to be financed. Proposals that call for increased taxes should be avoided as they are almost certainly doomed to failure. On the other hand, it might be an effective strategy to seek to displace special interests with weaker claims (in terms of merit and numbers in the electorate) on the federal budget. For example, the $10 billion in increased federal funding required to meet minimal national policy goals for ECCE with a parent choice plan could be obtained by targeting federal agricultural subsidies to millionaire farmers and corporations (Gardner, 1992). The political viability of this proposal might be increased by framing the issue as a choice between subsidies for the ultrarich and meeting the basic needs of young children. Adequate revenue could be obtained while still retaining subsidies for the few "truly needy" family farmers. Although the conventional wisdom is that special interests such as the farm lobby are too politically strong to challenge, encouragement for this strategy can be found in Keynes's dictum that the "power of vested interests is vastly exaggerated compared with the gradual encroachment of ideas" (Keynes, 1936, p. 383).

Notes

1. Data are not available on the distribution of government program costs by age of child for those programs that serve families with children from birth to adolescence. *Faute de mieux,* it was assumed that government program support by age of child was proportionate to use of nonparental care and education (excluding public elementary education). This seems eminently reasonable for programs such as Title XX and dependent care tax credits (the very small portion going to older dependents is ignored).

2. Theoretically, even if federal funds are earmarked, the state can shift its allocation of state funds to offset completely the effect of earmarking. Thus, the change to the SSBG need not have had any effect on spending patterns. However, in practice, federal earmarking is observed to have a substantial effect on state allocations, often called the "flypaper effect," that may result from the ways in which agencies make decisions generally (Wycoff, 1991).

3. One reason that California spends so much is that it is an extremely large state. Although it is one of the higher-spending states on a per capita basis, however, several others spend more per capita. By far the highest spending on a per capita basis are the District of Columbia and Massachusetts.

4. This strategy is not without costs. A professional organization is likely to raise costs above the competitive market level. The American Medical Association provides an excellent example of what happens when a professional organization strongly dominates a human service industry with government support (Starr, 1982).

5. These calculations are based on the number of three- and four-year-olds in 1990, which is expected to rise slightly to the next century before declining, and a poverty rate of 25 percent.

6. This estimate uses Willer's (1990) "full cost of quality" estimates, in which staff salaries are equivalent to those in the public schools. Although Willer computes cost-per-child figures for a program serving all ages of children under age five, cost per child was recalculated for a program serving only children ages three and four with a staff-child ratio of 1:9. It is assumed that 50 percent of all children are served at the all-day cost ($7,900), while 50 percent are served at half the all-day cost ($3,950). These figures tend to underestimate cost because they are based on 1988 salary data and do not adequately reflect the added cost of twelve-month salaries for public school personnel.

References

American Public Health Association and American Academy of Pediatrics. *Caring for Our Children — National Health and Safety Performance Standards: Guidelines for Out-of-Home Child Care Programs.* Washington, D.C.: American Public Health Association, 1992.

Barnett, W. S. "The Economics of Early Intervention Under PL-99-457." *Topics in Early Childhood Special Education,* 1988, *8*(1), 12–23.

Barnett, W. S. "Developing Preschool Education Policy: An Economic Perspective." *Educational Policy,* 1990, *4*(3), 245–265.

Barnett, W. S. "Some Simple Economics of Child Care." Unpublished paper, Graduate School of Education, Rutgers University, New Brunswick, N.J., 1991.

Becker, G. S. *A Treatise on the Family.* Cambridge, Mass.: Harvard University Press, 1981.

Berrueta-Clement, J. R., and others. "Changed Lives. The Effects of the Perry Preschool Program on Youths Through Age 19." Monographs of the High/Scope Educational Research Foundation, no. 8, Ypsilanti, Mich., 1984.

Besharov, D. J., and Tramontozzi, P. N. "Federal Child Care Assistance: A Growing Middle-Class Entitlement." *Journal of Policy Analysis and Management,* 1989, *8*(2), 313–318.

Bredekamp, S. (ed.). *Developmentally Appropriate Practice in Early Childhood Programs Serving Children from Birth Through Age 8.* (expanded ed.) Washington, D.C.: National Association for the Education of Young Children, 1987a.

Bredekamp, S. (ed.). *Accreditation Criteria and Procedures of the National Academy of Early Childhood Programs.* Washington, D.C.: National Association for the Education of Young Children, 1987b.

Bredekamp, S., and Willer, B. "Of Ladders and Lattices, Cores and Cones: Conceptualizing an Early Childhood Development System." *Young Children,* 1992, *47*(3), 47–50.

Chubb, J. E., and Moe, T. M. *Politics, Markets, and America's Schools.* Washington, D.C.: Brookings Institution, 1990.

Clifford, R. M., and Russell, S. D. "Financing Programs for Preschool-Aged Children." *Theory into Practice,* 1989, *28*(1), 19–27.

Cohen, D. K. "Governance and Instruction: The Promise of Decentralization and Choice." In W. H. Clune and J. F. Witte (eds.), *Choice and Control in American Education.* Bristol, Pa.: Falmer Press, 1990.

Dervarics, C. *Report on Preschool Programs.* Silver Spring, Md.: Business Publishers, 1992.

Escobar, C. M., and Barnett, W. S. "Costs of Early Childhood Special Education." In W. S. Barnett and H. J. Walberg (eds.), *Economic Analysis for Educational Decision Making.* Greenwich, Conn.: JAI Press, forthcoming.

Frede, E., Baron, P., and Lee, B. "The Psychometric Properties of Two Instruments Based on NAEYC's Guidelines for Developmentally Appropriate Practice." Paper presented at the annual meeting of the American Educational Research Association, San Francisco, Apr. 1992, pp. 20–24.

Gardner, B. L. "Changing Economic Perspectives on the Farm Problem." *Journal of Economic Literature,* 1992, *25,* 62–101.

Goodman, J. C., and Musgrave, G. L. *Controlling Health Care Costs with Medical Savings Accounts.* National Center for Policy

Analysis Policy Report no. 168. Dallas, Tex.: National Center for Policy Analysis, 1992.

Gormley, W. T., Jr. "State Regulations and the Availability of Child-Care Services." *Journal of Policy Analysis and Management,* 1991, *10*(1), 78–95.

Grubb, W. N. *Young Children Face the States: Issues and Options for Early Childhood Programs.* Consortium for Policy Research in Education, Rutgers University, New Brunswick, N.J., 1987.

Grubb, W. N., and Lazerson, M. "Child Care, Government Financing, and the Public Schools: Lessons from the California Children's Centers." *School Review,* 1977, *86*(1), 5–37.

Grubb, W. N., and Lazerson, M. *Broken Promises: How Americans Fail Their Children.* New York: Basic Books, 1982.

Hanushek, E. A. "The Impact of Differential Expenditures on School Performance." *Educational Researcher,* 1989, *18*(4), 45–51, 62.

Hofferth, S. L., Brayfield, A., Deich, S., and Holcomb, P. *National Child Care Survey, 1990.* Washington, D.C.: Urban Institute Press, 1991.

Kagan, S. L. *Excellence in Early Childhood Education: Defining Characteristics and Next-Decade Strategies.* Washington, D.C.: Office of Educational Research and Improvement Policy Perspectives, 1990.

Kagan, S. L. *United We Stand. Collaboration for Child Care and Early Education Services.* New York: Teachers College Press, 1991.

Keynes, J. M. *The General Theory of Employment, Interest, and Money.* Orlando, Fla.: Harcourt Brace Jovanovich, 1936.

McKey, R. H., and others. *Final Report. The Impact of Head Start on Children, Families, and Communities: The Head Start Synthesis Project.* Washington, D.C.: Department of Health and Human Services, 1985.

Marx, F., and Seligson, M. *The Public School Early Childhood Study. The State Survey.* New York: Bank Street College of Education, 1988.

Moore, E. K. "Child Care in the Public Schools: Public Accountability and the Black Child." In S. Kagan and E. Zigler (eds.), *Early Schooling: The National Debate.* New Haven, Conn.: Yale University Press, 1987.

Moore, M. T., Strang, E. W., Schwartz, M., and Braddock, M. *Patterns in Special Education Service Delivery and Cost.* Washington, D.C.: Decision Resource Corporation, 1988.

National Association for the Education of Young Children. "NAEYC—Our Organization, Present and Future: Issues for Discussion." *Young Children,* 1992, *47*(4), 69–71.

National Black Child Development Institute. *Excellence and Equity, Quality and Inequality: A Report on Civil Rights, Education and Black Children.* Washington, D.C.: National Black Child Development Institute, 1985.

Nelson, M. K. "Providing Family Day Care: An Analysis of Home-Based Work." *Social Problems,* 1988, *35*(1), 78–94.

O'Connor, S. M. "Rationales for the Institutionalization of Programs of Young Children." *American Journal of Education,* 1990, *98*(2), 114–145.

Phillips, D., and Zigler, E. "The Checkered History of Federal Child Care Regulation." In E. Z. Rothkopf (ed.), *Review of Research in Education,* no. 14. Washington, D.C.: American Educational Research Association, 1987.

Robbins, P. K. "Federal Financing of Child Care: Alternative Approaches and Economic Implications." *Population Research and Policy Review,* 1990, *9*(1), 65–90.

Rose-Ackerman, S. "Unintended Consequences: Regulating the Quality of Subsidized Day Care." *Journal of Policy Analysis and Management,* 1983, *3*(1), 14–30.

Sandfort, J. Unpublished data. Washington, D.C.: Children's Defense Fund, 1992.

Schweinhart, L. J. "Early Childhood Development Programs in the Eighties: The National Picture." High/Scope Early Childhood Policy Papers, no. 1, Ypsilanti, Mich., 1985.

Schweinhart, L. J., and Mazur, E. "Prekindergarten Programs in Urban Schools." High/Scope Early Childhood Policy Papers, no. 6, Ypsilanti, Mich., 1987.

Starr, P. *The Social Transformation of American Medicine.* New York: Basic Books, 1982.

Sugarman, J. L., and Sullivan, C. J. *The Future of Child Care and Development: A Prospectus Prepared for the Child Care Action Campaign.* New York: Child Care Action Campaign, 1992.

Turnbull, A. P. "Preschool Mainstreaming: A Policy and Implementation Analysis." *Educational Evaluation and Policy Analysis,* 1982, *4*(3), 281–291.

U.S. Bureau of the Census. *Statistical Abstract of the United States: 1980.* (100th ed.) Washington, D.C.: Department of Commerce, 1980.

U.S. General Accounting Office. *Child Care Government Funding Sources, Coordination and Service Availability.* Briefing report to the chairman, Subcommittee on Human Resources, Committee on Education and Labor, House of Representatives. Washington, D.C.: U.S. General Accounting Office, 1989.

U.S. General Accounting Office. "Early Childhood Education. What Are the Costs of High Quality Programs?" Briefing report to the chairman, Committee on Labor and Human Resources, U.S. Senate. Washington, D.C.: U.S. General Accounting Office, 1990.

West, J., Hausken, E., Chandler, K. A., and Collins, M. "Experiences in Child Care and Early Childhood Programs of First and Second Graders Prior to Entering First Grade: Findings from the 1991 National Household Survey." *Statistics in Brief.* Washington, D.C.: National Center for Education Statistics, 1991.

Willer, B. "Estimating the Full Cost of Quality." In B. Willer (ed.), *Reaching the Full Cost of Quality in Early Childhood Programs.* Washington, D.C.: National Association for the Education of Young Children, 1990.

Willer, B., and others. *The Demand and Supply of Child Care in 1990. Joint Findings from the National Child Care Survey 1990 and a Profile of Child Care Settings.* Washington, D.C.: National Association for the Education of Young Children, 1991.

Wolf, C. *Markets or Governments. Choosing Between Imperfect Alternatives.* Cambridge, Mass.: MIT Press, 1991.

Wrigley, J. "Different Care for Different Kids: Social Class and Child Care Policy." In L. Weiss, P. G. Altbach, G. P. Kelly, and H. G. Petrie (eds.), *Critical Perspectives on Early Childhood Education.* Albany: State University of New York Press, 1991.

Wycoff, P. G. "The Elusive Flypaper Effect." *Journal of Urban Economics,* 1991, *30*(3), 310–328.

Zigler, E. F. "Addressing the Nation's Child Care Crisis: The

School of the Twenty-First Century." *American Journal of Or-thopsychiatry,* 1989, *59,* 484–491.

Zigler, E. F., and Lang, M. E. *Child Care Choices. Balancing the Needs of Children, Families, and Society.* New York: Free Press, 1991.

Zimmerman, D. "Nonprofit Organizations, Social Benefits, and Tax Policy." *National Tax Journal,* 1991, *44*(3), 341–349.

7

How the World of Students and Teachers Challenges Policy Coherence

Milbrey W. McLaughlin, Joan E. Talbert

Introduction: Students as Contexts of Teaching

Policymakers, concerned citizens, and critics of the public education system worry about American students' academic performance. They fear that poorly prepared students will cause the nation to lose its competitive position in global markets and that, at home, disappointing school careers will block youth from productive futures as citizens, workers, and parents. These conversations, taking place in such disparate settings as state capitals, district offices, grocery stores, corporate boardrooms, and living rooms tend to the bottom line and construe students as "outputs," products of America's schools and classrooms.

Research for and preparation of this chapter was supported by funding from the U.S. Department of Education, Office of Educational Research and Improvement, to the Consortium for Policy Research in Education (CPRE) and to the Center for Research on the Context of Secondary School Teaching (CRC). Our thanks to Ann Locke Davidson for her thoughtful comments on an earlier draft and to Juliann Cummer for her assistance with manuscript preparation.

    The research upon which this chapter draws involves three years of field work and surveys in sixteen public and private secondary schools located in eight different communities and two states. The CRC sample includes diverse secondary schools — magnet schools, small public high schools, elite independent schools, alternative schools, large comprehensive high schools — located in urban and suburban communities. The student populations of the schools ranged from predominately middle- and upper-middle-class white students to "majority minority" schools that serve both neighborhood youngsters and students participating in desegregation plans.

Teachers' talk about students differs markedly from these bottom-line discussions. Teachers' perspectives and concerns about students center on students as "inputs," as the context for teaching and learning. The students who enter their classrooms bring with them attitudes, abilities, backgrounds, assumptions, life circumstances, and perspectives that matter fundamentally to how teachers conceive their professional tasks and how they go about the business of teaching.

This teacher perspective of students as "context" has not received a great deal of attention in the literature on teaching or educational research on schools and instruction. In process-product models of teaching and input-output models of school effects, students are conceived as the objects of educational "treatments," rather than as contexts that shape teaching practice and school organization.

This distinction between student as product and student as context of teaching matters enormously to our understanding of classrooms. Viewing the student as product directs attention to how students perform and away from what teachers do in response to the attitudes, behavior, competencies, and circumstances that students bring with them to the classroom.

By teachers' report, students constitute the most salient aspect of their workplace. Student factors frame teachers' work, their conceptions of teaching and learning, and so in turn influence fundamentally student outcomes. But our several years of observation and interviews in diverse secondary school settings show that teachers' thoughts about, and responses to, the young people sitting in their classrooms encompass two importantly different phenomena.

One facet of teachers' views about their students has to do with the *objective* reality of student factors. Factors such as language and culture, racial background, parents' economic and educational resources and other family circumstances, and academic ability and background present particular demands on teachers' instructional choices and classroom strategies. Students who come to class with scant proficiency in English, for example, present constraints and challenges to high school teachers radically different from those presented by their native-born peers reading and writing English at or beyond grade level.

Students whose parents follow carefully their progress in school bring resources to the classroom that are missing for their peers from zero-parent families or for those whose parents are indifferent or uninvolved in their education. These differences in the objective realities of students' backgrounds and life circumstances have implications for their educational needs.

A second aspect of teachers' perspectives on students has to do with the meaning of these objective facts, or the *subjective* reality they comprise for teachers. Most particularly, while the so-called "traditional student"—a white youngster from a middle-class family with conventional aspirations for college and career—is seen similarly by many teachers, nontraditional students—young people from ethnic or racial minority cultures, from dysfunctional or nontraditional families, from disintegrating and often violent neighborhoods; young people living in peer cultures surrounded by substance abuse, early and unprotected sex, dangerous or illegal peer activities—are seen differently.

An important observation of our center's research in diverse school settings is that a school-is-not-a-school-is-not-a-school, from the students' vantage point (Davidson, 1992; Phelan, Davidson, and Cao, 1992). Even the microclimates of departments within schools represent significantly different educational environments and support substantially different educational experiences and outcomes for students who, objectively, are similar (Siskin, 1992). Our data suggest that this is because teachers' subjective perception of today's students, of nontraditional students, varies enormously on such critical dimensions as assumptions about academic abilities and interests, possible futures, and quality as a learner. Teachers offer strategically different explanations for their students' uneven attendance, short attention spans, low levels of academic engagement or achievement, undone homework, or basic skills deficiencies.

These subjective constructions of students matter enormously to students, because they influence the ways in which teachers structure their pedagogy and curriculum. Bluntly put, some teachers see nontraditional students as drains on the system, not worthy of time, attention, or respect; still others see them as people of value and endeavor to understand and meet their needs. Yet a third group recognizes the strengths that others fail to see and builds on them.

In short, the student "outcomes" or the bottom line of such concern to policymakers and the public turns to a significant degree on how the word "student" is construed and constructed in contemporary schools and classrooms. Teachers' subjective interpretations of students' objective circumstances turns to a significant degree on the norms, values, and character of the up-close school-level or department community to which they belong.

This chapter takes up the question of students as context for what happens in school, and the ways in which educators' subjective interpretations of the realities students bring with them to school influence every aspect of the school environment. We focus on nontraditional students, because we believe these contemporary students present an immediate and unmet challenge and underused resource for the public schools. Further, we believe that the experiences of contemporary students highlight the significance for teaching and learning of features that have long characterized the nation's schools. The press of today's students on the system simply amplifies these features and their consequences for students.

First, we describe the *objective* conditions of today's students that have an impact on the school and classroom. We then illustrate the diverse *subjective* interpretations teachers can construct of these student features, particularly their academic strengths and weaknesses. Using interviews and observations, we show how teachers working in different settings view the same student in dramatically different ways and so construct fundamentally different conceptions of similar students as learners and as possible selves in the classroom.

Finally, we argue that these different constructions of "student" have little to do with different formal aspects of the school and much to do with the character of the professional community that defines the school (or department) culture. These different constructions by teachers within and between schools ultimately challenge the coherence of education policy in terms of its expected or hoped-for consequences for students. Similar policies, or bundles of policies, will affect students differently depending on the contexts in which they are interpreted and carried out.

Contemporary Students: Objective Realities

Teachers agree not only that students are the context of greatest salience but that the ways in which today's students differ from traditional (and some would say idealized) students of the past, and often not-so-distant-past, leaves them feeling ill prepared and uncertain about how to proceed in their classrooms and leads them to question their professional efficacy with contemporary students. Hardly an aspect of school setting, rhythm, or activities remains untouched by the changed realities of today's students.

Across our secondary school sites, veteran teachers comment that the students they teach today differ in important ways from the students of twenty, fifteen, or even five years ago. Today's students bring different cultures and languages to school, bring different attitudes and supports to the classroom, and are required to navigate competing pressures of family, peers, and community at the same time they function as students (Phelan, Davidson, and Cao, 1992).

The first thing teachers mention is the negative consequences of *changed family structure*. A Michigan teacher believes that "the biggest change [in today's students] is that there is a lot less support from home . . . not just here but across the country . . . a lot of kids have very little support at home, a lot of single parents . . . we have a lot of kids who don't even live at home . . . the biggest change is in family structure . . . these kids just don't have the things [in terms of family supports] the kids used to have." A California social studies teacher advises: "You gotta be sensitive to changes in society, and how they're affecting kids, you know, what they're coming into. For example, I never say 'Well, tell your parents' anymore because when you say 'parents' you've closed down 75 percent of these kids. If they like you and respect your opinion, it makes them feel like 'God, I'd better not tell him I live with my auntie, or a single parent, or someone else.' A lot of people aren't aware of it."

Public school teachers feel the dysfunctional consequences of today's changed family structures most acutely. Home life, according to many public school teachers, is the crux of the difficulties they encounter. Teachers tell of neglect, abuse, violence, and tragedy as daily events in the lives of many of their students. In the course of our field work, we heard from students about molestation, murder, drug and alcohol addiction, violence, economic stress, serious illness, suicides, and physical neglect — life circumstances with which their teachers had little or no experience and about which they usually had little knowledge. But these worries, pressures, and pain came to school and competed with teachers' efforts to engage, motivate, and teach.

Concern about *parental attitudes and lack of support* appears as another, related issue for many of today's students. Parents besieged by any number of the pressures experienced by today's families — unstable domestic situations, inadequate income, bleak job prospects, lack of support for child rearing, joblessness, homelessness — have little time or energy or sometimes taste for involvement in their youngsters' school life. Issues of cultural difference or conceptions of "establishment" power also inhibit parental involvement (Fine, 1991). In addition, parental attitudes about school frustrate many teachers. A math teacher deeply committed to her nontraditional students told us: "Parents fight us too on homework and spending time on school. For example, one father came to a back-to-school night and said, 'Is it just because all of these kids are so dumb that they get homework on weekends; is it just because you are mean you make them work on weekends?' The attitude that we have weekends off, we don't think on weekends, means that the weekend begins on Thursday, because half of them don't come on Fridays. So it is more than just an uphill climb."

Parents who themselves are alienated from school or other mainstream institutions can provide little of the support that teachers expect from traditional families. A biology teacher frustrated over her inability to make contact with parents — unreturned phone calls, unanswered notes, missed conferences — feels she is alone in her attempts to work with many students. Or that even when she is able to reach someone at home, support is not available: "A lot of times I contact the home and the home is completely apathetic or unable, dysfunctionally unable, to intervene [or provide support]."

Lack of parental involvement in homework, school affairs, or, more generally, the high school careers of their children shows up in undone homework, apathy about school, and insufficient support for student efforts, teachers say. Students from families with limited or no English-speaking adults face additional challenges. "The girl you just saw? She's like most of the kids in my [science] class [in terms of parental support]. She is getting a low grade and she is concerned. And she felt like nobody cared what she got anymore. She went on and on, using bad language about her father—something is wrong there. And her mom used to help her [before they immigrated], but can't anymore, because she really doesn't speak English. She feels all alone."

Relations with parents of contemporary students differ for other reasons from those many secondary school teachers have experienced in the past. For some parent groups, especially newly arrived Asian immigrants, "going to school" falls out of the bounds of cultural appropriateness. These parents decline to involve themselves in their children's educational affairs, or in traditional school-parent interchanges, not because of lack of concern and support for school but because of cultural norms. The consequence of the changed parent-school relations associated with contemporary students, teachers observe, is erosion of the kind of parent spirit and participation seen in the past.

Policies that bring students to the school campus affect the nature of students', as well as parents', participation in the school community. Schools whose students ride buses across town as part of an effort to integrate the district's schools find that the "tyranny of the bus schedule" erodes the community built by participation in extracurricular events. Neither students nor their parents travel across town to attend evening or weekend events; students tied to bus schedules (which become increasingly tight as district budgets shrink) find it difficult if not impossible to stay after school for practices or activities. Sports teams, performing arts groups, and music ensembles are affected by students' interests and talents, but also by the bus schedules and difficulty of engaging in extracurricular affairs. The discouraged head of a music department remarked that his program essentially had collapsed with the student transportation problems associated with desegregation; students could not come to practices and their parents did not come to performances. The drama chair in another school told the same story. This fracturing of school community was evident to teachers in all CRC sites where students were drawn districtwide, rather than from a neighborhood community. Busing schedules also make it difficult for students most in need of extra attention to stay after school, or to come early, for tutoring sessions.

Family mobility and student transience present serious problems for today's youth and their teachers. Children of both affluent and poor families are affected by the high levels of mobility typical in American society. A teacher in a Michigan school particularly troubled by high student mobility commented that some of the seats in his classroom had been occupied by three different students over a two-week period. Another stressed the frustration of this lack of stability in a class: "You know, you just pass out a book and get this kid started, and two days later this one is gone and another comes in and says 'where are we?' . . . you just can't ever catch up with all of them."

Student transiency related to poor attendance is a "student problem" raised most frequently (and most passionately) by public school teachers. Teachers in all public CRC secondary schools report that "attendance is horrendous." The frustration of a Michigan English teacher about failed lesson plans and incomplete work captures the sentiments we heard from teachers in all our sites: "No one yet has figured out how do a process [of developing a writing project for publication] with kids who are here for a day or two and then gone for a day or two . . . it is difficult in all literature classes to teach kids who are just not here."

A California science teacher, exhausted by her efforts to keep all her students on track, describes how absenteeism exponentially increases her work load:

So part of the load is just the course itself. . . . If all I had to do was to teach a course to students who were here every day, I would be very busy. And on top of that is student absenteeism, and then there are students who are present who need a lot of special attention. What happens if a student misses the first few assignments? I try to remind them whenever I can — lots of notes, every night I am writing little Post-its to remind students, and you just keep at it. And those things take an awful lot of time. I mean if all I had to do was keep up with day-to-day stuff that would be plenty, but I've got a student working on stuff from two months ago, and other students from several weeks ago, and other students . . . and they're all in different stages. So that absenteeism has been a horrible drain.

Teachers also point to ways in which the *academic backgrounds and skills* of today's students differ importantly from those of students in the past. A uniform complaint about today's adolescents, especially among public school teachers, was decline in taste for or skill in reading. Students in high school today typically spend little time with books and have little interest in reading. Teachers report that this feature of today's student shows up in the weak general knowledge students bring to class as well as their unwillingness or inability to read difficult (or lengthy) texts. Furthermore, a number of teachers agree with this math teacher's complaint: "Too many students today just don't like to think."

Significant shifts in *student demographics and language backgrounds,* particularly in California and other border states, present significant challenges for secondary school teachers. Today's classrooms are occupied by students with diverse cultural backgrounds and language skills in both first language and English, and in many schools, demographic changes in student body composition have been swift. Faculty at one of our sites have in little more than two years seen their student body change from predominately white, middle class to a student population in which approximately one-third have only limited English proficiency and close to one-half come from poor families.

Students with limited or no proficiency in English have problems with reading and writing of a different kind than do mainstream students with low reading achievement. And many schools and classrooms contain students from a wide diversity of language origins. Further, limited English proficient (LEP) students from the same language background can and do differ radically from one another in skills in their native language and in academics. California teachers in our study are overwhelmed by the cultures and languages that fill their classrooms, swift changes for which they have not been prepared. One teacher estimated that in her district (Mostaza) in 1990, one out of four students were LEP; projections for the year 2000 bring that ratio to one in two students enrolled in the district's schools. These fundamental shifts in student demographics occurred with breathtaking speed and require significant shifts in curricula. She observes: "The change has been phenomenal. Five years ago we were not under court order. Five years ago, we were 6 to 8 percent minority. Today we are about 56 percent nonwhite, so it is a significant change and it has been rapid. . . . In each of the two classes you observed, there are probably five — no, more like ten — who don't speak English. It used to be that you'd teach advanced mathematics courses because nearly everybody was going to college. Now it is much more basic."

Further, teachers comment that students often "pass out" of bilingual or sheltered English classes before they are competent to handle regular classroom demands. One science teacher remarks: "The two physiology classes are the only ones I have in which students can read or write. In my two regular biology classes, nobody speaks English. There are about ten different languages in those classes." A biology teacher in another California school notes (pointing to students in the classroom): "Now those kids really have no grasp of the English language; they really don't. But they are high enough so they pass the test [to move from sheltered classes]. But what do you do with them when they don't know English? Or like Juan there: he's an 11th grader, but he can't read. This [biology] text is written at about a 7th grade level. These students do not understand this textbook; they do not understand it. Their reading level is awful and their vocabulary . . . "

The school climate also responds to increased cultural diversity among students, and to a different sense of "we-ness" among students and faculty: different values, expectations, and perspectives. Schools respond differently to today's heterogeneous student body, as we will discuss below. But regardless of that response, the nature of today's campus community for many secondary schools differs dramatically from that of even the recent past in terms of the cultures, languages, ambitions, and expectations of the student body. Diversity sometimes brings contention among student groups, even in the most supportive campuses. A social studies teacher in a school noted for attention to ethnic diversity says: "There is a growing trend here at school. It's a militancy among students of color, and I just fear the backlash. A lot of white kids, kids of European ancestry, are afraid to speak up, because they feel they are going to get some kind of verbal or physical backlash."

Dysfunctional student behaviors and activities trouble teachers in all our secondary school sites. Involvement with drugs and gang violence prematurely end the high school careers of many youngsters, especially youth from lower-income, urban neighborhoods. In every school, teachers comment on the increasing number of teen pregnancies and the students they lose either figuratively or literally as a result. A government teacher complained that it is hard to stand up and talk about the Soviet Union "when you have five young ladies who are concerned about who is babysitting. It is difficult to get through about social concerns because they have so many themselves."

Sometimes the safety of the campus changes also, for the worse: "We're having problems here we have never had before. In the past two weeks, there has been a stabbing and a shooting on campus. One of my kids was shot yesterday by a pellet gun . . . it's getting to be like an inner-city situation."

An English teacher's dramatic recital of her students' personal problems represents student realities we heard about in many classrooms. "We have a number of students who have emotional problems. Linda has a history of being involved in gang violence. We just recently finished a case of child abuse where one of my students was placed in a foster home after being sexually molested by two older brothers. You may have noticed the kid who is small and has difficulty socializing. He witnessed the murder of his father by his brother. He sits at his desk all hunched into himself. I marked him absent for two weeks straight because he hunches at desk level and I could not see this kid."

Other factors compete with academics. Many lower-income youngsters, especially females, are unable to spend time on schoolwork because of heavy family responsibilities. Jobs take the attention and energy from students of all SES backgrounds, but most especially the less advantaged teen. A math teacher comments: "There seems to be a general decline every year in the level at which students are functioning. [But what do you expect] when you have students walking in [who] are just totally exhausted because they're working all weekend, or they have worked the night before until 10 or 11 o'clock at night . . . students that are putting in thirty hours a week just on their work. School takes a back seat real quick."

Contemporary Students: Subjective Constructions

Teachers' reactions to these difficult classroom conditions differ in ways that matter a great deal to students and to their chances for educational success. The following chorus of teachers' voices captures some of this diversity.

> The kid here is where the problem is today. There's nothing wrong with the curriculum. . . . If I could just get people that wanted to learn, I could teach and everything would be wonderful.

> These kids are just not real smart, a lot of them. And they don't really want to learn. They could care less about school; they're just putting in time.

These are kids here who really do want to do a good job, but they have seen so much and heard so much, that it is like they don't know what is right and what is wrong anymore. That perspective is gone. But they are basically really good kids.

My guys. They're very, very brave kids. They are trying to make it, and it is really difficult for them.

A lot of the reason these kids are poor achievers is not what a lot of educators say. They are not dumb or turned off or screw-ups. Mainly it is behavior problems, and they have poor study habits, they have poor or counterproductive support at home, lots of times. They bring all of those problems into the classroom and you lose a lot of study and teaching time.

Our interviews with a sample of students and their teachers and our observations of their classes provide numerous examples of teachers constructing different conceptions of a student, and of the frustration students experience in many classrooms. The teachers quoted above refer to the same youngsters, in terms of their objective characteristics — ethnic or racial background, socioeconomic status (SES), family background, and the like. Yet their interpretations of students' behavior and performance, their construction of "student," varies profoundly. Some teachers see today's students as lazy, unmotivated, academically untalented. Other teachers perceive contemporary students as different from traditional students but nonetheless "good kids," interested in learning and able to learn.

These teachers reach different assessments and frame different expectations for *figuratively* the same students, but we also found that different teachers construct different conceptions of *literally* the same student. Take the case of Johnnie Betts, an African-American freshman, a six-foot, barrel-chested young man (Davidson, 1992). His teachers see him in very different terms. Johnnie's English teacher says: "Johnnie first of all does not belong in a progress (remedial) class. He's too bright, as far as I'm concerned. Anyone who performs consistently this well . . . he's consistently way above or at where he should be. . . . " But Johnnie's social studies teacher says, "He is overachieving in here. I don't think he is tremendously bright. I think he should probably — I think if he ever goes into a regular class he will have problems. He is a street smart kid, an [illiterate student] who will do whatever it takes to get the job done." Observations of Johnnie in the English class showed a bright, engaged student, who readily offered verbal definitions for words, identified authors' use of similes, volunteered to read. In social studies, Johnnie sat quietly and offered little.

Across and within our school sites, we saw that students with similar characteristics, students who represented essentially identical "contexts" for teaching, experienced significantly different school or classroom environments as a consequence of these different teacher interpretations of them as student and learner.

Some teachers say: "These kids are stupid." "They can't do the work; they are troublemakers." "These kids don't care a damn about school." "They are animals." Other teachers say: "These kids are really bright, good people." "Once they feel comfortable, it's fun to see them get engaged and turned on." "I really enjoy these students because of their integrity, their honesty." "These kids [the students assigned to basic or low-track classes] aren't stupid. In fact, they are the best question askers and problem solvers of all of my students, even those in the AP class. Asking good questions and solving problems, after all, is the only way they can survive." These teachers acknowledge the social pathologies of neglect, abuse, disappearing community and family that affect their students in the classroom and try to understand their students' attitudes and behaviors in that context.

Responses to Today's Challenges

Among the schools in the CRC sample, teachers have thus responded to the demands and challenges of today's students in various ways. Some have given up, electing on-the-job retirement, and expect little from the students whose attitudes, behavior, or academic skills differ from the students they "used to have." Others have worked to maintain traditional standards and expectations. Still others have changed expectations or practices.

Many of the teachers who have given up or who try to find ways to continue traditional practices see the behavioral and attitudinal problems evident in their classrooms primarily as the students' problems, exacerbated by inadequate school or district discipline or "standards." Teachers who view today's classrooms this way frame solutions in terms of tougher rules and enforcement, rather than adaptation of their own practices or task conception. For example, a California math teacher with more than thirty years' experience believes "the kid here is where the problem is today. There is nothing wrong with the curriculum." The appropriate response in the mind of this teacher is "to kick butt and take names . . . be like a drill sergeant in the Marine Corps . . . the first guy that gets out of line . . . just give him the bum's rush right out the door."

Likewise, a Michigan physics teacher believes that the problems in the classroom result from "a lack of discipline overall, throughout the school, throughout the district. . . . Educators ought to start exercising control of the situation more. . . . These kids are hurting our programs because of their behavior, attendance, tardies. . . . [I think] we should make an example out of those 50 kids so that the other 1,050 will understand that we mean business . . . that we have some rules and we are going to follow them. Basically . . . those kids don't fit into what we are trying to do and we don't have the time, the energy, or the money to change our program to suit them. . . . Let's not sacrifice everyone, let's use that little group as an example."

Other teachers see the problem as one of lack of fit between traditional practices and the students they serve today. But beyond this general diagnosis, interpretations and responses differ in critical ways. A few teachers adopting this perspective believe that many of today's students "just can't cut it" and so lower standards, countenance missing homework and classroom inattention, and feel there is "just so much a teacher can do for these students." As a result, the academic value and content of these teachers' classrooms is diminished significantly for students, and these teachers often express cynicism about the efficacy of teaching for "those kids" and disengage themselves as their teaching becomes less satisfying. Students, too, find such classrooms boring. A teacher shared one student's perspective on the question of content and challenge: "Kids want to be challenged. A kid told me yesterday, 'I want to be here [in this college prep class]. I would rather learn something and fail this class than be in a regular class again. I'm sorry, but I will drop out of school if I am in a regular class again.'"

Other teachers cut back on instructional content and the work they expect of their students in an effort to boost classroom accomplishments. In particular, some teachers have given up on homework and focus on accomplishing the important things during classtime. For example, an English teacher in Michigan completely rethought her instructional strategy when the students in her classroom were failing: "I was looking over all their failures; it was no homework, no homework, no homework. So I found a book of plays and we started reading plays in classes . . . got them more involved, participating. I tried to keep written work to a minimum. . . . I am really pleased with the results."

Often, this retreat from standards and traditional academic quality signifies a well-meaning attempt to structure a classroom environment that today's students will find engaging and nonthreatening. However, we saw that in a few cases this retreat unfortunately signaled disrespect or disdain for the students themselves. For example, a California teacher formerly assigned to honors classes and now teaching lower-level sections certainly saw things this way as he talked about how the "lesser" students would be less work for him.

However, still other teachers who share the "lack of fit" diagnosis frame adaptation to these "new" students not as "less" traditional activities but as simply different: instructional content and pedagogy keyed to conventional standards and expectations but rethought in terms of the needs and motivations of today's students. Teachers adopting this conception of the problem and of their task have made fundamental adaptations in what and how they teach and in the structure of the classroom.

For instance, many teachers frustrated by student absenteeism believe that an effective response lies not in rules and stiff enforcement but in school and classroom strategies that minimize the disruption and time demands generated by a high level of absenteeism. One teacher says she has learned to put "all of the lessons on the board [so] whoever decides to show up will know where we are." One school has set up study tables and a peer tutoring program that is available anytime in the day or evening to help students make up missed assignments, and teachers send notices of daily assignments to this central "clearinghouse."

Many teachers attempting to construct different practices believe that today's students require a high level of individualization: "You need to write out notes that Eric needs to do this today, and Scott should be sitting by himself on such and such a chapter, and we need to help Marianne with the research chapter, and . . ."

A number of teachers have found success with cooperative learning strategies as ways both to attend to individual student needs and to keep the class on track. A mathematics teacher, who commented she would have never believed she would move from conventional teacher-controlled pedagogy, uses small groups and encourages students to help each other: "I really don't care how they learn it as long as they learn it. I encourage them to work together; I encourage them to talk to other people when they have older brothers and sisters and boyfriends and girlfriends. I don't care. The object is to learn. If someone can get it across better than I can, fine."

Teachers successful in engaging contemporary students in academic work also report rethinking conceptions of subject matter — moving from a canonical view of their subject and its knowledge base to broader objectives for learning in English or mathematics or social studies. For example, an English teacher, a veteran of Advanced Placement courses and a Shakespeare buff, outlines her perspective on the value of English for her nontraditional students.

> So, I see my job as really one of the basic levels
> of communication, the correctness of that commu-

nication, and hopefully I am able to instill in them enough experiences that they're able to come up with their ideas . . . give them enough literature that they're able to generate their own ideas in terms of reactions to that literature. And then, hopefully, along the line I can teach them to express those ideas correctly; so that when they get to expressing the ideas, it's done. They are indeed actually express-ing what they are thinking and able to use language for their own benefit, rather than being used by literature and by the language itself . . . not becom-ing a victim to the language. I think my kids feel comfortable enough to speak out and give their opinions.

This conception of English literature as communication, as opposed to English literature as command of Shakespeare, enables flexible response to students' skills levels and interests. It highlights the value of students' views and opinions and stands in contrast to traditional classrooms where mastery of facts define objectives and students' opinions count for little. For example, an English teacher in another setting told her class: "Right now you can't give opinions. I noticed you, Andrea, and others have a tendency to answer questions based on what you believe. It's a problem. They don't give a damn about what you think on the Citywides and other tests" (Fine, 1991, p. 38).

A common theme among teachers attempting to revise their classroom practices in light of the needs and realities of contemporary students is the need for personalization—of see-ing students as people and of letting students see teachers as human beings (McLaughlin and Talbert, 1990; Phelan, David-son, and Cao, 1992). An English teacher whose traditionally low-achieving students produce poetry, literary analyses, and telling essays says: "I may get a little crazy and silly, I guess, in my classes, but it's not without purpose. Because I think that if they can see me as a human being who's not different than they are, then maybe they can also see that what I am saying and what I'm giving them in literature and writing is not really all that different from what they should be doing. I think it is real important for them to see that literature doesn't have to be a foreign language."

A mathematics teacher whose low-track prealgebra class is able to construct quadratic equations says, "I think the whole name of the game is getting the kids on your side. To know them and to let them know that you care about what they're doing and that they're not just another body in the seat. That they have their own personality."

A social studies teacher points to the need to find out about possible causes for the negative behaviors and attitudes that students bring to class, and not "punish the victim." "If I see a kid not developing, I'll get to him and try to find out what's going on. And you might find out that, hey, the kid goes home and gets beaten every night, or that there might not be enough to eat. The point is that because of his environment, he comes to school less equipped than other kids. So should I put him down or call him a failure?"

Teachers successful at engaging contemporary youth in learning and academics also agree that the first step to developing effective classrooms for today's students is throwing out traditional practices:

> From the days I went to college, I mean you sit down, you read the book, you do the problems, and you start all over again. I — you know, I was able to do that and to do it successfully. But I don't think that's the way to teach [contemporary students]. And I don't think that is the way to inspire love of learning. As time goes by, I have much more tolerance for a lot of things [in my classroom] . . . for the freedom to be what you are, for the [personal] problems to be what they are. I can accept it and work with it. So it's kind of a, more of an approach to liv[ing] than to mathematics, but it works for math.

A social studies teacher successful with nontraditional students says: "Those people [teachers unsuccessful with contemporary students], they continue to teach in a traditional way. I think they're running head on into a student who is not like the student they taught back in the 60s or 70s or even the 80s. It's a different generation of Americans now, and they are products of the 80s. So we have to deal with them [in different ways]."

Using the example of a former gang member, an angry African American now doing B work in his college preparatory history course, this teacher underscores the importance of changing practices to better match students' motivation. "In a traditional classroom, I don't think he'd be very successful, because different things motivate him. I look at his report card and I see that teachers who have my style, he does well in. Other teachers who say 'answer the questions, do the worksheet, dadada,' he doesn't do well in."

Contrast this perspective with that of a biology teacher, frustrated with his inability to motivate or engage his class made up of students similar to the student described above. "[What kinds of things do you think work with these kids?] Paper-pencil work. Paper-pencil work. That way you just kind of keep on top of them all of the time."

Teachers also underscore the need to rethink traditional classroom management strategies in terms of effective responses to today's students. "Teachers [who are unsuccessful with contemporary students] come in and they try to lecture for fifty-five minutes to kids whose attention span might be ten. And, the other thing is that philosophy that a noisy classroom is an unproductive classroom. [But you've got to create a different kind of classroom for these kids. They resent traditional teacher-authority stuff.] You know, it's an evolution. It was an evolution for me. A lot of it is letting control go, you know, the control factor. You know, wanting kids to sit-in-their-seats-with-their-feet-on-the-ground, hands-on-the-table type mentality. No way."

Teachers' responses based on these constructions of the abilities and value of their students engender dramatically different outcomes for students. Not only is students' success or failure affected by teachers' classroom choices, the students also take away fundamentally different conceptions of themselves as learners, and of their possible futures. Our interviews with students, particularly those of different racial and ethnic backgrounds, reflect that they feel misunderstood, ignored, unvalued, invisible. A high-achieving Latina, angry about what she sees as prejudice toward Mexican students and lack of attention to their success, told us: "I think my teachers should learn another method of teaching, because the one they use is not very effective. I also would like them to realize we are intelligent, that we can do things, would like them not to discriminate against us, treat us like civilized persons, not like some sort of objects. Also I would like them to give us work and to explain how to do that work well" (Davidson, 1992).

Chester Finn (1987) asserts that students drop out by choice, and that the decision is a rational one. Although it is true that many adolescents elect to leave high school, for many of these youngsters, elements of this "choice" lie in these subjective responses of their teachers to them, their future goals, and their roles as "students." Many of the students failing in traditional classrooms where "standards" are rigidly maintained, bored in "dumbed-down" classrooms, or encountering failure after failure drop out because they see no respect or no future for themselves in the environment. Many of the teachers with whom we spoke were sensitive to the demeaning or nonsupportive messages many contemporary students receive in the school setting.

An English teacher in a school still responding to sudden and dramatic changes in the composition of the student body remarks:

> I am polite to my students. I am respectful of them.
> I think that's important because if I want them to
> be respectful to me, I need to show them how to
> do it. You know, I hear teachers talking in the
> faculty room about "students don't show any re-
> spect, these students are outrageous," going on and
> on about how disrespectful and rude, on and on
> about the kids. And then I turn right around and
> hear that teacher say something which either hu-
> miliates or puts down the student and I think,
> "What's the matter with you? Why don't you hear
> yourself? How can you turn around and say this

child is rude, and you turned around and were rude
to him?" To me it's just basic; it's the Golden Rule.

A science teacher in a comprehensive high school says, "A lot
of these kids, we don't realize that no one ever tells them they
are good, no one ever tells them. They hear all the time, they
hear when they screw up, they hear about it all the time. And
a lot of kids continue to screw up because that is the only kind
of attention they can get. There's no positive reinforcement."
A social studies teacher in a magnet school that enrolls students
from diverse cultures and a broad range of SES notes: "Sure
these kids have an 'attitude.' But maybe in the school years I
can turn it around, an attitude, and say, 'Yeah, you got a raw
deal, but you're still a good person and I value you. And I want
you to be part of my class. Because I am not evaluating you
based on the fact that you might be a battered child, or molested,
or whatever. That may be your evaluation of yourself, or you
may come in here with another set of expectations, but I know
you can do these things.' It takes a lot of energy."

Teachers such as those who speak on these pages also
recognize that what may appear to be poor performance, slow-
ness, or inability to catch on may actually be the manifestation
of many years of poor instruction and insufficient grounding
in basic skills. Teachers note that "the problems begin in the
elementary years, so that by the time they hit our doors, the
problems have accumulated." A math teacher stresses the extra
determination such youngsters need to succeed in high school.
"Their skills aren't as strong, so it's going to take them twice
as long to understand some of the algebra topic that we have,
and it's going to take them twice as much work, I think. And
so they are going to have to have even more desire to succeed.
It'll be tough. If they come in with a shaky foundation, I find
those students have the most trouble, because they are trying
to work with these abstract ideas, while they're also trying to
get the basics."

Teachers' interpretations of and responses to the objective behaviors, attitudes, and achievements of their students create dramatically different educational settings for students, from

classrooms alive with the energy of students and teachers and where students are valued and supported to classrooms where students are controlled through traditional strategies of discipline and punishment, or even criticism and sarcasm. At the extremes, today's students move from classrooms where hopes for a productive future are nurtured to classrooms where little is expected of them and failure is the norm.

Constraining Myths and Professional Community

What factors underlie these subjective responses to contemporary students? Many teachers' subjective responses to the objective realities of today's students are shaped by a number of constraining myths — half-truths or untruths that form responses to students and classroom choices. Five were prominent in our field work.

1. *These kids can't do it.* This myth is debilitating for both students and teachers — that the students who display little academic motivation or few abilities as conventionally conceived (the students who occupy the lower tracks in high schools) are incapable of higher-order thinking, or of critical thinking, or of conceptual understanding.
2. *The body of knowledge and skills my students must learn is relatively fixed.* Teachers holding canonical views of their subject matter perceive little significant flexibility in adapting their content or pedagogy to today's students. In this view, there is an agreed-on body of knowledge that must be conveyed to students; departure from this standard signifies lowering of standards or lesser classroom instruction.
3. *Rules and regulations get in the way.* Teachers who feel unsuccessful with contemporary students often hold bureaucracy as the villain and see rules and requirements as inhibiting their adaptations to the needs of today's students.
4. *Insufficient materials or resources are available.* Teachers often feel helpless in responding to the needs of contemporary students without special resources, such as bilingual materials or programs, which are in short supply in today's schools and classrooms.

5. *Either I write them off or burn out.* Teachers who attempt to develop effective strategies for working with today's students or for responding to their multiple and often difficult needs feel they are doing the best they can under the circumstances—that they cannot give any more. This myth is supported by evidence that some teachers become overwhelmed by students' needs; it serves as a rationale for writing off difficult students.

Teachers who subscribed to these views found it difficult if not impossible to imagine another "reality," anything different in terms of the life or the outcomes of their classrooms. Teachers defined their classroom expectations and practices in terms of these myths as objective facts rather than matters of perspective or interpretation.

Other teachers held different views about contemporary students, their subject areas, and their own abilities to respond effectively. Even teachers within the same secondary school setting differed in the extent to which these perceptions were held as valid and as guides to practice.

What made the difference? Across and within our sample of schools, the *character of teachers' professional community*—teachers' up-close workplace setting—had most to do with how teachers saw their students and constructed their role as teachers. The extent to which teachers subscribed to the constraining myths depended on two factors: the strength of their professional community and the extent to which their professional community reflected these beliefs, or challenged them.

Positive, supportive collegial relations play an acknowledged, important role in the Byzantine world of schools where teachers are segregated by assignment and by physical space. (See Little, 1982; Grant, 1988; Lieberman, 1990; Rosenholtz, 1989, as examples.) For most of the secondary schools we studied, the department was the professional community of greatest significance to teachers' norms of practice, conceptions of task, and attitudes about teaching and students (Siskin, 1990). Further, we saw that the character of departmental professional community varied significantly *within* the school. The substantial variation shown for departments on measures of collegiality means that teachers literally working across the hall from one another but in different departments may experience their workplace in critically different ways. For example, in one school teachers working in a highly collegial English department experience a workplace buzzing with daily conversations about joint projects, new materials to share, and plans for next week, next year, or tomorrow. Teachers in the social studies department, however, interact only in mandated department meetings, where they generally sit in sullen silence through the chair's announcements and pronouncements. So noncollegial is this department, faculty members have been unable to craft within a year a vision of instructional goals to guide the department's response to the new state frameworks. Such within-school differences in department culture and collegiality were evident in all but the mission schools in our sample.

Our 1991 survey data show that professional communities that are cohesive, highly collegial environments are also settings in which teachers report a high level of innovativeness, energy, enthusiasm, and support for personal growth and learning. Teachers who belong to communities of this sort also report a high level of commitment to teaching and to *all* of the students with whom they work.

These features characterize department communities (such as the English department described earlier) where teachers struggle collectively to examine their practices, to devise new ways of meeting today's students' needs and of supporting one another in efforts to change. Supportive collegial communities, committed to the success of all students, provide the necessary conditions to begin to mount collective challenge to constraining myths as explanations for unsuccessful student outcomes or disappointing classrooms.

In contrast to these collaborative communities of teacher-learners are settings where teachers report strong norms of privacy (and so low collegiality). In these workplace environments another sort of syndrome operates to reify and reinforce the constraining myths we have outlined. Teachers who characterize their workplace in terms of norms of privacy also say that they see their job as routine, their workplace setting as highly bureaucratized and rule bound. Teachers who belong to weak professional communities are more likely to see their subject matter as static or unchanging and so are unlikely to question the relevance of last year's lecture plans or the conceptions of knowledge or pedagogy learned years ago for today's students. These teachers are less likely to innovate, to report support for learning. They also are more likely to lower expectations for students, especially nontraditional students, and to report low levels of commitment to teaching.

The coexistence of opposing norms of practice and conceptions of students as learners within a single secondary school creates inconsistent support for students and sends conflicting messages about expectations and goals for the students' futures. Often it is the teacher who holds nontraditional students in the highest esteem and expects the most of them who struggles the most: "Nobody else around here believes in them, so when I hold them to high standards and expectations they feel picked on." A teacher who had worked to move a number of minority students into position for college-level classes said, "They felt I was being exceptionally hard on them. It became very personalized; it decimated the trust we had built." A teacher of a program designed to support the academic aspirations of minority youngsters angrily points out the multiple disadvantage this inconsistency creates for nontraditional students: "They're real special kids. They are going to go to college. But I think they've been cheated by the public schools because few of their teachers have ever felt they were worth it. They're going to go with maybe one year's worth of solid curriculum under their belts. They are going with the study skills they learned in the program, but for the most part they are terribly behind."

On the other hand, teachers in department communities with strong norms of privacy generally are unaware of supportive departments and proactive practice elsewhere in the school. They comment about the frustration of working in isolation. Comments about the frustrations of isolation were common in professional communities characterized by norms of privacy. Teachers expressed feelings of having to "do it all themselves" with no help or support from colleagues. A discouraged, experienced social studies teacher grappling with the demands of swift change in classroom demographics observed quietly: "Here you have to do it over and over again, by yourself, and you do it every day, forever. Why did I go into teaching? I don't know; not smart, I guess."

Teachers working in these sequestered and noncollegial settings receive neither challenges to their conceptions of practice and assumptions about students nor sufficient support for trying to do something different in response to today's students. They tend to stick with what they know, despite lack of student success or engagement and despite their own frustration and discouragement. These are the teachers who burn out, who believe teaching has become an impossible job, who wonder whether it is all worth it for today's students. Ironically, the absence of a strong, positive professional community has robbed many teachers of control.

Constraining myths steal teachers' autonomy as they locate control in the bureaucracy, in the canons of their subject matter, and in aspects of today's students. A strong professional community committed to creating effective educational environments for all students returns the control lost when teachers close their classroom doors to confront the realities of today's students alone. The costs of teachers' isolation in the past, when classrooms in most of America's secondary schools were composed of "traditional" students, appeared to be levied primarily on teachers (Lortie, 1975; Jackson, 1986). Today's classrooms show how real are the costs of teachers' professional seclusion for students.

Summary: Communities of Learners

Teachers say that contemporary students—the social values, shifts, dislocations, and changes they represent—present fundamental and difficult challenges to their practice, their conception of themselves as teachers, and their sense of professional reward and satisfaction. Today's teachers, for the most part, have not been trained to work with today's students. Teachers who feel little support for constructing new responses to students or for rethinking classroom routines from the perspectives of today's students, teachers who feel they are alone in their efforts to respond, are more likely to persist in orthodox conceptions of subject matter, to move toward reliance on control and authority as classroom strategies, and to view the "personal problems" of their students as outside their purview.

Teachers isolated in their classrooms not surprisingly feel disengaged, furious, resigned, and frustrated with their work. And in the schools we studied, collectives of teachers were the exception; individual teachers working hard (or just getting by) were the norm (see also Fine, 1991). Today's teachers are bombarded with demands. The pressures of meeting four or five classes of thirty students five times a week place a premium on just getting by, let alone trying to make some kind of personal connection with 150 youngsters, rethink curricula, experiment with classroom routines, learn more about the cultures and backgrounds of their diverse students, spend extra time with special needs students, or devise ways in which absent students can continue successfully in a class.

The challenges of contemporary students and contemporary school settings in fact represent more than most teachers can respond to effectively. That many (if not most) of the isolated teachers we encountered in the course of our field work sincerely could not imagine an alternative response to the objective demands of their students is not surprising.

Yet the significantly different interpretations of students' objective realities or circumstances associated with the strength and nature of teachers' professional community carry critically different consequences for students. We saw that not only do objectively similar students have significantly different classroom experiences and messages about self and future and support for development but conflicting messages and experiences envelop a single student as he or she moves through the day from classroom to classroom.

This subjective diversity in teachers' construction of "student" obviously affects the bottom line that most concerns policymakers and the public — students' academic performance and accomplishment. The moral dimension of these inconsistent subjective interpretations of "student" also cannot be ignored because of the different futures and assessments of worth they signal for students. Students make sense of themselves and consider their futures largely in the terms that others use to describe them. Many students blame themselves as inadequate and label themselves as failures because of differences in the messages and experiences provided in their school settings. "Objectification" of the "student problem" or the "student context" and educational responses constructed of subjective perceptions or constraints underestimate the abilities of both contemporary students and their teachers. Policy coherence as intended by reformers and policymakers ultimately is achieved or denied in the subjective responses of teachers — in teachers' social constructions of students.

References

Davidson, A. L. "The Politics and Aesthetics of Ethnicity: Making and Molding Identity in Varied Curricular Settings." Unpublished doctoral dissertation, Stanford University, Stanford, Calif., 1992.

Fine, M. *Framing Dropouts*. Albany: State University of New York Press, 1991.

Finn, C. E. "The High School Dropout Puzzle." *The Public Interest*, 1987, *87*, 3–22.

Grant, G. *Teaching Critical Thinking*. New York: Praeger, 1988.

Jackson, P. W. *The Practice of Teaching*. New York: Teachers College Press, 1986.

Lieberman, A. *Schools as Collaborative Cultures: Creating the Future Now*. Bristol, Pa.: Falmer Press, 1990.

Little, J. W. "Norms of Collegiality and Experimentation: Workplace Conditions of School Success." *American Educational Research Journal*, 1982, *19*, 325–340.

Lortie, D. C. *Schoolteacher: A Sociological Study*. Chicago: University of Chicago Press, 1975.

McLaughlin, M. W., and Talbert, J. E., with Kahne, J., and Powell, J. "Constructing a Personalized School Environment." *Phi Delta Kappan*, 1990, *72*(3), 230–235.

Phelan, P., Davidson, A. L., and Cao, H. T. "Speaking Up: Students' Perspectives on School." *Phi Delta Kappan,* 1992, *73*(9), 695–704.

Rosenholtz, S. J. *Teachers' Workplace: The Social Organization of Schools.* New York: Longman, 1989.

Siskin, L. *Different Worlds: The Department as Context for High School Teachers.* Stanford, Calif.: Center for Research on the Context of Secondary School Teaching, Stanford University, 1990.

Siskin, L. "Realms of Knowledge: Academic Departments in Secondary Schools." Unpublished doctoral dissertation, Stanford University, Stanford, Calif., 1992.

8

Systemic Reform and Educational Opportunity

Jennifer A. O'Day
Marshall S. Smith

Introduction: Context and Purposes

The concept of content-driven systemic school reform[1] has emerged over the past two years as a major policy alternative for education in the United States. It has appeared in federal legislation, as well as in procurements of the National Science Foundation and Department of Education, reports of national education councils and panels, and major documents of the National Governors' Association, the Business Roundtable, and the Council of Chief State School Officers. In addition, over half a dozen states are at various stages of implementing systemic reform strategies, while others are actively pursuing their development.[2]

The particular forms of these national and state strategies vary depending on the conception of systemic reform underlying them, but most share a common purpose: to upgrade

This work was supported by a U.S. Department of Education grant to the Consortium for Policy Research in Education (OERI-R117G10007), by the Spencer Foundation, and by the Pew Charitable Trusts. The views expressed in the chapter are the authors' responsibility and in no way should be construed as representing the views of the sponsors. We wish to thank many people for their direct and indirect help, especially Deborah Weil, William Taylor, Ralph Levine, David Hornbeck, Miriam Gonzales, Susan Fuhrman, Jane David, and David K. Cohen. All errors of fact, judgment, and logic are the responsibility of the authors.

250

significantly the quality of the curriculum and instruction delivered to all children. To accomplish this goal, the reforms require major changes in the way states and local school systems make and implement policy. Three such changes characterize an idealized version of the model of systemic reform described in this chapter.

1. Curriculum frameworks that establish what students should know and be able to do would provide direction and vision for significantly upgrading the quality of the content and instruction within all schools in the state. The frameworks and their periodic revisions would be the product of a broad, participatory process, one that effectively balanced the professional judgment of educators and scholars about what constitutes challenging and important material with the views of many individuals and groups about what is important for our young people to learn.[3]

2. Alignment of state education policies would provide a coherent structure to support schools in designing effective strategies for teaching the content of the frameworks to all their students. Novice and experienced teachers would be educated to understand and teach the new challenging content, and teacher licensure would be tied to demonstrated competence in doing so. Curriculum materials adopted by the states and local districts, as well as state assessments of student performance, would reflect the content of the curriculum frameworks. The integration of these and other key elements of the system would act to reinforce and sustain the reforms at the school building level.

3. Through a restructured governance system, schools would have the resources, flexibility, and responsibility to design and implement effective strategies for preparing their students to learn the content of the curriculum frameworks to a high level of performance. This flexibility and control at the school site is a crucial element of the system, enhancing professionalization of instructional personnel and providing the basis for real change in the classroom.

When fully implemented, this model of content-driven systemic reform would be a uniquely American adaptation of the educational policies and structures of many of the world's highly developed nations. It would marry the vision and guidance provided by coherent, integrated, centralized education policies common in many nations with the high degree of local responsibility and control demanded by U.S. tradition.

Such a system is, of course, a far cry from the way the educational enterprise currently operates in this country. Many problems and uncertainties stand between our present educational structure and a fully implemented model of this sort. Nonetheless, the model has gained considerable momentum in policy circles. Consequently, it is crucial at this point to step back and pose some tough questions about the possible effects such a system might have, both during and after its maturation.

Among the chief concerns — and the focus of this chapter — is the potential impact of systemic school reform on equality of educational opportunity. Because of the magnitude of the change represented by the reform model and the unprecedented diversity in the American populace, it is imperative to consider the following questions: How would minority, low-income, and limited-English-proficient students in the United States fare under such a system? Will these students be better or worse off than under the present structures? How will the distribution of resources be affected? How will such a system deal with cultural and linguistic differences? What kinds of safeguards could be established?

The answers to these questions are both complex and uncertain. We address them here by presenting an argument about what *could* be the relationship between systemic reform and educational equity.[4] Our core premise is that a systemic state approach for providing a more challenging content for all children and greater local professional responsibility for schools *could* provide the structure necessary to extend the reforms to all schools and all children. Under these conditions, it *could* raise the general level of achievement while also helping to reduce educational inequalities substantially. Although we find the argument compelling, our concern here is not to "sell it" but to understand better both the opportunities and potential problems posed by a systemic reform strategy. We address four parts of this argument.

1. Curriculum reform intended to improve the overall quality of schooling *for all children* is necessary for a healthy democracy in our diverse society.

2. A well-designed systemic reform strategy could provide an opportunity for extending reforms in challenging curriculum and instruction to all schools and all segments of the student population. Without a systemwide strategy, curricular reform runs the risk of simply "changing the rules of the game" while excluding from play poor and minority children in schools that lack the support and wherewithal to make the necessary but difficult changes in curriculum and instruction.[5]

3. The logic of systemic reform suggests powerful new policy instruments for promoting and sustaining equality of educational opportunity. Differences in appropriateness and quality of the curriculum and programs offered to different groups of students might be more easily exposed and addressed than under the present less coherent system. In addition, a coherent reform strategy suggests a number of legal and administrative mechanisms for helping to ensure educational equity.

4. Finally, even with technical and legal mechanisms to help ensure equal treatment, the legitimacy and effectiveness of a systemic approach will depend in large part on its ability to strike a balance between the common culture and common needs of society as a whole and the diverse perspectives, needs, and strengths of subgroups and individuals within it. The United States, like other nations, has not been particularly successful in achieving this kind of balance, which requires far more than "cookie-cutter" policies. However, we believe this balance could be facilitated by a system that combines a centralized vision and supportive infrastructure (top-down reform) with considerable responsibility, flexibility, and discretion at the local level (bottom-up reform).

Before we turn to an elaboration of the argument and discussion of countervailing possibilities, we need to establish the context within which we will consider the potential effects of systemic curriculum reform on poor and minority students. Of particular importance is our contention that recent gains made by minority and low-income children toward closing the achievement gap are currently in jeopardy.

Historical Context: Achievement Gaps, Trends, and Predictions

One of the least known stories in education is the dramatic gains made by African-American and low-income children in achievement test scores over the past two decades. These gains came during a time when the scores of white and affluent students stayed relatively constant. Table 8.1 and Table 8.2 show these gains on National Assessment of Educational Progress (NAEP) reading tests, narrowing the gap between their scores and the scores of white and middle-income students. The data from the NAEP show the gap closed by 30 to 60 percent from 1971 to 1988, depending on the grade assessed.

In an earlier paper, we argued that gains in the achievement of minority and low-income students were due both to improvements in their social conditions and to changes in the curriculum and instruction of the schools (Smith and O'Day, 1991a). In particular we showed gains in the early grades (measured at grade four), which we attributed to decreases in poverty, improved social conditions, and greater opportunities for minority and poor children in Head Start and elementary school programs such as Chapter 1. These gains were retained and enlarged in later grades (grades 8 and 12), which we attributed to a continuing influence of improved social conditions and to changes in the curriculum of schools. We went on to predict that these gains were in jeopardy due to changes both in social conditions and in instruction. Recent data indicate that our predictions may be accurate. We review briefly the data and the logic that led to these predictions.

Table 8.1. NAEP Reading Scores for White and African-American (AA) Students, Displayed by Testing Date and Age.[a]

Date of Testing	Age 9			Age 13			Age 17		
	White	AA	Difference	White	AA	Difference	White	AA	Difference
1971[b]	214	170	44	261	222	39	291	239	52
1975	217	181	36	262	226	36	293	240	53
1980	221	189	32	264	232	32	293	243	50
1984	218	186	32	263	236	27	296	264	32
1988	218	189	29	261	243	18	295	274	21
1990	217	182	35	262	242	20	297	267	30

[a]The scores are the reading proficiency scale scores — the standard deviation for the age 9 scores is about forty points, for the age 13 scores about thirty-five points, and for the age 17 scores about forty points.

[b]The 1971 assessment scores for whites included scores for Hispanics; the scores for whites for the other assessments did not.

Source: Mullis and others, 1991, pp. 331–333.

Table 8.2. NAEP Reading Scores for Advantaged and Disadvantaged Urban Students, Displayed by Testing Date and Age.[a]

Date of Testing	Age 9			Age 13			Age 17		
	Advantaged	Disadvantaged	Difference	Advantaged	Disadvantaged	Difference	Advantaged	Disadvantaged	Difference
1971	230	179	51	273	234	39	306	260	46
1975	227	184	43	273	230	43	305	259	46
1980	233	188	45	277	242	35	301	258	43
1984	231	192	39	275	239	36	302	266	36
1988	222	192	30	266	239	27	301	275	26
1990	227	186	41	270	241	29	300	273	27

[a]The primary sampling units were stratified into *extreme rural*, *disadvantaged urban*, *advantaged urban*, and *other*. We are using the data here from only the second and third strata.

Source: Mullis and others, 1991, pp. 313–315.

Effects of Changes in Social and Economic Conditions

Between 1960 and the early 1980s, the social and economic conditions of many minorities and the poor changed greatly for the better. The percentage of children in poverty decreased from 26.5 percent in 1960 to 18.3 percent in 1980, the health of infants and young children improved, preschool attendance rose dramatically, schools in the South desegregated, and the average education level of the parents of minority children increased. At the individual level, each of these factors has a small but positive relationship to achievement for poor and minority children. Taken together they appear to have contributed in a substantial way to the narrowing of the achievement gap between 1960 and the late 1980s (Smith and O'Day, 1991a).

Unfortunately, starting in the late 1970s and early 1980s, many of these trends reversed. In particular, more children now live in poor families[6] and poverty has become increasingly concentrated in inner-city schools; the average educational attainment of minority parents has leveled off; use of drugs by young and poor pregnant women has increased while public health care resources have declined; and the inner-city environment has undergone tremendous social deterioration (Smith and O'Day, 1991a; Wilson, 1987). In time, the cumulative effect of these social factors could be a substantial decrease in achievement of poor and minority students, especially those in inner-city schools.

Effects of Changes in Instruction

Our earlier analysis suggested a second major influence on the narrowing of the gap between the middle 1960s and the early 1980s. This period of time was characterized by a focus on achieving equality of educational opportunity through improving resources for minority and low-income students. In instruction, this focus manifested itself in an increased emphasis on basic skills and compensatory education.

The critical issue here is the emphasis on basic skills and its relationship to many commonly used assessments. By and large the instruction, curriculum, and tests for many low-achieving children were mutually reinforcing during a substantial part of this two-decade period. Many states instituted regulations requiring passage of minimum competency tests as a graduation requirement. These tests, like the reading and mathematics portions of standardized norm-referenced tests, emphasized recognition of facts, word analysis, mathematics computation skills, routine algorithmic problem solving, and little else. Moreover, teachers were generally comfortable with "effective" instructional strategies using controlled large-group instruction and plenty of drill and practice. Textbooks and other instructional materials were easily altered (watered down) to "meet the needs" of these students. Finally, the federal and state compensatory education programs provided a strong regulatory structure that required yearly testing and continuous emphasis on basic levels of reading and mathematics.

Taking all these factors together, it is not much of an overstatement to say that for many poor and minority students we had a de facto national basic skills curriculum. To a considerable extent all parts of the system were aligned—in much the same way they would be in what we describe as a systemic approach to education reform. Together with the improvements in social conditions, the "reform" seems to have worked, at least in part. The achievement levels increased, and because the scores of more well-to-do and majority students did not change during this time, the achievement gap narrowed.

However, just as policies toward improving the quality of social conditions for the poor and minorities changed in the 1980s, so did school reform policies. During the early and middle eighties, there was great emphasis on state-initiated top-down regulatory reforms, many of which had little to do with actually changing the nature of curriculum and instruction.

Toward the end of the 1980s, reforms began to focus more on changing schools and, at least in some places, on changing the nature of curriculum and instruction. Concern about the relative underachievement of U.S. students and their lack of improvement over the past two decades combined with developments in instructional theory to produce not only increased rhetoric about raising standards but also greater instructional emphasis on complex knowledge and skills. The reform focus turned toward teaching for understanding and improving students' ability to apply knowledge in novel situations. The new reforms emphasize language- and literature-based approaches to literacy instruction, process approaches to composition, complex problem solving in mathematics, and discovery and hands-on experimentation in science. New expectations for higher-order skills and knowledge have emerged, and assessments based on those expectations are being developed.

Although recent studies indicate that these new reforms will be difficult to implement even in the best of situations (Cohen, 1990; also see his chapter in this volume), work is proceeding on them and much of the policy talk and new assessment strategies assume the higher expectations that the reforms imply. This raises a particular problem with regard to educational equity, because resources for change vary greatly within the system. Schools with large numbers of relatively disadvantaged students typically have less discretionary money, fewer well-trained teachers, and more problems that drain attention and energy from implementing complex reforms. This fact, combined with the newness and complexity of the instructional approaches and content as well as the emphasis of many of the current reforms on school-by-school change, makes it unlikely that the reforms will reach the majority of schools with large numbers of disadvantaged students—at least not until well after they are implemented in more advantaged schools.

What Does the Future Hold
for Poor and Minority Children?

Because of the difficulty of implementing the reforms, particularly in schools with large numbers of disadvantaged students, it seems possible that a substantial new differentiation of curriculum will occur, albeit slowly, with a continued but diluted basic skills approach for the majority of low-income children and an increasing emphasis on problem solving and complex content for more advantaged students.

In terms of test scores, the emphasis in middle-income

schools on more complex and challenging material should lead over time to higher scores on the NAEP or other tests being developed to assess such material. We would expect this change to occur somewhat slowly, however, especially if the reforms continue to focus on school-by-school change.

In low-income schools, the worsening social and economic conditions could lead to lower scores and a widening of the achievement gap no matter what kind of assessment is used. Because the conditions began to deteriorate in the early 1980s, our earlier article predicted this effect might be seen quite soon. We also suggested that the widening of the measured gap could be exacerbated if the achievement measures place a greater emphasis on higher-order skills and content to which large numbers of poor students have not been given access.

The 1990 NAEP data were not available when our earlier article on equality was published. They are now and indicate results depressingly congruent with our analysis (Mullis and others, 1991). Among other trends, the data indicate the following:

1. Mean scores for white students in reading, math, and science were essentially unchanged in 1990 in comparison with 1988, continuing a two-decade trend of very modest improvement.[7] (See Table 8.1 for the reading scores.)

2. Scores in reading for African-American students fell between 1988 and 1990 at all three age levels. (See Table 8.1.) Between 1988 and 1990 the scores of African-American students in mathematics remained relatively constant at all three age levels, while in science they fell at the nine- and seventeen-year-old levels and remained constant at the thirteen-year-old level (Mullis and others, 1991).

3. The relative stability of the scores of white students and the decrease in scores of African-American students led to an increase in the size of the gap between 1988 and 1990. For the first time in two decades, the difference in reading achievement scores increased at all three age levels. (See Table 8.1.)

4. The gap is no longer continuing to close between the scores of urban advantaged and disadvantaged students. For the first time in many years, there was a clear increase between 1988 and 1990 in the gap for nine-year-old students and no reduction in the gap for thirteen- and seventeen-year-olds. For nine-year-olds the increase in the gap was substantial, over one-quarter of a standard deviation, and was contributed to equally by a drop in the scores of the disadvantaged and an increase in the scores of the advantaged. At ages thirteen and seventeen there were essentially no changes in the scores of either group. (See Table 8.2.)

What Do Recent Findings Suggest?

First, as social conditions have deteriorated, the momentum for improving educational opportunity, as assessed by both the changing emphasis of education reforms and the NAEP test scores, has dissipated. The declines in reading and science scores of African Americans are most certainly caused by a number of factors, including out-of-school influences. Reading scores are particularly sensitive to social and economic conditions, and African Americans are disproportionately affected by increases in the overall poverty rates and by declines in the quality of life in the cities.

A second conclusion is that, although schooling as we know it certainly cannot overcome all of the effects of inequities in the general social environment, the potential power of schooling and especially of a coherent curricular strategy to help provide equal opportunity should not be underestimated. The impact of the moderately well-aligned and coherent basic skills emphasis in the curriculum during the seventies and the early eighties appears to have been a significant contributor to the increase in African-American student scores; the decline in emphasis on basic skills in the late 1980s may have contributed to the recent decreases in their scores.

Third, the reform emphasis on more challenging content and skills either has not had much of an effect yet or the effect is not reflected on the NAEP tests.[8] As the reforms reach greater numbers of students within states and as assessments are changed to reflect the new content, we expect that there will be greater and more detectable effects on children's learning, just as there were in the basic skills movement. Unless these reforms are deliberately and aggressively implemented systemwide, however, we expect them to reach few schools of the disadvantaged.

Our best guess is that this combination of factors will continue to erode the relative quality of the education offered to less advantaged students until and unless the coherence and clarity of the back-to-basics movement is replaced with a similar coherence and clarity in support of the new, challenging content. Simply aligning tests and the curriculum will not be enough, however, as it was in the back-to-basics movement of the 1970s and 1980s. At that time, the components of the system were ready for the reform: teachers understood the basic skills content, the curriculum materials were already aligned with a fact- and skill-oriented approach, and the instructional strategies were routine and familiar. Today's emphasis on challenging content, by contrast, finds a system unprepared: most teachers lack the necessary depth of content knowledge, appropriate instructional materials are not available, and schools have little experience with the new forms of instruction. Creating coherence through alignment this time will require a much more focused and sustained effort by policymakers at all levels of the system.

Reform Goal: Challenging Content for All Children

At the heart of content-based systemic reform is the tenet that *all* children should have access to the new challenging content and, moreover, should be expected to learn this content to a high standard of performance. This tenet is based on two key assumptions of the current reform movement.

The first of these is that deep understanding of academic content, complex thinking, and problem solving are not only desirable and highly valued but have become *necessary* for responsible citizenship in our diverse moden society. The complex problems both of a modern U.S. democracy and of an interdependent world community require complex solutions and a citizenry able to grapple with differing perspectives and novel approaches. Moreover, many analysts link a perceived decline in the quality of human capital in this country, as measured by the relatively poor performance of U.S. students in international achievement assessments, to the nation's lack of economic competitiveness. Sustained economic recovery, they suggest, rests on an entire work force trained to creatively analyze, communicate, and resolve problems in production and service delivery.

We do not intend to recapitulate the arguments for the new content and pedagogy in any greater detail. What is important is that the need for instructional reform is taken for granted in most policy circles. Supporting language and arguments for such change pervade the texts of most reform documents, including the standards and reports of the National Council of Teachers of Mathematics (NCTM), the National Academy of Sciences, and the American Association for the Advancement of Science; the speeches of presidential candidates, governors, and chief state school officers; the publications of the Business Roundtable and the official documents of the National Education Goals Panel (1991) and NCEST (1992); and congressional legislation.

With the exception of a few skeptics who point to a lack of compelling data documenting the claims for curricular change, the argument seems to have captured the education, business, and political establishments. Even the skeptics agree that such a goal would be desirable as long as the trade-offs were not too great.

As official bodies endorse it at state and national levels, as organizations of experts design national and state content frameworks and standards, and as curriculum and test developers redesign their materials to meet the new criteria, the concept of challenging content and higher-order skills takes on an aura of official policy.

And with the aura of policy comes the responsibility of governments. Simple justice dictates that skills and knowledge deemed *necessary* for basic citizenship and economic opportunity be available to *all* future citizens—that is, access must be distributed equally, not just equitably.

But if there is a body of knowledge that citizens must grasp, or think they must grasp, so as to play their parts, then they have to go to school; and then all of them have to go to school. Thus Aristotle, in opposition to the practices of his own city: "the system of education in a state must . . . be one and the same for all and the provision of this system must be a matter of public action" (Barker, 1948, p. 370). . . . We can think of educational equality as a form of welfare provision, where all children, conceived as future citizens, have the same need to know, and where the ideal of membership is best served if they are all taught the same things [Walzer, 1991b, p. 244].

In line with the justice and equal access argument is the second key assumption of the reform movement: all children can acquire these skills. This means not only that "all children can learn," an oft-quoted platitude of many reform documents, but that *all children can learn challenging content and complex problem-solving skills.*[9] This assumption is supported by recent psychological theory and research that finds that all children engage in complex (higher-order) thinking tasks.[10] Moreover, "dumbing down" the material for the "disadvantaged" represents a clear denial of their opportunity to learn challenging material of the curriculum. "The most important single message of this body of research is that complex thinking processes — elaborating the given material, making inferences beyond what is explicitly presented, building adequate representations, analyzing and constructing relationships — are involved in even the most apparently elementary mental activities. Children cannot . . . become good writers [for example] without engaging in complex problem-solving-like processes" (Resnick, 1987, p. 45).

The assumption is also supported by existence proofs, examples of situations where students who are not expected to succeed do so when given the opportunity to learn particularly challenging material. Jaime Escalante's work with lower-income Mexican Americans in Advanced Placement mathematics is one of the better known examples. (See Mathews, 1988.)

If these assumptions are valid—that is, if the skills and content are considered necessary and if all children can acquire them—then it is the responsibility of our system and schools to make the relevant instruction available to all students. This does not mean that all children will achieve to the same degree. It does mean that teachers and schools should have the material and pedagogical resources to provide curricular access to all children. Expressed in terms of equality of opportunity, we might say that *access* to the necessary content should be (at least in theory) equally distributed, with the result that outcomes would be equitably distributed. Equity in the distribution of outcomes means that while outcomes would continue to differ, those differences would not be based on "educationally irrelevant" criteria such as race, class, gender, or language. Thomas Green refers to the argument underlying this notion as the "principle of fair benefit distribution."[11]

It is important also to note that ensuring access to the common content core does not necessarily mean all children receive exactly the same curriculum. Indeed, we would expect specific curricula to vary with the interests, backgrounds, and cultures of the students and possibly of their teachers and schools. Such diversity within a common core is an integral characteristic of systemic curricular reform. Achieving it, however, is neither straightforward nor easy.

First, there is great tension between responding to differences among students by providing them with different curricula and affording all children access to common challenging content. Not to accommodate student differences—differences in language, for example—could effectively deny access to large numbers of students. At the same time, such "accommodation," if taken too far, could itself result in substantially different opportunities for different students. For the reform to be successful, the approaches taken by all schools must be based on common curriculum frameworks and all students must be *expected* and *given the opportunity* to perform at the same high standards on a common assessment. But individual schools, to maximize the opportunities for their particular students, must be free to choose the instructional strategies, language of instruction, use of curriculum materials, and topics to be emphasized.

Second, different curriculum strategies may require different instructional materials and personnel, which in turn may require different dollar resources. We believe that in our already unequal world, disparities in fiscal resources should be tolerated only if they serve to equalize access to the desired content by providing more help to those students who need it the most.

Finally, in practice, we would not expect the impact of a strategy that emphasized a common challenging curricular approach to overcome all of the disparities generated by social class. This would occur only if there were a major redistribution of the opportunities outside of the schools. However, because differences in the complexity and challenges of *present* curricula are highly correlated with class, we expect that in such a new reform the relationship between class and outcomes will be substantially reduced over the long run.

Systemic Reform: A Strategy for Reaching All Schools

We have argued that improving the content of instruction is critical to improving the quality of schooling and that justice dictates that all children should receive a curriculum of common content and equal quality. The question at this point is whether a systemic reform strategy would provide poor and minority students more equal access to the new curriculum than would otherwise be available, and if so, how.

Logically, our response to this question has two parts. The first, that reliance on other strategies is unlikely to ensure change in many of the nation's neediest schools, is mentioned above and discussed more extensively in earlier publications (Smith and O'Day, 1991a, 1991b). Fragmentation of the current policy system serves as a major obstacle to educational improvement from either the top down or the bottom up. Multiple and conflicting messages from a variety of policy sources and short-term magic bullet approaches to change dilute the impact of centralized reform policies on classroom instruction. At the same time, the policy structure provides little support for generalizing or maintaining changes engendered by a more instruction-oriented school-by-school reform strategy. Without such support, schools with large numbers of already underserved students are particularly unlikely to be able to make the kinds of fundamental changes in instruction required by the new reforms. Where the changes do occur, it will be the result of the tremendous hard work, foresight, and knowledge of dedicated individuals in the affected schools. But personnel turnover, "burnout," and competing demands make the maintenance of such schools tenuous at best, and the history of school reform in the United States is replete with promising but eventually failed examples of school-by-school change. Even the newly forming networks of restructured schools, if forced to exist in the currently fragmented and unsupportive policy environment, will not be able to provide the infrastructure — to say nothing of the resources — necessary for sustained improvement.

Indeed, if public education is to change in a serious and productive way, it is not enough to convince a few leading schools about the need and direction for the change in the hope that these schools, by their example, will convince others to join the movement. Rather, the vision of change must be powerful enough to focus the public and all the levels of the governance system on common challenging purposes and to sustain that focus over an extended period of time. From these common purposes will stem the strategy and mechanisms to ensure the delivery of an equitable and high-quality public education for all the nation's children.

How would this strategy work? This brings us to the second part of our response. A common vision and set of curriculum frameworks establish the basis in systemic curriculum reform for aligning all parts of a state instructional system — core content, materials, teacher training, continuing professional development, and assessment — to support the goal of delivering a high-quality curriculum to all children. Over time a variety of important though informal effects should flow from the common vision and alignment.

Most important, the frameworks should make public a common, challenging set of expectations for what all children should know and be able to do. These expectations would apply equally to all schools even though the specific curricula of the schools may differ. We should stress again that the implementation of a common content vision along with variation in curricula across schools will not be a trivial task to work out. Indeed, if the nature of the differences in the school curricula vary by social class or cultural group, they might be politically explosive. The task should be seen up front as an *educational* endeavor, one that embraces discussion and controversy about the important social issues of what students should be expected to learn in a diverse democratic society. Although there is necessarily a political aspect to this undertaking, it would be a mistake to reduce it to primarily a power struggle among special interest groups, as this could fracture the community and any sense of common purpose. The task will be complicated further, of course, because over time the curriculum frameworks will have to change as content and pedagogical knowledge change and as the system learns what it does well.[12]

Despite these difficulties, the development and implementation processes themselves should help significantly to spread curricular reforms throughout the system. The developmental process itself should increase the awareness and interest of various education stakeholders in the content of instruction. Moreover, as their knowledge of the frameworks deepens over time, parents, student advocates, the press, and others in the public could help to reinforce the quality of the curriculum. For example, a well-known set of curricular expectations should aid parents both to assist their children in a more informed way and to monitor the quality of their schools. In addition, we might expect the press to be able to interpret assessment results better if the assessments were designed to measure the content and skills actually taught as part of the school curriculum. Careful, thoughtful reporting about the overall progress in a school system, rather than the sporadic, short-term, project-oriented coverage that is now so prevalent in the press, could be of tremendous value.

In addition to the reinforcing effects of public knowledge and pressure, alignment of the various components of the system should foster the spread of the reform through enhanced professionalization of the teaching force. We see this happening in two ways. First, teachers would in time have a common and well-understood body of content that they had been trained to teach and that would be reflected in their classroom curriculum materials, even commercially developed ones. The common content would be shared across classrooms and grades, enhancing professional conversation among teachers. The reinforcing effect of the alignment of the parts of the system and of enhanced professional conversation around a shared set of content goals should aid in the development of a serious professional community within many schools, facilitating the transfer of effective strategies from school to school (Smith and O'Day, 1991b; Lieberman and McLaughlin, 1992).

Second, new teachers and new professional development strategies brought into a school should add to the reinforcing effect. This would be unlike the present system where new teachers are often unprepared to teach the school's curriculum, especially if it has challenging content, and where experienced teachers often believe that professional development activities are irrelevant to their classroom efforts. By aligning the content of professional development with the content of the classrooms, the systems of teacher preparation and professional development would help to sustain and enhance the reform in the classroom, rather than undercut it as is typically the case now.

All these reinforcing effects could provide substantial benefits to schools with high percentages of low-income and minority youth, as well as to schools with more advantaged youngsters. Parents and advocates in low-income areas would have stronger ammunition to hold schools to high standards of practice and performance because they would have a much clearer sense about what to expect from their schools. Moreover, schools in predominately low-income areas are often buffeted by the whims of reformers and by erratic support systems. A clear and continuing vision, structure, and system of support could enhance the stability and coherence they need to be effective.

Standards for Schools and School Systems: Mechanisms Toward Achieving Equal Opportunity[13]

We have argued that a clear vision of the content schools should be prepared to teach, combined with coherent, supportive state policies, would encourage the growth of various reinforcing mechanisms to strengthen curricular reform. But are these enough to ensure that the reforms will reach all schools and all children? In the ideal "good society," we might not expect instant across-the-board implementation of a complex reform but we would expect fair implementation.

Unfortunately, we believe that in the absence of new deliberate policy, our history as a nation shows that such fairness is extremely unlikely. The deck will inevitably be stacked against minorities, the poor, and the least politically powerful and their schools (Kozol, 1991). Policy coherence may be a necessary prerequisite to systemwide reform, but we cannot imagine that it is sufficient.

How, then, might the playing field be evened out? What deliberate policy steps could be taken to help ensure that the schools of the poor and minorities receive an equitable distribution of resources designed to enable them to provide their students the opportunity to learn the desired content and skills? Should schools, school systems, and states be offered incentives, given technical assistance, and/or held accountable?

The approach most often suggested in current policy proposals is a performance-based accountability model with clearly defined outcome standards for schools.[14] The standards would be based on average levels of student performance and would specify a satisfactory gain over time or an absolute level of achievement. There are two conceptions of how performance-based accountability would work. One would operate on the fuel of good intentions and self-correction, assuming that schools and school systems will respond quickly and productively when they receive evidence of problems from outcome assessments. Advocates see a systemic curricular strategy as self-correcting because data from assessments that adequately measure the content that students are taught would provide corrective feedback to the schools.

This performance-based model is attractive because it involves a minimum of bureaucracy and regulation. However, although feedback mechanisms are an important component of any healthy system, they cannot be the sole mechanism for promoting equal opportunity to learn. Indeed, a solely performance-based strategy might be likened to closing the barn door after the horse is stolen. We know that many schools simply do not have the resources to provide the level of opportunity necessary for their students. We do not need to wait until we have clear outcome documentation of failure before addressing obvious problems.[15] Moreover, once failure is noted, there is no assurance in this model that schools of the poor would have the knowledge or other capacity to improve, nor is there any mechanism to stimulate outside assistance.

An alternative performance-based model would hold students and schools, and presumably school systems and even states, accountable for their respective performances. If they failed to meet a preestablished performance standard, some corrective action would be required. Conversely, if they met or surpassed their goals, they would receive a reward. Unlike the first model, this strategy would provide stimulating mechanisms for both continued improvement and corrective action, possibly including penalties. Judiciously used, it might be an important stimulus for equity, though it also would close the barn door too late.

There are, however, two deeper and more important problems with any simple performance-based accountability model that relies primarily on rewards and sanctions. The first of these is that the model assumes that low-achieving schools perform poorly because school personnel *lack the will* to improve. Rewards and sanctions are designed to stimulate that will, and in appropriate situations they may be quite successful. However, where limited capacity in preparation, resources, or personnel is a problem, as it is in many schools serving poor and minority students, such an approach is unlikely to yield meaningful results. Indeed, in the absence of sufficient resources or a clear idea of how to improve, the pressure to get more students to pass the examination may pull schools toward narrow "beat the examination" strategies rather than toward upgrading the quality of the curriculum and instruction.

The second problem is that it is essential for the public to see the accountability process as legitimate. When a performance-based accountability system uses punitive action in response to the failure of a school to meet its performance standards, the school and community must perceive the action as fair and justified. This means that the school must be seen as having had a reasonable opportunity to meet the performance standard. It is not legitimate to hold students accountable unless they have been given the opportunity to learn the material on the examination. Similarly, teachers or schools cannot legitimately be held accountable for how well their students do unless they have the preparation and resources to provide the students the opportunity to learn. A central question, then, is under what conditions might a school legitimately be held accountable for the performance of its students?

This question and our belief that performance standards alone are not enough to stimulate the education system to meet the needs of poor and minority students suggest to us the need for additional mechanisms. The NCEST report (1992) and the Education and Labor Committee in the U.S. House of Representatives came to the same conclusion.[16] Both groups recommended school delivery standards be established that include *inputs* as well as outcomes and that would (1) amplify the vision and structure provided by the curriculum frameworks and reform strategy for school improvement efforts by schools and school systems and (2) establish criteria for determining under what conditions students might legitimately be held accountable for their performance on "high-stakes" assessments.

In the following sections we develop a way of thinking about standards for schools that would meet these purposes. We do so recognizing the dangers involved. Given past tendencies toward governmental regulation in such matters, specification of inputs runs the risk of becoming a bureaucratic exercise that would in fact undermine the authority and responsibility of local school professionals for constructing the most effective school organization and instructional strategies for their students. We have tried to avoid this danger.

We have, however, included considerable detail both about what school standards might be and about how they might be used. This detail turns out to be quite useful for exploring exactly where we believe responsibility in a school system should lie and how standards might be used to foster equal opportunity. In fact, exploration of these issues led us to consider more specifically concerns about the relationship between a quality education and equal educational opportunity.

One way to look at this relationship in the context of systemic reform is to define a quality education as the opportunity to learn well the content of the frameworks. Equal educational opportunity might then be achieved by providing all students a quality education. In this context, school standards, by defining an opportunity to learn, become the operational specifications for both educational quality and equality, at least insofar as the content of the frameworks is concerned. Green (1982) described the underlying relationship as follows: "If we succeed in advancing the spread of educational excellence, then we will tend to resolve major problems of equity. The pursuit of excellence is more likely to produce gains in equity than policies in pursuit of equality are likely to produce gains in excellence. Or, to put the point in still other words, there is a stronger connection between seeking excellence and finding equity than between getting equality and getting excellence" (paraphrased in Green, 1991, p. 233).

Linking quality and equality provides a powerful but very general formulation. Two immediate qualifications should be made: first, schools would have to pass a quite rigorous standard to demonstrate that they were providing an "opportunity to learn" and second, we have provided a narrow definition of a "quality" education. For the purposes of this discussion, we have focused entirely on classroom learning in the context of the content in the systemic curriculum reform. Other important dimensions to school quality and equality deserve attention but are outside of the context of systemic curriculum reform; we would expect schools to vary on these dimensions but not to vary on providing all students the opportunity to learn.[17]

What Is Meant by School Standards in Systemic Curriculum Reform?

As we thought about how to conceptualize school standards, four guiding ideas emerged.

First, standards should be parsimonious and well focused. We are aware of the history of difficulties Americans and others have had in developing and implementing sensible quality standards. Too often they degrade into minimum standards and senseless bureaucratic exercises with long lists of easily measured but essentially meaningless elements (Wise, 1979). Parsimony, that is, few standards based on a clear and defensible conceptual model of what we want to assess, should help to combat this proclivity.

Second, within the context of content-driven systemic reform, the purpose of school standards should be to provide operational specifications for assessing whether a school is giving its students the opportunity to learn the content and skills set out in the curriculum frameworks. Focusing on the content of the frameworks provides the basis for both parsimony and rigor in standard setting.

Third, the use of school standards in a systemic curriculum strategy is predicated on a different way of thinking about the relationship between school inputs and student achievement outcomes — a conceptualization that offers substantial promise of allowing a clear linkage between inputs and outcomes.

To date, research has failed to find a consistent relationship between school resources and student achievement outcomes. One hypothesis about why this is so is that inputs and outcomes have been defined in such a way as almost to preclude the discovery of linkages that do exist. The basic problem is that, with the exception of the most elementary decoding skills in reading and of basic computation facts in mathematics, the U.S. education system lacks a common vision of what outcomes should be expected of our students. Textbooks offer one conception, standardized achievement tests another, and district- and school-designed curriculum materials a third. Different visions about what students should know and what schools should teach exist across districts in most states, across schools in most districts, and across grades and classrooms in many schools.

The corollary of this problem is that there is no substantive basis on which to determine quality of resources. For example, one measure of teacher quality commonly used is the teacher's educational attainment — or, more specifically, the presence or absence of a master's degree. However, if the coursework required for the higher degree is unrelated to the content the teacher actually teaches or to the tests the students take, it is not surprising that the teacher's attainment has little impact on student achievement.

A systemic reform strategy that aligns the fundamental elements of the education infrastructure (teacher training, certification, continuing professional development, curriculum materials, school curriculum, and assessment) provides a new and importantly different way of thinking about the essential resources and practices of a high-quality school. The common content and alignment of key components of the system provide a basis for identifying the necessary core of appropriate resources and practices and for determining whether they are of sufficient quality for providing all students the opportunity to learn the challenging material of the curriculum frameworks.[18]

Finally, our understanding of what the essential resources are and of what constitutes quality in curriculum and instruction will change as systemic reform is implemented and as we understand more about teaching and learning. It will therefore be important to view school standards as dynamic and supportive of the entire school system's learning to improve over time. They should be constructed and assessed in such a way that they both rely on and foster professional judgment.

With these guides in mind, we suggest a particular way of thinking about school standards in order to explore a difficult set of issues. Our own thinking on these issues is very much in the formative process and we in no way wish to imply that the formulation we give here is either the correct or the only one. We have included considerable detail in this discussion to sharpen and clarify the issues.

In our current conception, school standards would have three parts. They would spell out criteria for determining whether a school (1) has the essential human and other materials to offer all of its students the opportunity to learn the content of the curriculum frameworks to a high level of performance (*resource standards*), (2) actually implements a program of study likely to provide its students such an opportunity (*practice standards*), and (3) meets challenging goals, as measured by the percentage of students who successfully achieve a high performance level (outcome or *performance standards*). In the next three sections we explore some of the ways in which these three components of school standards might be further defined. In later sections we consider how the standards might be assessed and used for the purposes of school improvement and accountability.

Resource Standards. In the interest of parsimony we argue that only those resources deemed *directly* necessary for implementing the overall systemic strategy be included in the definition of resource standards. Obvious candidates include teachers and administrators knowledgeable of and able to teach the content of the frameworks and a planned school curriculum, professional development programs, assessments, and instructional materials and resources (such as laboratories), all in line with the frameworks. On the one hand, this highly targeted approach should help to guard against the kind of overregulatory "wish list" that might otherwise be generated by the exercise of defining school standards. At the same time, however, it excludes from the standards some resources that many people (ourselves included) believe every school *should* have.[19] The one exception to this criterion of a direct link between the frameworks and the standards is that we believe it critical to ensure through the standards that every school has a physically safe environment for all participants. Without that, little learning of anything but sheer survival techniques is possible.

Assessing whether the resource standards have been met for any given school would then be a matter of defining and addressing such questions as: Does the school have the necessary resources in sufficient quantity to make them *available* to all relevant staff and students? Are the resources *appropriate,* not only for the overall strategy but also for the specific students in that school? That is, are they aligned with the frameworks and in a form (for example, language) that will make the desired content and skills accessible to the students in that school? And finally, are the necessary resources *of sufficiently high quality,* both in content and in form, to enable the students to learn the content to a high level of performance? Are the resources sufficiently well managed to support instruction?

This approach to defining resource standards meets our guiding ideas: it focuses attention on curriculum and instruction and on the provision of an "opportunity to learn" for all students, it gives a strategy for keeping the number of standards small, and it provides a conceptualization that could guide system learning and improvement. It offers a focused alternative to the conventional generic assessment of resources used for accreditation or other school assessment purposes.

Practice Standards. A more complete understanding of whether a school provides all students the opportunity to learn the content of the curriculum frameworks would come from an analysis of the actual curriculum and related practices of the school. Addressing this issue will be a particularly challenging task in American schools in the context of the system we envision. In a school system where the curriculum is rigidly prescribed and where the school population is relatively homogeneous, the complexity of the task might be reduced, but that will not be the case in most American schools.

Our principal focus is on practices directly related to implementing the systemic reform. *This continues to place our attention squarely on the issues of curriculum and instruction in the classroom.* Effectively, the practice standards should parallel the resource standards but with attention to actual implementation. Most likely, schools will not be able to meet practice standards unless resource standards have also been met. These standards should address such questions as: Does the curriculum as taught in the school reflect the curriculum frameworks? Is the classroom curriculum and pedagogy powerful and appropriate to the needs and cultures of the particular students in the school? Does the school build on an understanding of the cultural, linguistic, and other strengths of its students? Do the professional development activities of the school focus on improving the capacity of the school to give all students the opportunity to learn the content of the curriculum frameworks?

We elevate two areas outside of the direct implementation of systemic reform elements as critical practice standards.

One, which parallels the resource standards, is that the work environment be safe for teachers and students. The other is that mutual respect among staff and students is encouraged and practiced. Safety and respect influence all interactions among individuals within a school. The absence of either of these two conditions makes productive classrooms extremely unlikely.

Defining the input side (resources and practice) of school standards as focused directly on the implementation of systemic reform would provide a very powerful mechanism for assisting in school improvement and for exposing true inequalities in opportunity among schools, far more powerful, we believe, than using conventional definitions of inputs.

Performance (Outcome) Standards. School input standards address the first two parts of our three-part conceptualization of school standards. School performance standards in a systemic reform strategy could provide a powerful gauge for determining whether students are actually learning the challenging content of the curriculum frameworks. The alignment between the curriculum and the assessment instrument would provide a degree of content validity to the measures well beyond that provided by current tests.

In the context of school standards, the concern is with the aggregate performance of a school's students. Does the school reach a satisfactory level of performance in providing all students the opportunity to learn the content of the curriculum frameworks to a high standard?[20]

An important design issue here is how to define "satisfactory level of performance." For example, a school might meet its performance standards either if the percentage of students who met high student performance standards improved by a set number of points or if some high, preestablished percentage of students met their student standards.[21] The first alternative would establish yearly goals for schools that initially had only a small percentage of students succeeding while the second would represent an ultimate target for all schools. A somewhat more sophisticated approach would address some important equity issues by defining acceptable school performance not only in terms of the total student body but also in terms of major subgroups within the school.

Other design issues regarding performance standards concern the nature of the assessments themselves. Puzzles as to how to develop appropriate assessments for use with challenging curriculum frameworks are receiving substantial attention in the United States and other developed nations. The impetus for concentrating on these issues arises from an important critique of the adequacy of conventional norm-referenced achievement tests for assessing the kinds of learning the new reforms seek to engender. Reformers believe that complex performance tasks and portfolios are more appropriate for the kinds of content and skills to be taught as well as more "authentic" — that is, more like the kinds of activities that should go on in the classrooms. Criticizing norm referencing for its reliance on ranking students, reformers argue for its replacement by "absolute" high standards of performance. [22]

These are exciting and important ideas, but they are far from fully conceptualized, much less developed and implemented. This is yet another reason why as states move to implement systemic curriculum reform they must be patient and deliberate and not sacrifice quality for urgency. A mismatch between the content and skills of the framework and those measured by the assessment or an assessment system that is poorly designed or unreliable will hurt all of the schools in the state but will hurt the schools of poor and minority students most of all.

Assessing and Using School Standards for School Improvement and Accountability[23]

It is one thing to think conceptually about what school standards might be. It is another to imagine how to implement a system that actually assesses and uses them. [24] A number of important issues have to be addressed at the very outset of this process.

One set of issues concerns the inherent difficulty of conceptualizing and measuring the standards. Recognizing that teachers must be knowledgeable about the frameworks, for instance, is clearly not the same as operationalizing criteria and standards to assess that knowledge. And once we determine whether a teacher is sufficiently knowledgeable (that is, meets the resource standard for knowledge), how then do we determine if he or she is meeting the practice standards for teaching? And how do we then aggregate this information to the level of the school? Suppose five teachers out of forty fail one or another of these standards; has the school failed to meet its standards? To address these difficult questions will require deep understanding of schools and school systems.

Part of the difficulty of designing and measuring standards arises from the importance of addressing equity concerns throughout the process. The new approaches to student assessment, for example, pose a variety of problems. The psychometric characteristics of performance tasks and portfolios and other forms of authentic tasks are largely unknown. In particular, their sensitivity to bias due to circumstances extraneous to schooling is essentially unstudied. Other problems arise in the assessment of resource and practice standards. For instance, it will be necessary to determine the appropriate resources in schools with very diverse student bodies. Who will make such determinations? Will suburban teachers be able to fairly assess inner-city schools that have very different kinds of students than those with whom they are familiar? Equity issues will have to be addressed at every stage of the design, development, and implementation of school standards and, indeed, of systemic curriculum reform.

A second set of issues concerns the broader conceptualization of who will perform the assessments. In our view, the assessment of school standards must rest primarily on professional judgment, that is, on careful investigation and reflection by teachers and other practicing educators about whether a school has appropriate high-quality resources and practices to offer all its students an opportunity to learn the desired content. Four advantages of a professional model for standard assessment come to mind. First, the complexity of what's being assessed — particularly the practice standards — requires the experience and judgment of professionals. Those less knowledgeable would be more likely to reduce the assessments to mechanical and largely useless checklists of traditional school inputs. Second, for the assessments to have an impact on actual instruction, they must be seen as legitimate by the instructional staff in the schools. Teachers are more likely to respect and respond to suggestions made by other professionals after a thorough investigation of the specific content of their school than to results of a more quantifiable evaluation. Third, the assessment process itself has the potential for becoming a source of high-quality professional development for those involved. Professionals on review teams would learn not only from the experiences of those they review but also from collaboration amongst themselves. Moreover, they would serve to spread knowledge about common problems throughout the system, advancing the understanding of those both at the school site and beyond. Finally, such a model would provide an avenue for keeping the standards themselves dynamic, for professionals would be more likely to identify problems that arise in the definition or application of specific standards and would be more able to suggest appropriate changes.

A third set of issues concerns the ways in which the standards are used and their resulting impact on the system as a whole. We have argued that the purpose of school standards should be to improve curriculum and instruction, and more specifically to help ensure that all students have an equal opportunity to learn the desired content to a high level of performance. Logically this can happen in three ways: through self-generated improvement as part of the normal functioning of the organizational unit or individual; through special system-generated efforts aimed at improvement (soft accountability mechanisms); and through a strong accountability structure involving rewards and sanctions designed to motivate or force improvement.

Self-Generated Improvement. First, the standards can provide guides and targets for all levels of the system in their day-to-day functioning. This is based on the notion that it is the *professional responsibility* of all actors in the system to help ensure that the school standards are met. Thus, the primary question at each level would be: How does this policy, resource allocation, or practice enhance or detract from the ability of the schools to meet the school standards? A powerful by-product of this question is that it would keep all levels focused on issues of curriculum and instruction. It could also help to foster continuity in policy across changes in superintendents, school boards, principals, and teachers.

In addition, the various levels of the governance structure and individuals within those levels would have particular *administrative responsibility*, both for the activities of their own level or unit and for those of their subordinate levels. Thus, the state would be responsible for ensuring to the best of its ability that the districts had the resources necessary to help all schools in their jurisdiction meet the resource standards. The district would have a similar responsibility in relation to the school, within the constraints imposed by the state. The school, depending upon the degree of authority it exercised over such issues as personnel selection and curriculum design, would be responsible for making decisions that enhanced its ability to meet the school standards.

Within such a structure, all levels and units would engage in self-generated improvement efforts as part of their normal functioning, not unlike the organizational learning and improvement that are part of any successful organization. One focus of these efforts at the district and state levels would be to make certain that schools with low-income and minority students received a fair shake. In this regard, superintendents of local districts could especially benefit from regular, independent information about whether their schools were meeting the standards. In large urban systems, moreover, the introduction of curricular continuity and of supportive school standards could in itself go a long way toward establishing the groundwork for sustained improvement.

At the level of the school, school standards could establish understandable and challenging targets in their efforts to improve instruction and opportunities for all their students. The standards could provide a focus in the development of school plans, shape internal decision making about the use and purchase of key resources, and supply models for improving classroom practice. They could also furnish supportive rationales for schools in their efforts to obtain necessary resources and technical assistance from districts and states.

In all these efforts, the general goal would be to create

a climate where the system as a whole was continually learning and improving. Additional means of fostering this goal could also be incorporated into the very design and assessment of school standards. One way to do this would be to think of the standards, like curriculum frameworks, as continually evolving as new knowledge is developed. Another would be to involve as many practicing teachers as possible in the design and assessment. The deliberate involvement of large numbers of teachers and other school professionals in system-maintenance and improvement tasks should help create a common culture that continually focuses on the quality of the curriculum and instruction. Finally, school standards could help design system standards for school districts and states.

System-Generated School Improvement: Soft Accountability. Efforts to improve individual schools may also come from outside the schools themselves, generated by system mechanisms or public pressure. We believe these soft accountability efforts could profit from the guidance of school standards as well.

System-generated improvement efforts would be specific proactive steps taken by districts and states to achieve the standards in all schools. They would involve specific activities and programs focused directly on ensuring that all schools have the resources and technical assistance to meet the school standards. We do not have a "formula" for the right mix of state and local activities to make up this support system, but we do have a series of ideas about important components. We also believe it would be effective to concentrate on those schools needing the most help while assisting schools throughout the system.

One component of the support structure would be general system activities and programs. For example, states and districts should take steps to ensure that school professionals have access to high-quality continuing professional development programs focused on assisting them to meet the school standards — that is, to understand the core content, to design and implement effective curricula and instructional strategies, and to organize the school in ways that support high achievement. The state might encourage or otherwise stimulate state higher education institutions to develop appropriate programs and, with the assistance of local teachers, might recommend or even certify programs developed by vendors outside the system.

The state or local district could also underwrite the basic costs of teacher networks as well as other relevant professional development programs. In systemic curriculum reform, schools and teachers may be more likely to benefit from the experiences of other teachers and schools working on the same problems, which could happen on a regular basis through teacher networks, professional development activities run by the district, and other ways of sharing information (Lieberman and McLaughlin, 1992).

A more aggressive district or state strategy would involve continuous monitoring of how well the schools were meeting the standards. One purpose would be to track schools' performance over time, both as a check on the overall system and as a trigger for technical assistance when needed. This type of monitoring could easily be centralized at the district and state levels.

Another purpose would be to understand more deeply the needs of schools so as to provide supportive services and resources. This would require knowing which schools met the school standards and analyzing why some failed to meet them. One strategy would be to have regular school reviews by teams of experienced teachers drawn from outside districts, to assess the appropriateness and quality of a school's resources and practices. Reviews might occur at regular intervals (for example, every three years) in areas of high need and less often elsewhere. They could be triggered by particularly low school performance on the student assessments. The results of the reviews could be used to provide feedback to the schools, to indicate to districts the schools' needs for assistance, and, under extreme circumstances, to trigger stronger accountability mechanisms.

A different strategy could be borrowed from overseas. School inspectors in Ireland, England, or France are former teachers who work for the central authority, the Ministry, serving as technical advisers and quality-control monitors for a group of schools. They conduct professional development activities, oversee and evaluate the progress of novice teachers, assist schools in obtaining resources, and work with principals and teachers to improve their schools. If implemented in the United

States in the context of a commonly shared curricular strategy, a system of inspectors could be a powerful source for sharing ideas and enforcing common standards; inspectors could also operate as a professional force in the political arena. Their role in the system could combine the functions mentioned above with the function of a warning system for schools that are not meeting the standards. Indeed, in times of scarce resources the inspectors might focus on areas where schools are deemed less likely to have the capacity to meet the school standards. In cases where strong action is recommended, an inspector's evaluation and recommendations might be augmented by those of a review team to provide independent judgment.

Monitoring strategies could keep the issues of school improvement and school quality continually at the front of the state's agenda. Any monitoring strategy, however, would have to have a high level of credibility, based on the quality of the reviewers. It would also need the clear backing of the district or state, which would have to take the results seriously and act on them quickly, if necessary.

In our view, self-generated and system-generated improvement should be the cornerstone use for school standards. When such improvement efforts fail to produce the needed results, however, stronger accountability mechanisms may be required.

Strong Accountability: Using Rewards and Sanctions. Earlier we argued that a strong accountability model would require school standards to operate fairly. We are now ready to imagine how such a model might work. This section considers issues of both student and institutional (school and district) accountability and how these might play out within the state education system.[25] The next section considers how school standards might influence ways in which institutions external to the regular state education system (state and federal courts and federal legislation) might hold the state and local education agencies accountable for providing equal opportunity to all students.

The central purpose of a strong accountability strategy should be to improve teaching and learning. The assumption of accountability strategies is that rewards and punishments based on the degree of success in achieving clear standards will motivate both students and educators to high levels of performance. *High stakes* in theory will increase motivation and performance. Another purpose of accountability is to protect students. When other methods of school improvement fail to ensure that the schools offer all students the opportunity to learn, the public must be able to hold the district and state accountable.

Fair Student Accountability. The typical conception of student accountability is that a student's future educational or occupational opportunities should rest at least to some extent on whether he or she has met a preestablished performance standard on an assessment. In practice, we hope that the process in the United States would be more complex. At a minimum, we argue that assessments used for student accountability should not occur until late in the school career, that high-stakes decisions should involve additional information beyond that contained in the assessment, and that there should be second chances for students who do not succeed.

In addition, we believe one other condition is necessary if student assessments are to have any legitimate role in high-stakes decisions: students must have had the opportunity to learn well the material on the assessment. We have presented ethical arguments for the notion of *legitimate accountability*. Those arguments are further supported by recent developments in psychometric theory regarding test validity. Sam Messick and others hold that a test is not in itself valid or invalid, but instead validity resides in the way a test is used and in the effects it has on the individuals and institutions that use it. They term this new approach *consequential validity* (Messick, 1989; Linn, 1991).

The criteria for determining the consequential validity of an assessment will vary, depending on the intended use, but for most purposes (especially those involving accountability) the criteria would include concepts highly congruent with the basic components of systemic reform and school standards. These include curricular relevance (the assessment should reflect the curriculum), instructional opportunity for all students (opportunity to learn the curriculum), instructional sensitivity (assessment performance should be sensitive to variation in the quality and content of instruction), and generalizability (on replication, the assessment should produce the same results). These four criteria would all be necessary for an assessment to have consequential validity as part of a student or school accountability system. In a systemic curricular strategy, we believe a high-quality, curriculum-based assessment would be more likely to satisfy the criteria for consequential validity (and therefore for legitimate accountability) in a school that had met the school standards.

There is also some legal precedent supporting the ethical and psychometric arguments we have presented. During the late-1970s minimum-competencies era, a federal court of appeals in Florida in *Debra P. v. Turlington* (1981) upheld a lower-court decision that restricted Florida's use of a minimum competency requirement for graduation. There were two parts to the decision. One was due process: *all* students were entitled to adequate notice and the opportunity to prepare for the test before suffering adverse consequences. The other was equal protection: African-American children who had been educated in segregated, constitutionally inadequate schools could not be made to suffer adverse consequences for the inferior education that had been foisted on them.[26] If the assessments in a systemic curriculum reform are used for high-stakes accountability for students, school standards could provide legal criteria for assessing whether students had been provided due process and equal protection.[27]

School Accountability. Accountability, whatever the target, might be said to have both a positive and negative face. With regard to school accountability, there are many good reasons for taking positive action when a school succeeds in passing the school performance standards. Rewards, particularly those shared by an entire staff, can help keep morale high and stimulate ongoing improvement. We are primarily concerned here, however, with the darker side of school accountability.

Although schools cannot be held *legally* accountable for the failing performance of their students (legal responsibility rests with the state and local school boards), it might be reasonable for districts and, under certain circumstances, states to hold schools *administratively* accountable.[28] In the section on school improvement, we considered some ways in which districts and states would exercise moderate means of holding schools administratively accountable. But what about situations in which school improvement activities fail to help the school meet the school standards? Could districts and states exercise a stronger form of accountability?

Certainly a school should only be held accountable if it has the resources to meet the school standards. If the resource standards have been met and the school has a reasonable degree of autonomy and flexibility, a district or state might legitimately hold the school accountable for meeting the performance and practice standards. If the school failed to improve after continuous assistance, "high-stakes" action might be called for. One approach would be to protect the students by providing them resources to transfer to other schools. While this strategy might help individual students, it leaves many questions unresolved, including what to do with the existing staff. Another approach would be to "reconstitute the school" — that is, replace all of the instructional staff including the principal and engage a new faculty with the responsibility for bringing the school up to standards. This approach would be taken only after repeated efforts at school improvement had failed. This strategy has been used in San Francisco in the context of a desegregation case (*San Francisco NAACP v. San Francisco Unified School District*, 1983). In Kentucky, a similar strategy is available to the state when a school does not meet certain performance standards (Kentucky Reform Act of 1990).

We sympathize with the reasons for this approach. Too often, the schools of the poor have been allowed to fail their students without any consequence. But a number of questions plague us. Would the "old" staff be fired? Would they be distributed throughout the system? From where would the new staff be drawn? How would this work in a small system? Would the measures for assessing whether the school could legitimately be held accountable have to be psychometrically stronger than the assessments used to trigger school improvement efforts?

District Accountability. A district derives from the state the legal responsibility for making sure that all of its schools are meeting the school standards, and ultimately it is the state that must hold districts accountable. But as in the case of school accountability, there is a "legitimate accountability" issue for districts as well. The district must have access to sufficient resources to provide all of its schools the opportunity to meet the school standards, a particularly important issue in schools with large numbers of low-income and minority students. These schools are often in districts that do not have access to the necessary resources.

Assuming that the state is doing its share to provide the resources, however, is it legitimate and reasonable for the state to hold its districts accountable for ensuring that schools in their jurisdiction meet the school standards? States, including New Jersey and California, have taken some steps along these lines in recent years, though in most instances the measures of accountability were fiscal and not educational.

Ultimately, the problem is "What the devil do you do?" Taking funds away from the district does not seem reasonable to us, and the human resources are not available to "reconstitute" the district. Removing some authority from the school board and replacing the superintendent have been the primary strategies to date. The private sector might be providing another alternative: in some cases educational and management consultant groups have offered to take over responsibility for managing a troubled district out of its problems. These and other strategies require exploration.

The Use of School Standards by Institutions External to the School System

A final use for school standards involves actions that could be taken by courts, legislatures, and advocates against a district or state for not providing equal opportunity. School standards provide a measure of equal opportunity. If the assessments of school standards were at least partially open to public scrutiny, the level of public accountability would be greatly enhanced.

State and federal courts and legislatures have struggled for years to define equal opportunity. Traditionally, governments and courts have focused on the equality of finances and generic, easily defined school resources. School finance reform has emphasized equality of expenditures, within certain parameters of political and fiscal feasibility. The educational arguments for desegregation and for eliminating tracking are often based upon equalizing the resources available to all students, including the curriculum and student composition.

Courts and legislatures could redefine their understanding of equal educational opportunity in the context of a systemic curricular strategy. We have argued that equal opportunity for poor and minority students would be achieved when their schools meet the standards for providing all of their students the opportunity to achieve a high standard of performance on assessments based on the curriculum frameworks. Of course, providing this opportunity may require very different strategies for different students. Specifically, to meet the school standards, schools of the poor and otherwise less advantaged may require more and quite different resources than schools of the more advantaged.

The basis for moving to this redefinition of equal opportunity is grounded in ethical arguments, embedded in the ideas about resource and practice standards for schools, and supported by arguments for legitimate accountability and consequential validity.[29] The reformulation rests on two interrelated points: (1) the alignment and coherence of the proposed system around challenging curriculum standards, which provides a way of relating education standards for schools to student opportunity to learn the curriculum; and (2) a conception of equality of opportunity as being met through provision of opportunity to learn.

Some examples should help. At the state level, conceptions of the "right to an education" and equal opportunity are deeply embedded in many state constitutions. In New Jersey, for example, the state constitution requires that all students receive a "thorough and efficient"[30] education. In a case argued before the New Jersey Supreme Court, *Robinson v. Cahill* (1973), the complainant originally argued that the "thorough and efficient" clause required the state to provide enough money so that each child could undertake the ordinary duties of citizenship and had the minimum education so that he or she may be able to read, write, and function in a political environment. The court found that the amount of state funds allocated to education was inadequate to yield the mandated equal opportunity (Tractenberg, 1974, pp. 312, 315; Yudof, Kirp, van Geel, and Levin, 1982, pp. 609–610). Seventeen years later the case, now called *Abbott v. Burke* (1990), was brought back to the New Jersey Supreme Court, which unanimously ruled that the "thorough and efficient" provision had continued to be violated. This time the court argued not only for fiscal equality but for equity in services and programs for students in poor urban districts.

A second example is *Edgewood Independent School District v. Kirby* (1989). In this case, the Texas Supreme Court reversed a court of appeals decision and upheld a district court ruling that found that the state school financing system violated both the state constitution's equal protection provision and its "efficiency" mandate. "The court found that the state foundation program did not cover 'even the cost of meeting the state-mandated minimum requirements'" (Taylor and Piché, 1990, p. 14). Although the focus of the court's decision was on finances, the amount of financing necessary was traced back to state education requirements. "The court cited specific ways in which rich districts were superior to poor ones. It noted disparities in foreign language, pre-kindergarten, math and science, and extracurricular activities" (Taylor and Piché, 1990, p. 14).

While courts have struggled with the concept of equality of opportunity in school finance cases, as represented by states' equal protection clauses and phrases such as "thorough and efficient," there is typically no agreed-on framework for understanding what equality actually means in practice. It has been left to legislatures to try to accomplish the generalized lofty principles, but the results are generally based on vague definitions of services and programs, politics, and monetary constraints.

Equality of opportunity is defined earlier in this chapter, not as a common level of generic resources but as the provision of the resources and practices necessary to provide all students the opportunity to learn the content of the frameworks. In a systemic curriculum reform, the opportunity to learn is defined in terms of the school standards. The determination of whether a student receives the kind of education required by many state

constitutions could rest on whether the student is in a school
that meets the school resource and practice standards. We believe that these standards could be a more powerful lever for
providing educational opportunity to poor and minority students
than those typically used in school finance cases.

Because there are dimensions to equal schooling other than
those covered by a systemic curriculum strategy, we would not
expect the school standards to constitute all of the criteria necessary for satisfying a requirement such as New Jersey's "thorough
and efficient" clause. However, we would expect that such criteria
would form the core definition. To meet other needs fiscal criteria
would probably be required as well. We are intrigued with
Clune's conception of a substitute for the prevailing use of "fiscal
neutrality" in school finance cases (Clune, 1992). Clune argues
for a three-part remedy consisting of "1) a base program of
substantial equality of spending throughout the state . . . 2) a substantial amount of compensatory aid based on a realistic needs
assessment of children in poverty . . . [and] 3) 'performance-
oriented policies designed to increase the effectiveness of educational spending'" (Clune, 1992, pp. 733–734). Our conception
of systemic curriculum reform would retain Clune's first two
parts and substitute criteria based on the school standards for
his third part.[31]

Finally, a concept related to equality of opportunity, comparability, appears in Title I (now Chapter 1) of the Elementary and Secondary Education Act of 1965. Before a district
receives Chapter 1 funds, it must show that the Chapter 1 schools
in the district receive the same level of foundation support as
non-Chapter 1 schools. In effect, Chapter 1 requires "equality
of resources" across the schools within districts. But just as *equality
of opportunity* is defined generically in school finance cases, so
too is *comparability* defined in Chapter 1 law and regulations.
As a consequence, there are striking differences in the quality
of resources and the ways they are used between Chapter 1 and
non-Chapter 1 schools within districts. An alternative, in the
context of systemic reform, is to define comparability as requiring that all students be offered the opportunity to learn, as assessed by their school meeting the school standards.[32]

Diversity and Democracy

Thus far we have focused our attention on the importance of providing all students an equal opportunity to learn an agreed-upon core of common content. We have touched only briefly on issues of diversity within or beyond that core. Yet such issues are critical to any treatment of educational equity. The content of a public school curriculum is a statement of the values and norms of the society as well as a product of educational expertise. In a democracy as diverse as ours, it is essential that we ask *whose* values and norms are represented in that statement and what the process has been for its creation.

In the past, answers to these questions may have been — or at least appeared to be — rather straightforward. Because of American traditions of local control, arguments about what schools should teach were generally confined to localities. At this level, participants in the discussion were often of similar traditions and beliefs — either because the local populations were fairly homogeneous or because large subpopulations of children were segregated within or excluded from the public system of education.[33] Even where school populations reflected greater cultural, linguistic, or religious diversity, the political disenfranchisement of large groups often resulted in decisions being made by fairly homogeneous groups of leaders about how best to educate (and often "Americanize") other groups.

In the last half century, however, the situation has changed significantly. As the demand for social, political, and economic equality among groups has broadened and deepened, as larger units — including states and massive urban school districts — have assumed more responsibility for structuring the curriculum, and as affected populations within those jurisdictions have become increasingly diverse, debate over curricular content has sometimes been quite intense, erupting periodically along racial, religious, or ethnic lines and often being linked to issues of political power and cultural legitimacy.

Recent cases in point include the controversies over the adoption of history textbooks in California and the report of the New York State Social Studies Review and Development

Committee (1991). National debates over multicultural education and Afrocentric curricula are other examples of this phenomenon.

Justice, Legitimacy, and the Curricular Core

That such controversy should exist in a democratic society is hardly surprising. Our acceptance of it stems in part from the supposition that individuals are socially constituted — that is, as they mature, they internalize the traditions, roles, and understandings of their communities, which often differ in significant ways. Our acceptance also derives from the modern view that much of what we call knowledge is itself socially constructed, with schools being a primary mechanism for legitimizing certain knowledge constructions over others. Given these two underlying suppositions, as well as the unprecedented diversity of the student population in U.S. schools and the historical pattern of dominance of certain "communities" over others, it seems inevitable that the development of a common curriculum would be an arena for political struggle.

It also seems inevitable that debates about the nature of curricular content would assume even greater significance within the context of content-driven systemic reform. The systemic strategy we have described takes content frameworks as the driving force and kingpin for the entire system. States adopting such a strategy would be expected to develop common frameworks in all areas of the curriculum, including controversial subjects such as history, social studies, literature, and science. As those frameworks take on a larger role in shaping the nature of schooling, their salience to all stakeholders in the educational enterprise necessarily increases. And so should the controversy.

We believe this controversy can be a positive and productive force in the reform movement. The legitimacy and effectiveness of a systemic curricular approach will ultimately rest in the ability of the system to establish challenging curricular goals while striking a creative balance between the common culture and needs of the whole society on the one hand and the diverse perspectives, needs, and histories of subgroups and individuals on the other. This is the essence of the concept of liberal

justice.[34] Broad and deep public debate over the nature of the
frameworks is, we believe, essential to establishing that balance,
which in turn provides the basis for eventual public acceptance
of the frameworks and the reforms. Without acceptance by
diverse parts of our society, the reforms will not gain legitimacy
and will fail the very students we are addressing.

The resolution of controversy over how schools will respond to the substantial diversity in our society is by no means
assured, however. Theoretically, a range of possible responses
exists—all the way from separatism based on distinct cultural
heritage to a monolithic suppression of differences.

One way of thinking about these issues is to adopt the
liberal justice view that social policy should be "neutral," that
is, straightforwardly respectful of differing views within a democratic context. Educational philosopher Kenneth Strike argues
that neutrality consists of two parts: no one is inherently deserv-
ing of better treatment than anyone else, and people are entitled to their own conceptions of their own good (Strike, 1991,
pp. 205–206).

One implication of this definition is that everyone is entitled to equal opportunity—or, in our terms, equal access to
an opportunity to learn the content of the frameworks. We have
focused most of our discussion up to this point on this implication. A second implication, however, concerns the nature of the
content itself. In this regard, Strike's definition of neutrality
would place "two requirements on schools. First, schools should
not be vehicles for enforcing parental conceptions of a good life
on children. . . . As they progress toward citizenship, children
have a right to develop a conception of their lives that may, if
they choose, depart from that of their parents. Second, schools
must provide education in such a way that children can explore
various conceptions of a good life, but without committing the
school to some official definition of what that life is and without
arbitrarily restricting the range of options to be explored" (Strike,
1991, p. 207). This view of social justice provides criteria for
considering differing ways for resolving conflicts over the nature of public school curriculum.

How might the criteria for social neutrality be met? Strike

argues that people are formed by various traditions, that this process is already well under way when students enter school, and that educational institutions must respect and aid in the process of enculturation. But to be neutral, they must do so by aiding and respecting a variety of cultures and traditions. He proposes a "pluralistic dialogue" model of schooling to meet his criteria for neutrality while assisting in the process of enculturation (1991, p. 214). The model seeks depth and coherence in the curriculum, while acknowledging the complexities of perspectives that our nation's diversity generates.

In this model (as in some current conceptions of multicultural education), school curricula and instruction would be designed to foster dialogue among people of various cultures and about the nature and perspectives of various traditions. The purpose of this dialogue would be two-fold. On the one hand it would build students' tolerance of cultures and perspectives different from their own. At the same time, it would give students both a substantive basis and the analytical tools for a critical consideration of their own traditions and values. Such an approach would aid students in forming their own "conceptions of the good life." Moreover, because it is congruent with constructivist notions of teaching and learning, it may have the added benefit of developing critical thinking skills, also a goal of the reform movement (Banks, 1991). We note that this model does not argue for treating all cultures and traditions uncritically, and it would specifically exclude certain traditions, cultures, and cultural claims if they are unjust (Rawls, 1988; Strike, 1991) or unsupported by evidence through rational appraisal, such as claims of particular historical occurrences or creationism.

The "pluralistic dialogue" model is attractive, if somewhat idealistic. Indeed, it provides promise for moving toward a more coherent and challenging curriculum on the one hand while simultaneously respecting various cultural perspectives on the other. We recognize that implementing it would represent an extraordinary challenge, different from but at least equal to that of implementing well the standards of the National Council of Teachers of Mathematics or other similar content frameworks.

An intriguing aspect of Strike's model of schooling is that it views schools and their students as undergoing the same learning process that we hope the society will undergo as it works its way toward the goal of legitimate curriculum frameworks. The way decisions are made about the content and pedagogical strategies of the frameworks is critical to their legitimacy. There must be strong and continuing input from all the various stakeholders to ensure both the legitimacy of the content and the political buy-in of the stakeholders.

Flexibility and Choice Within the Common Curriculum Frameworks

A basic premise of the reform we have sketched is that the structure and support provided by the system would allow substantial professional discretion and responsibility at the school building and classroom level. Obviously this discretion would apply to all areas outside the core content, but it must also apply in meaningful ways to the core itself. Within the context of the core frameworks, the system needs to ensure flexibility and choice in content and pedagogy. This has a number of implications.

One implication is that the content of the frameworks should be specific enough to provide serious substantive direction to schools and districts but not so specific as to inhibit creativity and professional discretion. There must be room for flexibility and choice in topic if the content is to reflect the interests, abilities, and traditions of the teachers and students. Such flexibility would allow teachers to adjust the content in ways that would make it more meaningful to and thus more fully engaging for their specific students as they worked toward common understandings and skills. For example, Asian, African, Latin American, and European literature might each be studied to give students an understanding of how literature influences and is influenced by culture, experience, and social forces. Similarly, graduates in a California fishing community may be more knowledgeable about coastal ecology than students in Palm Springs, who in turn may be far better versed in the weather, biology, and botany of desert regions. The trick will be to establish serious choice within the context of coherent frameworks.

A second implication is that the time frame for the frameworks would need to incorporate sufficient flexibility that the teachers and schools were not locked into rigid instructional sequences. School professionals must be able to allocate instructional time and to sequence topics in ways appropriate to the topics themselves, the structure and resources of the school, and the needs and interests of the students. The NCTM Standards and several of the California frameworks are laid out in three-to-four-year blocks for this reason; teachers and schools then develop specific curricula to guide instruction year by year.

Finally, within the context of the systemic strategy, it is essential to ensure flexibility and choice in the selection, adaptation, and development of instructional materials and of pedagogical strategies, based on professional knowledge and decisions at the local school level. Teachers must be able to meet individual learning needs of students in order to provide equal access to the core. For example, they must be able to make the content linguistically accessible for LEP and other nonstandard-English-dominant students. The choices must be based on professional judgment, not centralized policy, as teachers and schools are in the best position to assess and respond to the strengths and needs of their students. This implies an organization in which great authority for the instructional plan and process rests at the school site (such as for refining content, determining pedagogy, and hiring appropriate personnel).

Concluding Thoughts

We have barely scratched the surface of a complex and very important set of issues. Students from poor and minority groups face a very uncertain time in U.S. education. Their economic and social conditions are deteriorating without relief in sight, and the progressive curriculum reforms, if carried out one school at a time, will almost certainly place them at an even greater relative disadvantage.

Our thesis has been that systemic curriculum reform offers an alternative that might have a strong positive effect on equal opportunity. Curriculum frameworks that contain challenging content and that are developed in the spirit of open discussion among diverse groups could provide direction for major curriculum reform for all schools and their students. As part of our argument we have suggested a way of defining equality of educational opportunity that could have substantial implications for ensuring equitable treatment of all students by guiding school improvement efforts and providing leverage for courts and advocates. At the same time we have raised many more questions than we have answered. Our gravest concern is whether there is sufficient commitment in our society to significantly and directly address the problems of educational equity through any sustained and coherent strategy.

Notes

1. Our conception of *systemic school reform* was set out some time ago in a book chapter of the same name (Smith and O'Day, 1991b). It is similar to the one put forth by Susan Fuhrman in the introductory chapter of this book and to the formulation of David K. Cohen's under the label *coherent instructional guidance*. William Clune in his chapter in this book uses a somewhat different definition. Many of the basic ideas underlying systemic school reform have been around for a long time. California has been pursuing parts of a systemic curriculum reform strategy for some time. The structure and policies of the educational systems in many other economically advanced nations are shaped by something like systemic curriculum reform and, as Arthur Powell describes in his chapter in this book, a coalition of private schools followed a somewhat similar strategy in the decades prior to 1940. Only in recent years have U.S. researchers begun writing about this type of reform. However, we do not know of any other extensive treatment of equity issues in the context of systemic school reform.

2. For example, the conception of systemic school reform in this chapter closely resembles that used as the basis for the Systemic State Initiative (SSI) of the National Science Foundation (NSF), which now has major projects in science and mathematics in over twenty states, for the analysis of systemic reform in the National Council on Educational Stan-

dards and Testing (NCEST) report (1992), and for the structure and content of the school reforms or legislation in Arkansas, California, South Carolina, and other states. In addition, this conception of systemic reform served as the basis for parts of two federal bills (S2 and HR4323), which passed their respective houses and the conference committee but failed to get a final vote in the 102nd Congress. An education bill containing similar provisions is likely to be introduced early in the 103rd Congress.

We have emphasized state rather than national systemic reform because states have the constitutional responsibility for public education in the United States and, with the local agencies that are granted authority through state constitutions, the practical responsibility of providing over 92 percent of the funding.

3. Over the past year the terms *curriculum frameworks* and *content standards* have often been used interchangeably to refer to state or national specifications of what students are expected to know and be able to do. The NCEST report (1992) and the National Council of Teachers of Mathematics (NCTM) (1989) use content standards, while we in our earlier papers (Smith and O'Day, 1991a, 1991b) and others have adopted curriculum frameworks, the term used in California. At some point the language should be standardized. We use curriculum frameworks for state-level documents and content standards for national-level documents such as those established by the NCTM.

4. We have chosen to structure this chapter around an argument about the way the reform might work, rather than consider a variety of separate issues, for two major reasons: the form and logic of the argument are important to consider and the issues and steps in the argument are not truly independent. One of the consequences of this strategy is to illuminate how far we have to go to analyze seriously our assumptions and understandings of how the reforms might actually work. We suggest in these notes some of the places where new analyses and data are necessary.

5. An opposite danger, of course, is that a poorly imple-
    mented systemwide strategy of curriculum reform might
    bring the quality of curriculum and instruction to a low
    common level for all students by forcing rigidities on the
    schools or bowing to political pressures to set low com-
    mon standards.

6. The decrease in poverty between 1960 and 1980 was not
    strictly linear. The percentage of children in poverty reached
    a low of 14.4 percent in 1973 and was already on the in-
    cline again by 1980. By 1987, it had reached a level of
    20.6 percent and was climbing. In 1987, 25 percent of all
    children under the age of six were living in poverty (Smith
    and O'Day, 1991b, p. 57).

7. Only for nine-year-olds in mathematics does the gain over
    the past fifteen years for white students approach a third
    of a standard deviation. None of the other comparisons
    for whites in reading, mathematics, or science for nine-,
    thirteen-, and seventeen-year-olds shows a gain in size
    more than 0.2 standard deviations over the trend line. See
    Mullis and others, 1991.

8. Even though the NAEP is not specifically aligned with the
    curricula of any given state and continues to be primarily
    a multiple-choice or short-answer assessment, we expect
    that it will be moderately sensitive to effects of curricula
    that emphasize challenging content. The new NAEP as-
    sessments in math are based generally on the NCTM stan-
    dards, as are the emerging frameworks in a number of
    states. Moreover, the NAEP frameworks for reading as-
    sessment increasingly emphasize the comprehension and
    analysis of meaningful text, as do many of the new state
    frameworks. Thus there is a growing emphasis on chal-
    lenging content for the curriculum policies of many states
    and the NAEP frameworks.

9. *All* should be modified here to *the very great majority*. We
    estimate that 2 to 4 percent of all children have handicaps
    severe enough to restrict their capacity to learn the kinds
    of material we are considering.

10. See Bereiter and Scardamalia, 1985; Chi and others, 1989; Glaser, 1984; Peterson, 1986; and Stigler and Stevenson, 1991.

11. Green elaborates on the concept of fair benefit distribution as follows:

> The educational system will distribute its benefits unequally, and it will do so no matter how the system is organized and no matter how "benefits" are defined. The fact is that some people will do well in the system and some will not do so well. . . . [However], the system must distribute its educational benefits on the basis of the distribution of educationally relevant attributes in the population. . . . By "educationally relevant" . . . I mean relevant to the grounds on which a particular distribution of educational benefits might be regarded as just or unjust. . . . The logic of our thinking shows that we normally regard choice, tenacity, and ability to be educationally relevant attributes of the population in the sense defined and that we do not regard class, sex and race in the same light [1980, p. 49].

> To illustrate. That those who attain least often in high school are likely to be those of lower social status is often taken as evidence that the distribution of high school attainment is unjust. By advancing this claim, we are declaring, in effect, that social class is an educationally irrelevant attribute of the population. It is not the sort of thing that should determine the distribution of educational benefits. Distribution according to social class is unjust. On the other hand, that the Amish typically benefit less than others from the educa-

tional system is not viewed as unjust because it is said to result from choice flowing from religious convictions embodied in a long cultural tradition. And neither is it considered unjust that some benefit more than others because they try harder or persist more. Even though class is declared to be irrelevant in this sense, the exercise of choice and perseverance is not [1991, p. 227].

12. An interesting observation here is that it may be relatively easy to make serious changes in an aligned system simply by changing the frameworks and allowing the alignment ripples to work through the system. It would certainly be easier to make changes than in the present loosely coupled system operating in most states. When the changes are constructive, this is a very positive attribute.

13. Over the past twenty-five years, the nation has struggled over what it means by terms such as *equity* and *equality of opportunity* in education. For some recent thinking about these issues, see Kirp, 1992; Walzer, 1991a, 1991b; Green, 1991; Strike, 1991; and Jencks, 1988.

14. Others argue for a second form of self-correction: schools should be set free to let the market place determine their fate. We are skeptical about solutions predicated on "choice" for the poor and minorities, especially because of the relative vulnerability of these groups in our society.

15. Measuring the progress of a school on assessment outcome standards is not as straightforward a task as might be imagined. Witness the massive debate now going on in the country over how and when and for what purposes to test students.

16. In the NCEST report (1992), school standards were called *school delivery standards*. See especially Appendix E. Since this report was released, the issues of what school delivery standards are, how they might be measured, and how they might be used to protect the poor have received extensive debate in the Committee on Education and Labor

in the U.S. House of Representatives, the National Governors' Association, and other policy circles. See especially the legislative and committee report language of HR4323.

17. Systemic curriculum reform provides a very specific context for school standards. If a local school or system wanted to maximize other outcomes than those suggested by the systemic curriculum reform (such as service, sports, creative arts, and so on), other school standards would be appropriate.

18. This argument provides us with what we think is an important insight about why the U.S. quantitative school-effects literature is so bereft of significant results. Production functions that related school inputs to school outcomes in the United States showed that there were few significant relationships (Hanushek, 1986). Since the measures used on the outcome side of the equation have essentially been designed to be independent of the characteristics measured on the input side, it should not be surprising that the regression weights are distributed around zero. But in the future, if the key input parts of the system, especially curriculum materials and teacher professional development, are aligned with each other and with the key outcomes, there could be a major change in the results of production functions. If both sides of the equation (inputs and outcomes) are aligned, we might expect a much more substantial relationship between the two sides than we have seen in the past. Obviously, the measures would change. For example, we now assess teacher quality by counting the number of courses teachers take. In the future we might use teacher knowledge of the content of the curriculum frameworks as one proxy for teacher quality. Another input measure might be the fit of the content of the textbooks to the frameworks. Neither of these measures makes sense in American education now; they would, however, in a system that had a coherent curricular strategy. We believe that these "new" measures would have substantially larger coefficients than the ones generally found now. We should be able to examine the accuracy of this insight by

looking at production function results from other nations where the assessments and the inputs are both aligned with a common curricular framework.

19. For example, we have not included as necessary resources a library, or a teachers' room with a separate desk and phone for each teacher, or the human support necessary to allow teachers to have at least one period per day to plan their work together. Though these other resources may be justifiably viewed as *necessary* for the instructional program to succeed in many settings, they are not directly part of the systemic curriculum reform and it should be within a school's discretion to allocate certain resources for these or other expenditures it deems more effective in meeting the needs of its students.

20. Assessments of student success in achieving the curriculum goals might be made at various times during the student's career. The NCEST report (1992) suggests assessments at grades four, eight, and twelve. See also Smith and O'Day, 1991b.

21. See Independent Commission on Chapter 1 (1992) and also a proposal from the New Standards Project to the Pew Charitable Trusts, January, 1992.

22. The rejection of norm referencing is not a new idea in testing in America. The basic skills movement of the 1960s and 1970s spawned minimum-competency, multiple-choice, criterion-referenced testing with a single standard established for passing. Interestingly, these tests also met the criteria established for the kind of assessment preferred in the new reforms. Although the minimum-competency test questions were typically single answer, quick response, and multiple choice, they were appropriate for measuring the content and were also "authentic" in their representation of the instruction. But on another dimension, the reasons for rejecting norm-referenced testing now are different than they were twenty-five years ago. At that time, criterion testing was used to try to bring the achievement floor up for the lowest-scoring students. The assumption, however, was still prevalent that many students simply

could not learn complex material. This time around, the prevailing assumption is that, given the opportunity, *all* students have the capacity to achieve very high standards.

23.   The conference versions of House Bill 4323 and Senate Bill 2 (refer to note 2 for explanation) required the development of national school standards. Over time the nation will have to work out the relationship between national school standards and school standards developed at the state level.

24.   A number of groups around the nation are struggling with the issues of designing a system that uses school standards. Of note are the New Standards Project at the University of Pittsburgh's Learning Research and Development Center and the National Center on Education and the Economy in Rochester, New York, and the Chapter 1 Commission based at the Council of Chief State School Officers.

25.   Some accountability advocates argue for holding individual teachers accountable beyond the methods presently used. (See Bridges, 1990.) We have indicated that in school improvement efforts teachers may be given special training and even "gently" reassigned, but a more rigorous degree of *high-stakes* accountability for tenured teachers seems unlikely. We dismiss the idea of holding individual teachers accountable for their students' performances for a variety of reasons, the most important being that the task of preparing students for high performances is a collective task of many teachers and administrators within a school. There is no feasible and general way of sorting out individual specific contributions and, if there were, it might inhibit collaborations among teachers, which would probably lead, on average, to a reduction in the quality of the pedagogy.

In one other way a teacher might be held accountable in the context of school standards. Teachers should know and be able to teach the content of the frameworks to some standard. It should be feasible to hold existing and new teachers to at least a resource standard of knowing the content and skills of the frameworks, if they have been given sufficient opportunity to learn the relevant material.

26. See also Yudof, Kirp, van Geel, and Levin, 1982, pp. 390–401 and McClung, 1979. Information is also from a personal communication with William Taylor.

27. There would continue to be some difficult questions in the design of a student accountability system even with this formulation in place. For example, should a student have the opportunity to take an assessment and get "credit" even if the school does not meet the school standards? We think the answer to this question is yes.

28. We understand that accountability is usually thought to rest on individuals rather than groups. We use the notion of school accountability here to emphasize the *collective responsibility* of the entire staff to provide all students in the school with the opportunity to learn the desired content.

29. One problem with this argument is that it would rely on a coalition of the poor, minorities, philosophers, and psychometricians to be the primary supporters. Not a likely possibility.

30. The idea of an efficient education takes on substantial meaning in a systemic curricular reform. One of the concepts in systemic reform is that a clear set of goals and a vision about where the system is going and what standards need to be met will serve as a guide for allocating resources throughout the system. Resource-allocation decisions (among different curricula, about how to organize a school to use school personnel better, and so on) would be substantially driven by a clear conception of the curricular goals, rather than by often conflicting and vague general conceptions of the goals of the school.

31. Clune (pp. 734–735) suggests three kinds of performance-oriented strategies: a *systemic* approach, an *accountability* approach, and an *organizational* approach. We believe that the systemic strategy we have proposed incorporates both the systemic and the accountability approaches suggested by Clune. His organizational approach combines arguments for both parental choice and for decentalization, concepts that are clearly related but not necessarily the

same. We also believe that we have incorporated the advantages he cites for decentralization in our formulation.

32. In the federal General Education Provisions Act and the local applications section of Chapter 1, there is language requiring equal educational opportunity under the law.

33. For example, the Chinese in California, African Americans in the South, Mexicans in the Southwest, and Native Americans throughout the country have faced such discrimination.

34. *Liberalism* here refers to the line of political thought developed by such sources as Hobbes, Locke, Mill, Ackerman, and Rawls. According to Strike, "The central problem of political liberalism is to provide a principled way of distinguishing the legitimate range of civil authority from that sphere over which the individual is autonomous" (1991, p. 196). We have used Strike's analysis as a basis for our discussion of liberal justice in this section.

References

Abbott v. Burke, 119 N.J. 287, 575 A.2d. 359 (1990).

Ackerman, B. A. *Social Justice in the Liberal State.* New Haven, Conn.: Yale University Press, 1980.

Banks, J. A. "Multicultural Literacy and Curriculum Reform." *Educational Horizons,* spring 1991, *69*(3), 135–140.

Barker, E. (Trans.). *Aristotle: The Politics.* Oxford: Oxford University Press, 1948.

Bereiter, C., and Scardamalia, M. "Cognitive Coping Strategies and the Problem of 'Inert Knowledge.'" In S. F. Chipman, J. W. Segal, and R. Glaser (eds.), *Thinking and Learning Skills: Research and Open Questions.* Vol. 2. Hillsdale, N.J.: Erlbaum, 1985.

Bridges, E. H. *Managing the Incompetent Teacher.* Eugene: University of Oregon, 1990.

Chi, M. T. H., and others. "Self Explanations: How Students Study and Use Examples in Learning to Solve Problems." *Cognitive Science,* 1989, *13,* 145–182.

Clune, W. H. "New Answers to Hard Questions Posed by

Rodriguez: Ending the Separation of School Finance and Educational Policy by Bridging the Gap Between Wrong and Remedy." *Connecticut Law Review,* 1992, *24,* 721–755.

Cohen, D. K. "A Revolution in One Classroom: The Case of Mrs. Oublier." *Educational Evaluation and Policy Analysis,* 1990, *12*(3), 327–345.

Debra P. v. Turlington, 474 F.Supp. 244 (M.D. Fl 1979), *affirmed in part* 644 F.2d 397 (5th Cir., 1981).

Edgewood Independent School District v. Kirby, 777 S.W.2d 391 (Tex. 1989).

Glaser, R. "Education and Thinking: The Role of Knowledge." *American Psychologist,* 1984, *39,* 93–104.

Green, T. F. *Predicting the Behavior of the Educational System.* Syracuse, N.Y.: Syracuse University Press, 1980.

Green, T. F. "Excellence, Equity and Equality." In L. S. Shulman and G. Sykes (eds.), *The Handbook on Teaching and Policy.* New York: Longman, 1982.

Green, T. F. "Distributive Justice in Education." In D. Verstegen and J. Ward (eds.), *Spheres of Justice in Education: The 1990 American Education Finance Association Yearbook.* New York: Harper Business, 1991.

Hanushek, E. A. "The Economics of Schooling." *Journal of Economic Literature,* 1986, *24,* 1141–1171.

Jencks, C. S. "Whom Must We Treat Equally for Educational Opportunity to Be Equal?" *Ethics,* 1988, *98,* 518–533.

Kirp, D. L. "Among School Children: The Equities in the Schoolhouse." Paper prepared for the Center on Organization and Restructuring of Schools, University of Wisconsin, Madison, 1992.

Kozol, J. *Savage Inequalities.* New York: Crown, 1991.

Lieberman, A., and McLaughlin, M. "Networks for Educational Change: Powerful and Problematic." *Phi Delta Kappan,* 1992, *73,* 673–677.

Linn, R. "Technical Considerations in the Proposed Nationwide Assessment System for the National Education Goals Panel." Paper prepared for the Resource Group for Goal 3 for the National Education Goals Panel, Washington, D.C., 1991.

McClung, M. "Competency Testing Programs: Legal and Educational Issues." *Fordham Law Review,* 1979, *47,* 651–712.

MacIntyre, A. *After Virtue.* Notre Dame, Ind.: Notre Dame University Press, 1981.

Mathews, J. *Escalante.* New York: Holt, Rinehart & Winston, 1988.

Messick, S. "Meaning and Values in Test Validation: The Science and Ethics of Assessment." *Educational Researcher,* 1989, *18*(2), 5–11.

Mullis, I. V. V., and others. *Trends in Academic Progress: Achievement of U.S. Students in Science, 1969–70 to 1990; Mathematics, 1973 to 1990; Reading, 1971 to 1990; and Writing, 1984 to 1990.* Report prepared by the Educational Testing Service under contract with the National Center for Education Statistics, Office of Educational Research and Improvement, U.S. Department of Education (report no. 21-T-01). Washington, D.C.: U.S. Government Printing Office, 1991.

National Council of Teachers of Mathematics. *Curriculum and Evaluation Standards for School Mathematics.* Reston, Va.: National Council of Teachers of Mathematics, 1989.

National Council on Education Standards and Testing. *Raising Standards for American Education: A Report to Congress, the Secretary of Education, the National Education Goals Panel, and the American People.* Washington, D.C.: U.S. Government Printing Office, 1992.

National Education Goals Panel. *The National Education Goals Report: Building a Nation of Learners.* Washington, D.C.: National Education Goals Panel, 1991.

National Governors' Association. *From Rhetoric to Action: State Progress in Restructuring the Education System.* Washington, D.C.: National Governors' Association, 1991.

New York State Social Studies Review and Development Committee. *One Nation, Many Peoples: A Declaration of Cultural Interdependence.* Albany: New York State Education Department, 1991.

Peterson, P. "Selecting Students and Services for Compensatory Education: Lessons from Aptitude-Treatment Interaction Research." Paper delivered at the Conference on the

Effects of Alternate Designs in Compensatory Education, Washington, D.C., June 1986.

Rawls, J. "The Priority of Right and Ideas of the Good." *Philosophy and Public Affairs,* 1988, *17,* 251–276.

Resnick, L. B. *Education and Learning to Think.* Washington, D.C.: National Academy Press, 1987.

Robinson v. Cahill, 62 N.J. 473, 303 A.2d 273 (1973).

San Francisco NAACP v. San Francisco Unified School District, 576 F.Supp. 34 (N.D. Cal. 1983).

Serrano v. Priest, 5 Cal.3d 584, 487 P.2d 1241, 96 Cal. Rptr. 601 (1971).

Smith, M. S., and O'Day, J. A. "Educational Equality: 1966 and Now." In D. Verstegen and J. Ward (eds.), *Spheres of Justice in Education: The 1990 American Education Finance Association Yearbook.* New York: Harper Business, 1991a.

Smith, M. S., and O'Day, J. A. "Systemic School Reform." In S. Fuhrman and B. Malen (eds.), *The Politics of Curriculum and Testing.* Bristol, Pa.: Falmer Press, 1991b.

Stigler, J. W., and Stevenson, H. W. "How Asian Teachers Polish Each Lesson to Perfection." *American Educator,* Spring 1991, pp. 12–20, 43–47.

Strike, K. A. "Liberal Justice: Aspirations and Limitations." In D. Verstegen and J. Ward (eds.), *Spheres of Justice in Education: The 1990 American Education Finance Association Yearbook.* New York: Harper Business, 1991.

Taylor, W. L., and Piché, D. L. "A Report on Shortchanging Children: The Impact of Fiscal Inequity on the Education of Students at Risk." Prepared for the Committee on Education and Labor, U.S. House of Representatives, U.S. Government Printing Office, Washington, D.C., 1990.

Tractenberg, P. L. "*Robinson v. Cahill:* The 'Thorough and Efficient' Clause." *Law and Contemporary Problems,* 1974, *38,* 312–332.

Walzer, M. "On Distributive Justice." In D. Verstegen and J. Ward (eds.), *Spheres of Justice in Education: The 1990 American Education Finance Association Yearbook.* New York: Harper Business, 1991a.

Walzer, M. "Education." In D. Verstegen and J. Ward (eds.),

Spheres of Justice in Education: The 1990 American Education Finance Association Yearbook. New York: Harper Business, 1991b.

Wilson, W. J. *The Truly Disadvantaged: The Inner City, the Underclass, and Public Policy.* Chicago: University of Chicago Press, 1987.

Wise, A. E. *Legislated Learning: The Bureaucratization of the American Classroom.* Berkeley: University of California Press, 1979.

Yudof, M. G., Kirp, D. L., van Geel, T., and Levin, B. *Kirp & Yudof's Educational Policy and the Law.* (2nd ed.) Berkeley, Calif.: McCutchan, 1982.

9

Conclusion:
Can Policy Lead the Way?

Susan H. Fuhrman

Designing more coherent education policy has become a national priority. At this writing, at least half the states are developing or considering sophisticated, challenging curriculum frameworks detailing what students should know and be able to do. Simultaneously, states are creating assessments that reflect the content of the frameworks, or that measure student outcomes that will eventually be folded into frameworks. Curriculum policy and assessment cohere. Several states are beginning to take the next step by aligning teacher licensing and staff development with curriculum frameworks as well. The federal government is assisting states with these efforts. For example, the National Science Foundation's Statewide Systemic Initiatives Program and the U.S. Department of Education's national Eisenhower Program aid states in incorporating professional development into curriculum reforms in math and science. Furthermore, the development of national standards as an outgrowth of the national education goals adopted in 1990 gives the entire U.S. system a sense of direction and a basis for coherent policy development.

The chapters in this book indicate that designing more coherent policy will be extremely challenging. Political factors promote fragmentation, central instructional guidance runs counter to our tradition of deferring decisions about teaching and learning, and important inconsistencies within schools thwart coherency efforts. Furthermore, as difficult as the policy

313

reforms will be, the new expectations for teaching and learning at the heart of coherent policy proposals require even more profound changes. We are hoping for unprecedented changes in attitudes and approaches to instruction and to learning and suggesting that we encourage those changes with unprecedented political consensus and coordination. But in addition to probing the problems, the authors focus on several key aspects of coherent policy design that contain within them some ideas about improving its prospects. They identify forces that might generate support for reform over the long term, while the slow process of classroom change is unfolding. The predominant note is one of hope, as it surfaces in four themes that span the chapters: the cultural basis of improved teaching and learning, the importance of professional development for teachers, the potential of non- or extragovernmental bodies for promoting political stability and improving practice, and the varied purposes of coherent policymaking.

Culture and Educational Improvement

Ths book focuses on policy; many of the authors, however, stress that policy cannot improve teaching and learning without broader societal reinforcement. David K. Cohen and James P. Spillane, who take up the issue most directly, argue that employers and college admissions officials do not provide clear incentives for student effort. With some exceptions, such as the elite colleges, most colleges and most businesses send very weak signals about the importance of strong academic performance, in contrast to other nations where these consumers join with policymakers and educators to provide more coherent instructional guidance. An even greater contrast concerns the extent to which intellectual work is valued in the broader culture. While other nations take academic accomplishment very seriously and support it, American families, students, and teachers demand and accept much less than best effort.

Although he provides a similar assessment of the ways Americans undervalue learning, Arthur G. Powell describes a linked system of independent schools, colleges, and the College

Board that triumphed over anti-intellectualism. The colleges (in Cohen's and Spillane's terms, the consumers) were the linchpin of the system, providing the major incentive for students by requiring examination passage for admission. It was also important that parents were integral partners in assuring that incentives aligned to promote academic achievement. Parents wanted their children to attend the best colleges. Although they had many reasons for choosing elite private schools over other precollegiate educational options, the fact that these schools prepared students for admission to preferred colleges made parents supporters of their academic demands. The values were shared.

For more coherent policy to succeed in improving education, surrounding societal influences must also corroborate the policy efforts. One benefit to the current movement to coherent policy is that it includes mechanisms, such as the South Carolina Curriculum Congress I refer to in Chapter One, for involving the public and professionals in discussions about providing direction for the educational system. Creating a system of consistent incentives for academic achievement requires the type of public education such efforts entail. As Jennifer A. O'Day and Marshall S. Smith point out, widespread public discussion is important in creating legitimacy for new standards and in determining the balance between the common culture and the perspectives of subgroups. It is particularly encouraging that many professional associations are undertaking their own consensus-building efforts that influence the environment surrounding educational policy, although it will be important for the many independent efforts currently under way to coordinate with one another. These societal developments make it more likely that politics as usual can be put aside in service of more policy coherence. Policy efforts need broader cultural support, but also widespread societal discussion provides impetus to and greater leverage for policy efforts.

Professional Development: The Indispensable Ingredient

Intertwined with concerns about societal support is the worry that teachers, who are after all part of the broader culture, lack the knowledge base to provide more challenging instruction. Cohen and Spillane find that recent reforms demand much greater depth and sophistication in grasp of academic subjects than most teachers possess. Even if they had better understanding of their disciplines, most teachers would be unfamiliar with the more active, collaborative instruction envisioned by new curriculum frameworks and related policies. Furthermore, teachers may need to change their views of students as well as their views of curriculum and instruction, according to Milbrey W. McLaughlin and Joan E. Talbert. If the nontraditional students who are becoming a majority in many schools are seen as "drains" on the system rather than individuals of value, no improvement in instructional guidance will suffice to meet the overarching goal of higher standards for all students. Finally, if teachers are not prepared to teach to new standards, students cannot be expected to achieve them. As O'Day and Smith assert, the opportunity to learn the material in curriculum frameworks from well-prepared teachers is the foundation for justice and legitimacy. Yet, as Richard F. Elmore makes clear, districts have not focused much on curriculum and instruction. How is the extensive, sophisticated professional development that appears necessary to be provided?

William H. Clune gives examples of state-supported professional development programs that are integrated with curriculum policy efforts. California provides networks of and workshops for teachers as well as training for superintendents and principals in school improvement related to the curriculum goals. New York uses a system of turnkey training to gradually educate teachers in new curriculum materials once they are adopted. An important professional development experience can occur through teacher involvement in the setting of new curriculum goals and related policies. For example, Powell tells us that thousands of independent school teachers actively participated in creating and grading the College Board examinations.

The importance of professional development in the movement toward coherence is underscored by the efforts of national professional bodies to use standards for what teachers should know to leverage improved teaching and learning. The National

Board for Professional Teaching Standards (NBPTS), an independent body composed primarily of teachers, is defining competencies for teachers in some thirty areas of expertise, in elementary and secondary education as well as early childhood. Similarly, the National Council of Teachers of Mathematics (NCTM) developed *Professional Standards for Teaching Mathematics* that include expectations for what teachers should know and be able to do as well as for the content and nature of professional development.

Finally, professional standards can be an important unifying influence in the field of early childhood education. As W. Steven Barnett describes, faced with so many funding sources and providers, early childhood advocates are attempting to specify a common core of knowledge for the profession of educators. The knowledge would be a basis for defining the profession and for determining levels of preparation and specialization required of each position.

Bypassing Government

The National Association for the Education of Young Children's efforts to professionalize early childhood education extend beyond defining knowledge for teachers and caregivers. Barnett points out that the group has also established standards for practice and developed a voluntary national accreditation system based on peer visitation and validation of standards. Several authors suggest similar nongovernmental efforts to bring more coherence to elementary and secondary education efforts. Two advantages are cited for the use of extra- or nongovernmental bodies to establish and oversee standards and related policies.

First, such groups or boards could enlist professionals as members. Professional bodies can have great legitimacy; their expertise accords them significant authority. Consequently, the standards they promulgate would enlist significant cooperation in the field. As McLaughlin and Talbert indicate, professional communities can have strong influence over norms of practice, conceptions of task, and attitudes about teaching and students. Professional leadership, for example, provided credibility to the

College Board's standards and assessment system described by Powell.

Second, extragovernmental bodies that would maintain membership and authority across electoral cycles enhance political stability, making necessary refinements and protecting reform momentum and coherence over time. Clune notes the political coherence provided by South Carolina's special institutions that report on reform goals and the role played by Chicago's reform coalition that evaluates success, makes adjustments, and shields the reforms from political and legal disruption. In my chapter on politics, I cite recent state willingness to experiment with such bodies as a sign that policymakers are searching for ways to overcome political instability.

The idea of bypassing government has some drawbacks, however. As Cohen and Spillane indicate, bypass operations can increase complexity rather than streamline, adding to regulations themselves or inciting existing governments to outregulate or outmaneuver them. For example, new standards and related instructional policies could be created by a body that had no authority to remove all the existing policies that would conflict with the reforms.

Should new entities be prescriptive, with legal authority over schools and districts, or voluntary, relying on professional respect and suasion? The notion that such agencies would represent and energize the profession may be most compatible with the voluntary posture: that is, new entities would establish standards, exams, and the like that schools could "choose" to use. Presumably the "best practice" seal the standards and exams carried would engender widespread adoption, a model that would parallel the College Board's prewar system. As it was a voluntary operation, only those who shared the values of the system participated. Hence the system operated from a basis of consensus.

The voluntary model is particularly appropriate for national standard setting, given the American desire to avoid federal control of education. The model entails no federal statutes or regulations. The independent, intergovernmental National Education Goals Panel would certify content and performance standards in key subjects. The National Board for Professional Teaching Standards is working on voluntary certification of experienced teachers, already licensed by states.

However, many reformers hope that state and local governments will formally adopt student standards, focus student assessment and staff development on them, and incorporate the teacher standards into their own legal licensure requirements. It is hard to see how state-level standard-setting bodies could operate entirely on a voluntary basis, even though specific elements of the instructional guidance system could be promulgated as guidelines rather than mandates. Would governments seeking accountability give schools the option of participating in new, more ambitious instructional guidance systems? If they did, how could schools serving disadvantaged students be held to the same high standards as schools with more advantaged student bodies? Given the tendency of districts to focus narrowly on state rules, as Elmore points out, could voluntary standards get and sustain their attention?

If it were voluntary, through what mechanism would the new body's recommendations supersede all the existing layers of policy, as Cohen and Spillane ask? Current policies that support traditional and unimaginative instruction could easily overwhelm and undermine the reforms under discussion in this book. But never before in this nation have we successfully eradicated existing policies prior to forging off in new directions. Even though the emerging societal reinforcement, growing professional support, and broad appeal of coherent policy suggest a realignment of political factors that might make such unprecedented policy reduction possible, the elimination of past policy requires action by appropriate authoritative institutions.

At the state level the challenge will be to marry the respect accorded voluntary professionally derived standards with legal authority. For example, a new body could make decisions that are then enacted through appropriate authorities following the body's deliberations. Might not professional involvement in policy design give the policies more authority than traditional political products, even though political bodies play a role in policy promulgation? The incorporation of professionally derived standards into legal requirements is similar to O'Day and Smith's proposal for inspecting school provision of opportunity to learn, in which teams of professionals would review school resources and practices in a nonpolitical, nonbureaucratic manner. However, their findings would trigger governmental consequences, such as increased technical assistance.

It appears likely that policymakers and educators will be debating questions about appropriate policymaking mechanisms, about the relations between governance and instruction, for some time to come. The debates, like discussions of what should constitute common standards for all students and for teachers, are important aspects of improving schooling in public education.

Coherent Policy: One Message with Varied Purposes

We have argued that the movement toward more coherent policy has slim prospects unless professional and public participation in establishing educational direction is strengthened. But it is also true that the movement promotes professional and public participation, which can be seen as a worthy aim in and of itself. The notion of coherent policy serves a number of purposes, and, therefore, has widespread appeal.

Improving teaching and learning is at the heart of coherent education policy. The reforms discussed in this book aim at that end through the establishment of ambitious goals, the alignment of policies so that teachers and schools receive consistent pressure and support for enhanced instruction, the provision of sufficient flexibility to schools to meet the goals, and the incorporation of extensive professional development. Applying the concept also involves enlisting the participation and support of parents, higher education, and employers who provide incentives to students.

But the ideas about coherent policy also serve other purposes. The authors argue that in order to influence instruction in desired directions, policy must be designed in ways that also address a number of political challenges. For example, more coherent policies from the state could focus the attention of districts, as Elmore argues. In the process of achieving academic

goals and assuring district cooperation, the reforms would energize districts in a way that could have a number of benefits.
I have argued that consensus about goals and more unity within
the political community surrounding education would shore up
policymaker support and enhance education's position vis-à-vis
other services. Also, coherent policy design requires reaching
consensus on common goals and on accommodating the views
of diverse subgroups in society, through debates that are healthy
for our society, as O'Day and Smith point out. Powell reminds
us that battles about standards and precise content were once
the serious intellectual debates that characterized discussions
about schooling, and he suggests they might be again.

A more coherent policy structure would provide a way
to join two overarching goals of American education that are
often seen as contradictory: equity and excellence. O'Day and
Smith's chapter argues that common, challenging standards
should be used to promote systemwide excellence. Reinforcing,
integrated policies could provide the infrastructure necessary
to achieve equal opportunity for students and schools in reaching the standards. Such an integrated structure and clearly articulated standards could provide a basis for comparing the quality of educational inputs, such as the quality and appropriateness
of curricular materials, the adequacy of teacher preparation,
and so on. Such comparison is more educationally relevant than
a simple comparison of fiscal resources; it speaks to how resources are allocated rather than simply to amounts of dollars.
Both courts and legislatures could use more meaningful definitions of equity.

Coherent policymaking has multifaceted appeal. This is
not to suggest that benefits such as revitalized school districts
or better equity measures are spinoffs or by-products that happen along the way to improved instruction. At work here is not
serendipity but a policy approach that deliberately anticipates
challenge and opportunities. The design suggestions in this book
take into account what would be necessary to recruit governments and society in a coordinated improvement effort, with
strategies crafted to appeal to many interests on many levels.
Perhaps the widespread state and national activity around these

ideas indicates that the appeal is working, although initial interest in more coherent policy is no guarantee that better, more integrated policies will be created, sustained, or successful. The fitting note on which to end this book is not that coherent policies as we have described them are likely to revolutionize instruction but that the professional, public, and political cooperation their design entails can have far more influence on instruction than any policy mechanism and can generate long-term support for the lengthy process of instructional change. Crafting more coherent policy will be extremely difficult, but the process can have widespread and long-range benefits for improved schooling.

Name Index

323

Subject Index

A

Abbott v. *Burke,* 291, 308

Accelerated Schools Project, 138

Accountability: assessing standards for, 279–289, 306–307; legitimacy of, 271–272, 286, 289; and local districts, 98–99; performance-based, 26, 270–272, 303; and rewards and sanctions, 271, 285–289, 306–307; soft, 283–285; strong, 285–289, 306–307

Achievement, student: and systemic educational policy, 125–140; trends in, 254–262, 301

Administration, and responsibility for standards, 282, 287–288

Admission to college: history of, 174–175; and independent schools, 153–174; and student incentives, 143–144, 150–166

Advanced Placement (AP) Program: and ability to learn, 264; and instructional guidance, 54; and student incentives, 145, 171–172, 174

Aid to Families with Dependent Children (AFDC), 188, 190, 197, 203

America 2000, 138

American Academy of Pediatrics, 201, 214

American Association for the Advancement of Science, 20, 263

American Medical Association, 213

American Public Health Association, 201, 214

Anti-intellectualism, impact of, 73–74, 145

Arizona: instructional guidance in, 49; policy coordination in, 18

Arkansas, policy coordination in, 18, 300

Assessments: appropriate, 279, 305–306; characteristics of, 130; and College Board standards, 161–163; and instructional guidance, 51–56, 78–79; professional model for, 280–281; for systemic educational policy, 129–130, 134

Association of Teacher Educators, 201

Associations: and College Board standards, 158; and instructional guidance, 61; and policymaking, 17–18, 20–21

At-Risk Child Care Entitlement, 185

Australia, governance and instruction in, 39, 40, 45, 52, 73